GENESIS 1-3

FOUNDATIONS OF THE FAITH

Bruce W. Newcomer, Thd.

Big Bend Publishing

Paperback ISBN: 979-8-9993560-1-7 All rights reserved.

All rights reserved. This book or any portion thereof may not be reproduced or used in any manner whatsoever without the express written permission of the publisher, except for the use of brief quotations in a book review.

"Scripture quotations are from the ESV® Bible (The Holy Bible, English Standard Version®), © 2001 by Crossway, a publishing ministry of Good News Publishers. ESV Text Edition: 2025. The ESV text may not be quoted in any publication made available to the public by a Creative Commons license. The ESV may not be translated in whole or in part into any other language. Used by permission. All rights reserved."

Layout and cover design by Bruce W. Newcomer

Contact at: bigbendpublishing@gmail.com

Contents

Also by	1
Dedication	2
Preface	4
Introduction	10
1. In the Beginning God - The Ultimate Foundation	23
2. The Goodness of Creation and the Nature of Reality	43
3. The Image of God: Human Dignity and Design	71
4. Male and Female He Created Them: God's Design for Humanity	100
5. The Sabbath Pattern: Rest, Worship, and God's Rhythm	134
6. The Garden of Delight: God's Provision and Presence	161
7. Covenant Foundations in Eden	189
8. Marriage: The First Human Relationship	217
9. The Serpent's Strategy: Deception, Doubt, and Disorder	247
10. Humanity's Rebellion: The Anatomy of Sin	264

11.	The Curse and Its Consequences	291
12.	The First Gospel: Hope in the Midst of Ruin	323
13.	Created for Glory, Broken by Sin, Redeemed by Christ	350
14.	Foundations for a Faithful Life in a Confused World	375
15.	Foundations That Hold: Living Faithfully in God's Story	397
About the author		421

Also by
Bruce W. Newcomer, ThD.

Lessons in Christianity
Rooted in Grace: POEMS of the REFORMED FAITH
Foundations of Faith: Genesis 1–3

To My Beloved Wife:
You have walked beside me through valleys I never imagined we would traverse together. Through the sleepless nights of cancer treatments, through the daily battles that test faith, through the thousand small moments where your courage humbled me, you have shown me what it means to trust the God who makes all things new. Your faithfulness in suffering has taught me more theology than a dozen commentaries. This book exists because you lived these truths when they cost you everything. I love you more than words can express, and I thank God for the precious gift of walking with you through this broken world toward the glory that awaits us both.

To My Seminary Students:
You sat in my classrooms, wrestling with texts that challenged comfortable assumptions, asking questions that sharpened my own understanding, and pressing me to make ancient truths relevant for a confused generation. You taught me as much as I taught you. Many of you now serve in pulpits and on mission fields, proclaiming the truths we studied together. This book is my final lecture to you. Guard the foundation. Stand firm on Scripture. Love the people God gives you. And never forget that the doctrines we debated are not abstractions but living realities that transform how we face each day.

To My Professors:
You shaped my mind, challenged my assumptions, and modeled what it means to pursue truth with rigor and devotion. You taught me that sound doctrine must serve the church, not exist in academic isolation. You showed me how to handle Scripture with care and conviction. Whatever is good in these pages flows from what you invested in me. The errors are mine alone. Thank you for your faithfulness to the Word and to the generations of students you trained to love it.

GENESIS 1-3

Soli Deo Gloria

Preface

The phone call came at 2:00 a.m. A father, his voice breaking, told me his young daughter had just announced she was pregnant and planned to have an abortion. "She says it's just tissue," he whispered. "She says it's not really a person yet. How do I answer that? How do I tell her what life really is when the whole world is telling her something different?"

I have received variations of that call more times than I can count. The details change: a wife questioning whether her marriage matters if she's unhappy, a college student convinced that science has disproven the Bible, a businessman wondering if his work has any real meaning, but the root issue remains constant. We live in a generation that has lost its foundation. We no longer know who we are, why we are here, or what any of it means. And when we lose our foundation, everything else crumbles.

This is why I have written this book. Not because I possess some novel insight into Genesis that previous generations missed. Not because I have discovered some hidden truth that the church fathers overlooked. But because the truths of Genesis 1 through 3, ancient and unchanging as they are, speak with urgent clarity to the confusion of our particular moment. These opening chapters of Scripture answer the questions that torment our age: What does it mean to be human? What is the purpose of sexuality and marriage? Why is the world so broken? Is there any hope for restoration?

The insights you will encounter in these pages come from Scripture alone, not from my own wisdom. I am simply pointing you to what God has already revealed, to truths that have sustained the faithful for millennia. My prayer is that as we walk together through these foundational chapters, you will discover, or rediscover, the solid ground beneath your feet.

What This Book Will Show You

This book traces three essential themes that flow from Genesis 1 through 3, themes that provide the framework for all of Christian faith and life.

First, the authority and clarity of God's Word in creation. When God spoke, worlds came into being. His Word is both creative and revelatory; it makes reality and makes reality known. This means that what God says in Genesis is not mythology or poetry to be interpreted around, but authoritative truth that defines reality itself. Everything we believe about who God is, what He requires, and how we should live rests on the foundation that God's Word is true, clear, and binding. In our age of confusion about identity, sexuality, and purpose, we desperately need the clarity that comes from submitting ourselves to Scripture's authority rather than trying to make Scripture submit to our preferences.

Second, the image of God establishes human dignity, design, and calling. You possess worth that was not earned but bestowed. You were designed with intentionality, male or female, according to God's purposes. You have been given meaningful work to do and a relationship with God to steward. These truths provide the only coherent foundation for understanding everything from marriage and gender to the sanctity of life and the meaning of work. When our culture reduces human beings to accidents of evolution or collections of self-determined identities, Genesis declares something infinitely better: we are image-bearers of the eternal God, creatures of immeasurable worth because of whose image we carry.

Third, the reality of the fall and the necessity of redemption through Christ. Sin is not a minor problem requiring minor adjustments. It is cosmic treason that has corrupted every dimension of human existence and subjected all creation to futility. We cannot fix ourselves. We cannot evolve into something better. We need a Savior who can accomplish what we cannot. Genesis 3:15 promises that One who will crush the serpent's head, and the entire Bible unfolds the story of how God keeps that promise through Jesus Christ. This is the gospel in seed form, the first announcement that God has not abandoned His creation but is working to restore what sin has broken.

These three themes are not abstract theological concepts to be debated in seminary classrooms. They are living truths that touch every aspect of your daily existence: your marriage, your work, your suffering, your hope. My goal is not to win arguments but to equip you to live faithfully in a world that has lost its way. I want you to see that Genesis is not optional background information but essential truth that makes sense of everything else Scripture teaches.

What to Expect

We will move through Genesis 1 through 3 slowly and carefully, pausing to consider implications that are easy to miss when we rush through familiar passages. Some chapters will require you to think deeply about doctrines you may have never considered. Others will call you to examine whether your own beliefs align with what Scripture actually teaches or with what our culture assumes.

I write as a pastor and theologian who has spent many years in the trenches of ministry, in seminary classrooms preparing future pastors, in pulpits proclaiming God's Word, and in counseling sessions walking with people through the hardest questions life poses. I have seen what happens when believers build on the foundation of Genesis and what happens when they try to build without it. The house built on sand collapses when storms come. The house built on rock stands firm.

You will find that I make no apology for holding firmly to what Scripture teaches, even when that teaching contradicts the spirit of our age. I believe God created the world in six days and rested on the seventh. I believe Adam and Eve were real historical persons. I believe the fall was an actual event that brought real consequences. I believe these truths not because I am naive about science or indifferent to scholarship, but because I trust that the God who created all things has spoken clearly about how He did so, and His Word deserves our full confidence.

At the same time, my aim is not to attack you or anyone else who struggles with these truths. If you have questions or doubts, you are not my enemy. If you have absorbed ideas that contradict Genesis, you are not beyond hope. I was once confused about many of these things myself. God was patient with me as I worked through them. I will strive to extend that same patience to you.

A Word of Hope

The message of Genesis 1 through 3 is ultimately a message of hope. Yes, we are fallen. Yes, the world is broken. Yes, we face an enemy who seeks our destruction. But God has not left us to our ruin. Before Adam and Eve were driven from the garden, before they experienced the full weight of the curse, God promised a Redeemer. The seed of the woman would come. The serpent would be crushed. What was lost would be restored, and more.

That promise has been fulfilled in Jesus Christ. He is the Second Adam who succeeded where the first Adam failed. He crushed the serpent's head through His death on the cross and His resurrection from the grave. He is making all things new, reversing the curse, restoring the image of God in His people, and preparing a new creation where we will dwell in His presence forever.

This is why Genesis matters. This is why we cannot afford to compromise on these chapters or treat them as negotiable. They tell us who God is, who we are, what went wrong, and how God is making it right. They give us solid ground in a world of shifting sands.

My prayer for you as you read is simple: May God open your eyes to see the glory of His truth in these ancient words. May He anchor your soul in the bedrock of His unchanging revelation. May He give you courage to stand firm when others fall away. And may He grant you the joy of living according to His design rather than the misery of chasing the lies our culture peddles.

The foundations hold. They have held for thousands of years. They will hold for you. Build your life on them, and when the storms come, and they will come, you will stand.

Grace to you and peace from God our Father and the Lord Jesus Christ, who gave himself for our sins to deliver us from the present evil age, according to the will of our God and Father, to whom be the glory forever and ever. Amen. (Galatians 1:3-5)

Bruce W. Newcomer, ThD.

Soli Deo Gloria (Glory to God Alone)

Introduction

The young woman sitting across from me in my office had tears streaming down her face. Her question came out in a broken whisper: "How can God call this good?"

She had just miscarried for the third time. The grief was crushing her, and beneath the grief lurked something even more dangerous: doubt about God's character, doubt about His goodness, doubt about whether the world He made had any meaning at all.

I have sat with countless people asking variations of the same question. Sometimes they ask it after burying a spouse. On other occasions, after watching their church split over issues that previous generations never imagined debating. Sometimes after simply looking at the brokenness of our world and wondering if there is any coherent explanation for the chaos.

Almost every time, I find myself returning to the same place: Genesis 1 through 3. These opening chapters of Scripture are not quaint origin stories or ancient poetry meant to comfort primitive people afraid of thunder. They are the foundation of everything. Remove them or reinterpret them into something less than historical reality, and you do not merely lose three chapters at the beginning of your Bible. You lose the entire structure of biblical Christianity. You lose the framework that makes sense of suffering, sexuality, identity, morality, redemption, and hope.

The woman in my office needed more than sympathy. She needed the truth. She needed to understand that the goodness God declared over His creation was real and remains real, that the brokenness she experienced was not part of His original design. I explained that her grief was appropriate because death is an enemy, and that though we still feel its sting, someone (Jesus our Savior) has defeated this enemy, and that a day is coming when someone will wipe away every tear and restore the original goodness in a glorified form. But I could not give her any of that without Genesis.

The Crisis of Our Moment

We live in a time of profound confusion. The culture around us has lost its moorings, drifting from one definition of reality to another with dizzying speed. What was considered settled truth a generation ago is now called bigotry. What was recognized as mental illness a generation ago is now celebrated as identity. What was understood as the murder of innocents a generation ago is now defended as healthcare.

The church has not remained unaffected. Many believers find themselves unable to articulate why certain things are wrong or right beyond "the Bible says so," which feels increasingly inadequate when pressed by neighbors, coworkers, or their own children. We have a vague sense that Christian morality matters, but we struggle to explain why it matters or how it connects to reality itself.

This confusion did not appear overnight. It came through a slow erosion of the foundation. Over the past century, many

Christians have made peace with the idea that Genesis could be read as poetry, allegory, or theological reflection rather than actual history. The motivation seemed innocent enough. Science appeared to demand an ancient Earth. Academic respectability required distance from "fundamentalist literalism." Why fight battles over the age of rocks when we could focus on more important matters like the resurrection of Jesus?

But ideas have consequences. When we reduce the opening chapters of Genesis to symbolic truth or mythological framework, we inadvertently communicate that the Bible's truth claims are negotiable, that Scripture must bow to the authority of contemporary science or scholarship, and that the historical details matter less than the spiritual lessons we extract from them.

This seemingly small compromise created cracks in the foundation. Those cracks have now widened into chasms. If Genesis 1 through 3 is not historical, then on what basis do we insist that gender distinctions are real rather than socially constructed? If Adam was not an actual person, then how did sin enter the world, and why do we need a last Adam to reverse what the first Adam did? If death existed before the Fall, then how was death the wages of sin, and what precisely did Christ's death accomplish? If marriage between the first man and first woman was not a historical event but merely a story illustrating spiritual principles, then why should marriage be limited to one man and one woman today?

The questions multiply. And many Christians find themselves unable to answer them coherently because we have been trying to build a house on a foundation we no longer fully believe.

The Purpose of This Book

I write this not as a scientist attempting to prove young earth creationism or as an apologist defending Genesis against evolutionary theory. Others have done that work ably, and I commend it to you. I write instead as a pastor and theologian who has spent decades studying Scripture and walking with people through the consequences of both believing and disbelieving what Genesis teaches.

My purpose is to show you how Genesis 1 through 3 provides the essential foundation for every major Christian doctrine. I want to demonstrate that these chapters are not optional or peripheral but absolutely essential for understanding who God is, who we are, why the world is broken, and how redemption works.

We will examine how these opening chapters establish the doctrine of God's sovereignty, His creative power, His right to define reality, and His good purposes for His creation. We will see how they define what it means to be human, created in God's image with dignity, purpose, and moral responsibility. We will trace how they explain the origin of evil without making God its author, the nature of temptation, the mechanics of the Fall, and the devastating consequences that followed.

Most importantly, we will discover how Genesis 1 through 3 sets up the entire redemptive storyline that runs through Scripture. Genesis 3:15's promise, often called in Greek *protoevangelium* or for first gospel, establishes the pattern of crushing and being crushed that culminates at the cross. The failure of the first Adam creates the necessity for the last Adam. The closing of Eden points forward to the opening of the New Jerusalem. The curse pronounced in Genesis 3 explains why Revelation 22 carefully notes that "no longer will there be anything accursed."

Without these foundational chapters, the rest of Scripture becomes disconnected scenes rather than a coherent story. With them, everything clicks into place.

How We Lost Our Way

Before we dive into the text itself, I need to address how the church arrived at this moment of confusion. Understanding where we went wrong will help us appreciate why recovering these truths matters so urgently.

For most of church history, Christians read Genesis 1 through 3 as a straightforward historical narrative. Yes, they recognized figurative language where appropriate. Yes, they acknowledged interpretive questions about the length of days or the exact mechanics of creation. But they universally affirmed that these chapters described actual events involving real people in actual history.

Augustine wrestled with how to understand the creation days. Calvin acknowledged difficulties in reconciling the two creation accounts in Genesis 1 and 2. The Reformers debated fine points of interpretation. But none of them questioned whether Adam and Eve were historical persons, whether the Fall was an actual event, or whether death entered the world through sin.

The shift began in earnest during the 19th century as evolutionary theory gained prominence and as higher critical methods of biblical interpretation spread through European universities and eventually to America. Scholars proposed that Genesis 1 through 3 was compiled from multiple sources, borrowed from ancient Near Eastern myths, or written centuries after Moses to address concerns of the Jewish community after the exile.

Some Christians resisted these ideas entirely. Others attempted a middle path, arguing that Genesis could be historically true in its theological claims while being flexible in its scientific or historical details. Still others embraced theistic evolution, proposing that God used evolutionary processes to create, and that Genesis was never intended to tell us how or when God created but only that He did.

Each compromise seemed reasonable in isolation. Each appeared to preserve what mattered most while making peace with contemporary scholarship. But collectively, they communicated something deadly: that Genesis was negotiable.

By the mid-20th century, many evangelical institutions that once held firmly to Genesis as history had softened their stance. Old earth creationism became acceptable. The historicity of Adam became debatable. The interpretation of Genesis became a matter of Christian freedom rather than doctrinal necessity.

I watched this shift during my own theological education. Professors who affirmed biblical inerrancy in principle would nevertheless suggest that Genesis 1 through 11 belonged to a different genre than the later historical narratives. They assured us we could maintain evangelical credentials while reading these chapters as theological reflection on creation rather than journalistic reporting of events.

The problem is that the rest of Scripture does not read Genesis this way. Paul treats Adam as a historical person whose actions had real consequences. Jesus references the creation of male and female as establishing God's design for marriage. The genealogies trace Jesus back through Abraham to Adam with no hint that they switch from history to mythology somewhere along the line.

Either the biblical authors were mistaken about Genesis, or our modern reinterpretations are mistaken. We cannot have it both ways.

Why This Matters Now

The chickens have come home to roost. The compromises made by previous generations have borne fruit in ours, and the fruit is bitter.

When we teach young people Genesis is negotiable, we should not be surprised when they conclude that biblical sexuality is negotiable too. When we communicate that Scripture must bend to accommodate scientific consensus, we should not be shocked when they decide it must also bend to accommodate cultural consensus about gender, identity, and morality.

The progression is logical. If humans evolved from lower life forms rather than being specially created, then we are fundamentally animals with no transcendent purpose or dignity. If death existed before sin, then death is natural rather than an enemy to be defeated. If Adam was not historical, then inherited guilt makes no sense, and neither does Christ's substitutionary atonement. If marriage was not instituted by God in Eden, then it is a social construct subject to redefinition.

I have watched this progression play out in the lives of people I love. The college student who embraced theistic evolution eventually concluded that biblical morality was culturally conditioned. The seminary student who reduced Genesis to theological poetry eventually denied penal substitutionary atonement because inherited guilt from Adam seemed unjust. The pastor who preached that Genesis describes who created but not how or when eventually performed same-sex weddings because the creation ordinance of marriage seemed culturally relative.

Not everyone who questions aspects of Genesis follows this trajectory. God's grace is bigger than our theological missteps. But the pattern appears often enough to be undeniable. Compromise Genesis, and everything else becomes vulnerable.

Conversely, I have watched robust faith in Genesis produce robust faith in everything else Scripture teaches. The scientist who believes God created *ex nihilo* (Latin for "out of nothing") has no trouble believing God raised Jesus from the dead. The physician who affirms that God created humans male and female sees gender dysphoria as a result of the Fall rather than an identity to be celebrated. The counselor who understands that death entered through sin can help grieving people distinguish between natural grief and despair.

Genesis is not merely one doctrine among many. It is the foundation that supports all the others. Get it wrong, and the entire structure becomes unstable.

The Shape of What Follows

This book will walk through Genesis 1 through 3 with careful attention to what the text actually says and how it functions within the larger biblical storyline. We will move slowly, pausing to consider implications that are easy to miss when we rush through familiar passages.

In the opening chapters, we will examine the doctrine of creation itself: what it means that God spoke the universe into existence, why creation from nothing matters, how the six days of creation reveal God's character, and why the seventh day of rest points to our ultimate hope.

We will then consider what it means to be created in God's image. This is not a minor detail but the foundation for human dignity, moral responsibility, gender distinctions, marriage, work, culture-making, and stewardship. Understanding the image of God is essential for addressing nearly every ethical question the church faces today.

From there, we will trace the tragic arc of Genesis 3: the serpent's temptation, Eve's deception, Adam's rebellion, the immediate consequences of sin, and the curse that fell on creation. We will see how this chapter explains everything wrong with our world while carefully preserving God's goodness and justice.

But we will not end in darkness. Genesis 3 contains the first promise of redemption, the cryptic prophecy that the seed of the woman would crush the serpent's head though his own heel would be struck. This promise sets the trajectory for the entire biblical story, pointing forward to the One who would succeed where Adam failed and undo what Adam broke.

Throughout, we will keep one eye on the text and one eye on the rest of Scripture. We will see how the New Testament authors understood and applied Genesis. We will trace connections between creation and new creation, between the first Adam and the last Adam, between the garden we lost and the garden-city we will gain.

My goal is not merely to convince you that Genesis is historical, though I believe it is. My goal is to show you why it matters, how it connects to everything else you believe, and what difference it makes for living faithfully in a confused and confusing world.

A Personal Word

I need to confess something before we begin. For years, I avoided diving deeply into Genesis. Not because I doubted its truth but because engaging with it seriously felt like opening a can of worms. I knew that thoughtful engagement with these chapters would require me to take positions on contested issues, to make arguments that would draw criticism from both liberal scholars and some conservative friends, and to follow implications that made me uncomfortable.

It was easier to focus on other texts. The Gospels seemed safer. The Epistles felt more directly applicable. The Prophets offered rich preaching material without the complications.

But pastoral ministry does not allow us to avoid hard questions indefinitely. People I cared about were deconstructing their faith, and Genesis was always near the center of their deconstruction. Young people I had taught were leaving the church, convinced that science had disproven Christianity, when what they meant was that evolutionary theory seemed incompatible with Genesis.

I realized I had been failing them by not equipping them to understand why Genesis matters. I had given them Jesus without giving them the foundation that makes sense of why Jesus came. I had preached about sin and salvation without grounding those concepts in the reality of what happened in Eden.

The woman in my office, whose tears I mentioned at the beginning, forced my hand. When she asked how God could call this good while she held her miscarried baby, I knew that "God works in mysterious ways" was not enough. She needed the full story: God created everything good, death was not part of His original design, sin broke what God made, death is an enemy we are right to hate, Christ has defeated that enemy, and the resurrection promises that God will restore the goodness we lost and even exceed it in glory.

But I could not give her that story without Genesis. So I went back to these ancient chapters with fresh urgency, determined to understand them deeply enough to help people ground their faith on bedrock rather than shifting sand.

What I discovered transformed not only my teaching but my own faith. I found that Genesis answered questions I had not known how to ask. It explained the tensions I had learned to live with but never resolved. It connected the dots between doctrines I had treated as separate. It gave me a framework for understanding everything from gender confusion to environmental ethics to the purpose of work.

More than that, it deepened my worship. Seeing God create by the mere word of His power filled me with awe. Recognizing His care in forming Adam from dust and breathing life into him moved me to gratitude. Understanding what was lost in the Fall and what Christ came to restore kindled a hope that burns brighter than ever.

This is what I want for you. Not merely intellectual understanding, though that matters. Not merely answers to hard questions, though you will find some of those here. I want Genesis to become part of your bones, shaping how you see yourself, your neighbors, your world, and your God.

An Invitation

The chapters that follow will require something of you. They will require you to slow down and pay attention to details you might usually skip. They will require you to set aside assumptions, even comfortable ones, and let Scripture speak on its own terms. They will require you to follow arguments to their conclusions even when those conclusions challenge the contemporary consensus.

Most of all, they will require that you come with humility. None of us approaches Genesis without preconceptions. We have all absorbed ideas from our culture, our education, our churches, and our personal preferences. We must be willing to have those ideas tested and, where necessary, corrected by Scripture itself.

I approach this task aware of my own limitations. I am not a scientist, though I have studied enough science to understand the basic questions at stake. I am not an expert in ancient languages, though I have worked in Hebrew and Greek enough to consult the experts responsibly. I am not a professional philosopher, though philosophical questions inevitably arise when discussing origins and meaning.

What I am is a pastor and teacher who has spent a lifetime studying Scripture and watching its truth transform lives. I have seen what happens when people build on the foundation of Genesis and what happens when they try to build without it. I have watched the house built on sand collapse and the house built on rock stand firm.

My prayer is that this book will help you build on rock. That it will equip you to face the hard questions with confidence. It will give you a framework for understanding yourself and your world that coheres with reality because it comes from the One who made reality.

The journey will be challenging at points. Some chapters will require careful thought. Some implications will discomfort you. Some applications will call for changes in how you think or live.

But I promise you this: if you persevere to the end, you will not be the same. You will see connections you missed before. You will understand why certain debates matter so much. You will be able to help others who are struggling with the same questions you once struggled with.

And most importantly, you will see more clearly the glory of the God who created everything by the word of His power, who made you in His image for His purposes, who did not abandon you when sin broke everything, and who has been working since Genesis 3:15 to crush the serpent and restore what was lost.

That is the story Genesis tells. That is the story we need to recover. And that is the story that makes sense of everything else.

Let us begin.

Chapter One

In the Beginning God - The Ultimate Foundation

"In the beginning, God created the heavens and the earth." Genesis 1:1.

Four words in Hebrew. Ten in English. The most foundational statement ever penned. Everything that follows in Scripture, every doctrine we hold, every truth we confess, stands or falls on these opening words.

I have read Genesis 1:1 thousands of times. I have taught it in seminary classrooms and preached it from pulpits. I have quoted it in counseling sessions and cited it in theological debates. Yet I never cease to marvel at its profound simplicity. In a single sentence, Moses demolishes every false worldview and establishes the only foundation capable of bearing the weight of reality.

The verse does not argue for God's existence. It assumes it. The verse does not defend creation against competing theories. It declares it. The verse does not ease us gently into theological complexity. It confronts us immediately with the ultimate truth: God is, and everything else exists because He spoke.

This is where we must begin because this is where God began. Not with man. Not with sin. Not with redemption. With Himself.

Before the Beginning

"In the beginning, God."

Stop there. Linger over these four words. Before the beginning mentioned here, before anything else existed, God was. The verb "created" comes second because God is first. Eternally first. Necessarily first. Supremely first.

This foundational truth separates biblical Christianity from every other worldview. Atheism begins with matter and energy existing eternally, then adds vast stretches of time and chance to explain everything else. Eastern religions begin with an impersonal force or cosmic consciousness that emanates reality. Ancient Near Eastern creation myths begin with warring deities or primordial chaos that even the gods must navigate.

Genesis begins with God. Personal, eternal, self-existent God. Not an impersonal force floating through the cosmos. Not a philosophical idea conjured in the minds of ancient peoples seeking to explain the unexplainable. Not an emergent property of nature that somehow bootstrapped itself into being. God, a living, conscious, sovereign God.

The Bible never attempts to prove God's existence because it treats His existence as the precondition for proving anything at all. Think carefully about this: how could we trust our own reasoning processes if our minds were merely the accidental byproduct of mindless, purposeless processes grinding away over eons? How could we claim to know anything truly and certainly if truth itself were not grounded in an eternal, unchanging, and utterly reliable reality that stands outside the flux of temporal existence? The very act of reasoning requires a foundation that atheism cannot provide.

This foundational reality is precisely what the Apostle Paul meant when he wrote to the Colossians: "For by him all things were created, in heaven and on earth, visible and invisible, whether thrones or dominions or rulers or authorities—all things were created through him and for him. And he is before all things, and in him all things hold together" (Colossians 1:16-17). Notice the comprehensiveness of Paul's declaration. God does not merely exist alongside creation as one being among many, however exalted. He precedes it absolutely, upholds it constantly by the word of His power, and gives it meaning, purpose, and direction. Everything finds its origin, sustenance, and ultimate goal in Him.

I remember sitting with a graduate student who had absorbed the modern secular narrative so thoroughly that he could not escape its gravitational pull. He wanted to believe in God, he said, but science had made God unnecessary. The universe explained itself. Natural laws accounted for everything.

"Tell me," I asked him, "where did those natural laws come from?"

He paused. "They just are."

"And the mathematical precision that allows those laws to function with such exactitude that we can predict planetary motions centuries in advance?"

"That is just how things work."

"But why do things work that way? Why is there something rather than nothing? Why does that something follow orderly, predictable patterns rather than chaotic randomness?"

He struggled. Every answer he offered simply pushed the question back one step. Eventually, he said what honest atheists must say: "I do not know."

This is the point. The atheist worldview cannot ground itself. It rests on borrowed capital from a theistic universe. It assumes rationality without accounting for where rationality comes from. It depends on order without explaining why order exists. It appeals to truth while denying any ultimate standard of truth.

Genesis 1:1 cuts through all this confusion. In the beginning, God. Not as one explanation among many. As the only explanation that makes sense of everything else.

The God Who Is There

But which God? The philosophers' abstract first cause? The deists' distant watchmaker who wound up the universe and walked away? The god of modern therapeutic religion who exists primarily to make us feel better about ourselves?

No. The God who created the heavens, and the earth is the God who reveals Himself throughout Scripture. The God of Abraham, Isaac, and Jacob. The God who delivered Israel from Egypt, gave the law at Sinai, and judged His people for their sins. The God who became incarnate in Jesus Christ, died for sinners, and rose again in triumph. The Triune God: Father, Son, and Holy Spirit.

This matters immensely. We cannot separate Genesis 1 from the rest of the biblical revelation. The God of "I AM WHO I AM" to Moses is the same God who said, "Let there be light." The creative Word through whom all things were made is the Word who became flesh and dwelt among us (John 1:1-14). The Spirit who hovered over the waters in creation is the Spirit who convicts of sin, regenerates dead hearts, and seals believers for the day of redemption.

The doctrine of the Trinity, which is foreshadowed in Genesis 1, though not fully revealed until the New Testament. When God said, "Let us make man in our image" (Genesis 1:26), He spoke as one who is eternally plural in persons yet singular in essence. The Father creates through the Son by the Spirit. All three persons of the Godhead participate in the work of creation, each according to His particular role in the divine economy.

I emphasize this because some want to accept a generic creator god while rejecting the specific God of Scripture. They find creation easier to swallow than incarnation. They prefer natural theology to special revelation. But Scripture gives us no such option. The God who created is the God who saves. To reject the latter is ultimately to lose the former.

Creation Ex Nihilo

"In the beginning, God created the heavens and the earth." Genesis 1:1

The Hebrew word *bara*, translated "created," appears only with God as its subject in the Old Testament. This is not the word for making something out of existing materials, like a potter forming clay. This is the word for bringing something into existence out of nothing.

The doctrine has a Latin name: *creatio ex nihilo*. Creation out of nothing. God did not shape preexisting matter. He did not organize primordial chaos. He spoke, and what did not exist came to be.

This truth demolishes dualism. There is no eternal matter independent of God that limits His creative freedom. This truth demolishes pantheism. Creation is not an extension of God's being but something distinct that He freely chose to make. This truth demolishes process theology. God does not evolve along with creation or depend on it for His own actualization.

The New Testament confirms what Genesis implies. "By faith we understand that the universe was created by the word of God, so that what is seen was not made out of things that are visible" (Hebrews 11:3). The visible came from the invisible, not through natural processes working on existing material, but through divine fiat.

Paul puts it even more directly: "For by him all things were created, in heaven and on earth, visible and invisible" (Colossians 1:16). Not some things. All things. Not rearranged. Created. Nothing exists apart from God's creative will.

This should stagger us. We are creatures who can only work with what already exists. A painter needs canvas and pigments. A musician needs instruments and sound waves. An architect needs materials and physical laws. Even our most creative acts involve arranging and combining existing elements.

But God created without any such raw materials. There was no "before" for Him to work with because time itself is part of creation. There was no space He occupied because space, too, came into being at His word. When God said, "Let there be light," He was not flipping a switch in a preexisting electrical system. He was calling into existence both light and the capacity for light to exist.

I sometimes ask students what existed before God created. The question itself reveals a limitation in our thinking. "Before" is a temporal category, and time is created. The answer is not that nothing existed before, as if there was an empty temporal moment preceding creation. The answer is that God exists eternally, without beginning or end, and He freely chose to create within the temporal framework He Himself established.

This distinguishes the Christian doctrine of creation from every ancient myth and modern speculation. The Babylonian *Enuma Elish* begins with gods emerging from primordial waters, with creation resulting from divine conflict and the dismemberment of defeated deities. Greek philosophy often posited eternal matter the gods shaped but did not create. Modern naturalism assumes matter and energy as eternal givens.

Only Scripture presents creation as the free act of an eternal, personal God who depends on nothing outside Himself.

The Word of Power

How did God create? The answer runs throughout Genesis 1 like a refrain: He spoke.

"And God said, 'Let there be light,' and there was light" (Genesis 1:3).

"And God said, 'Let there be an expanse in the midst of the waters'" (Genesis 1:6).

"And God said, 'Let the waters under the heavens be gathered together into one place'" (Genesis 1:9).

Ten times in Genesis 1, the formula appears: "And God said." Creation comes into being through divine speech. God does not labor or struggle. He does not experiment or adjust. He speaks, and it is so.

This reveals something essential about God's relationship to creation. His Word is performative. When human beings speak, our words describe reality or express our thoughts. When God speaks, His words create reality. His speech is power.

The Psalms celebrate this truth: "By the word of the LORD the heavens were made, and by the breath of his mouth all their host" (Psalm 33:6). Not through strenuous effort but through effortless speech. Not through long ages of gradual development but through immediate accomplishment. "For he spoke, and it came to be; he commanded, and it stood firm" (Psalm 33:9).

This connection between God's Word and creative power threads through Scripture. The same Word that created sustains: "He upholds the universe by the word of his power" (Hebrews 1:3). The same Word that brought light into darkness brings spiritual light to darkened hearts: "For God, who said, 'Let light shine out of darkness,' has shone in our hearts to give the light of the knowledge of the glory of God in the face of Jesus Christ" (2 Corinthians 4:6).

The Word incarnate is Himself the agent of creation: "All things were made through him, and without him was not any thing made that was made" (John 1:3). The eternal Son, the Word of God, spoke creation into existence. He is both the means of creation and the wisdom by which it was ordered.

This should transform how we read Scripture. The Bible is not merely a book containing information about God. It is

God's Word, carrying His authority and power. The same God who spoke worlds into existence speaks through Scripture to reveal Himself, to transform hearts, and to accomplish His purposes. To disregard Scripture is to disregard God Himself. To doubt Scripture's trustworthiness is to doubt whether God's Word accomplishes what He intends.

The God of Order

"In the beginning, God created the heavens and the earth. The earth was without form and void, and darkness was over the face of the deep. And the Spirit of God was hovering over the face of the waters" (Genesis 1:1-2).

Verses 1 and 2 establish the initial conditions. God created the raw materials of the earth, which at this point lacked order and fullness. The Hebrew phrase *tohu wabohu*, translated "without form and void," describes an unorganized, uninhabited state. Not chaos in the sense of random disorder fighting against order, but simply the initial stage of a process that God would complete.

What follows in Genesis 1:3-31 shows God systematically organizing and filling what He has made. Days one through three address the formlessness by establishing order: separating light from darkness, waters from waters, sea from land. Days four through six address the emptiness by providing inhabitants: luminaries for day and night, fish and birds for waters and sky, animals and humans for the land.

The pattern reveals God's character. He is not chaotic or arbitrary. He works according to wisdom and purpose. He creates structures, then fills those structures with appropriate inhabitants. He establishes laws, then populates His creation with beings who function according to those laws.

This is the foundation of all science. The scientific method depends on the assumption that the universe operates according to consistent, discoverable laws. But where did that assumption come from? Not from nature itself, which simply is what it is. The assumption came from Christian theology.

The early scientists, many of them devout believers, investigated nature because they believed a rational God had created an orderly world that reflected His wisdom. Johannes Kepler described his astronomical discoveries as "thinking God's thoughts after Him." Isaac Newton saw his work as uncovering the mathematical principles by which God governed creation. Even those who later abandoned Christian orthodoxy borrowed their confidence in natural order from a Christian worldview.

Ironically, modern naturalism, having rejected the Creator, struggles to account for the very order it depends on. If matter and energy are all that exist, arranged by chance over billions of years, why should we expect consistent natural laws? Why should the future resemble the past? Why should mathematics, an abstract system of logic, correspond so precisely to physical reality?

The Christian has answers. We expect order because God is orderly. We trust natural laws because God upholds all things by His powerful Word. We discover, upon careful reflection, that mathematics describes physical reality with such stunning precision not by accident or evolutionary necessity, but because the same divine Logos, the Word who was with God and was God, who structures and orders our rational minds also structures and orders the entire cosmos. The correspondence between abstract mathematical principles and concrete physical phenomena points not to mere chance, but to a single divine Mind behind both the laws of thought and the laws of nature.

This is not an argument for abandoning scientific inquiry. It is an argument for recognizing its proper foundation. Science works because Genesis 1 is true.

The Crown of Creation

The creation week builds toward a climax. Light, sky, land, vegetation, celestial bodies, sea creatures, birds, land animals. Each stage is good. Each stage prepares for what comes next. And then, on the sixth day, God created humanity.

"Then God said, 'Let us make man in our image, after our likeness. And let them have dominion over the fish of the sea and over the birds of the heavens and over the livestock and over all the earth and over every creeping thing that creeps on the earth.' So God created man in his own image, in the image of God he created him; male and female he created them" (Genesis 1:26-27).

Here we encounter the most controversial statement in all of Scripture for modern ears. Not because ancient people questioned it. They knew humans were special. Every culture distinguished between people and animals. The controversy arose when evolutionary theory challenged humanity's unique status and postmodern philosophy deconstructed the very concept of human nature.

But Genesis allows no ambiguity. Humans alone are made in God's image. Humans alone receive the divine breath of life directly from God (Genesis 2:7). Humans alone receive dominion over creation. Humans alone are addressed directly by God.

We will explore the meaning of the image of God more fully in later chapters. For now, we need only recognize what Genesis 1:26-27 establishes: humanity occupies a unique place in creation. We are not simply highly evolved animals. We are not accidents of cosmic chance. We are not interchangeable with other species. We are image-bearers, created by God for relationship with Him and responsibility before Him.

This truth grounds human dignity in the bedrock of divine creation itself. Every person who draws breath, regardless of ability or disability, appearance or lack thereof, age whether fetus or elderly, achievement or apparent failure, bears God's image stamped upon their very being. Every person deserves respect, protection, and justice not because of what they contribute to society, not because of their economic utility, not because of their intelligence or productivity, but because every person represents the Creator Himself. This is not a dignity we earn or a value we achieve; it is inherent in our creation.

To assault a human being, therefore, is to assault one who bears God's image. To devalue human life, to treat it as disposable or merely instrumental, is to dishonor the God whose image that life reflects. This truth stands as an absolute defense against every ideology that would reduce human worth to utilitarian calculations. It condemns slavery, which treats image-bearers as property. It condemns abortion, which destroys image-bearers in the womb. It condemns euthanasia, which determines that some lives are not worth living. It condemns racism, which elevates some image-bearers above others based on nothing more than melanin. The image of God is not distributed according to our preferences or prejudice; it is stamped on every human without exception.

This truth also grounds human responsibility with unshakable certainty. We are not autonomous beings, answerable to no one but ourselves. We are accountable profoundly, unavoidably accountable to the One who spoke us into existence. God made us for His purposes, not our own, and we will give an account for how we live, for the choices we make, for the way we steward the life He entrusted to us. This is not oppressive oversight; it is the natural relationship between Creator and creature, between the Potter and the clay.

The modern insistence on absolute personal autonomy, the relentless rejection of any authority outside the self, the declaration that each person is the ultimate arbiter of truth and morality, stands in direct and defiant opposition to the foundational revelation of Genesis 1. We are creatures, not creators. We are made, not self-existent. We have freedom, yes, genuine freedom to make meaningful choices, but it is freedom within the boundaries established by our Maker, freedom that operates within the design specifications of our Creator. To claim autonomy from God is to deny the very foundation of our existence. It is to live a lie, however culturally celebrated that lie may be.

The Seventh Day

"And on the seventh day God finished his work that he had done, and he rested on the seventh day from all his work that he had done. So God blessed the seventh day and made it holy, because on it God rested from all his work that he had done in creation" (Genesis 2:2-3).

God rested. Not because He was tired. The Creator of the universe does not suffer fatigue. He rested because His work was complete and perfect. Nothing needed addition or correction. The rest of the seventh day declares the sufficiency of what God had made.

This rest also establishes a pattern for human life. God did not create us for ceaseless activity. He built rhythm into the created order: work and rest, labor and worship. The Sabbath principle predates the Mosaic Law. It is woven into the fabric of creation itself.

When God gave the fourth commandment to Israel, He grounded it in creation: "Remember the Sabbath day, to keep it holy. Six days you shall labor, and do all your work, but the seventh day is a Sabbath to the LORD your God. On it you shall not do any work, you, or your son, or your daughter, your male servant, or your female servant, or your livestock, or the sojourner who is within your gates. For in six days the LORD made heaven and earth, the sea, and all that is in them, and rested on the seventh day. Therefore the LORD blessed the Sabbath day and made it holy" (Exodus 20:8-11).

The Sabbath principle reaches both backward and forward through redemptive history, anchoring us in the truth of who God is and who we are. Looking backward, it points us to creation itself, to that seventh day when God ceased from His labor and declared His work complete. It reminds us, week after week, generation after generation, that God is the sovereign Creator and we are His finite creatures. We did not make ourselves. We do not sustain ourselves. We exist because He spoke us into being, and we continue to exist because He upholds all things by the word of His power.

Looking forward, the Sabbath anticipates something even greater than creation rest, the ultimate rest that comes only through faith in Christ. Our weekly Sabbath observance, however we practice it under the new covenant, testifies to a profound spiritual reality: our work does not save us, our efforts do not establish our worth, our productivity does not define our identity. The writer of Hebrews captures this beautifully: "So then, there remains a Sabbath rest for the people of God, for whoever has entered God's rest has also rested from his works as God did from his" (Hebrews 4:9-10). The rest God offers in Christ is not merely physical refreshment or temporary relief from labor. It is rest from the crushing burden of trying to earn God's approval through our own righteousness, from the futile attempt to justify ourselves through moral achievement or religious performance.

This matters profoundly in our frantic, breathless age. We live immersed in a culture that not merely encourages but actively esteems constant productivity, relentless activity, perpetual motion. Our society measures human worth by measurable output, assigning value to people based on what they produce rather than whose image they bear. We exist in a system that never stops and never rests, that treats stillness as failure and quiet as emptiness to be filled. We check email and tweets compulsively throughout the day, in line at the grocery store, at red lights, in the bathroom, the moment we wake, and the last thing before sleep. We consume entertainment endlessly, scrolling through social media feeds that refresh faster than we can process their content, bingeing television series into the early morning hours, filling our minds with constant noise and distraction. We fill every single moment, every potential silence, every possible pause with some form of activity, terrified of what we might discover in stillness. The very idea of rest, genuine rest that involves actual cessation of labor and productivity, feels dangerously like weakness in a world that celebrates strength, or shameful waste in an economy that demands maximum efficiency from every human resource.

But God rested. Not because His creative work was somehow inadequate or incomplete, not because He had exhausted His divine energy and needed to recuperate like we do after a long day's labor, but precisely because His work was absolutely, utterly, unquestionably perfect. The creation was finished. Nothing remained to be added or adjusted. Everything existed exactly as He intended it.

And we, created in His image, rest not primarily to recover depleted strength or restore exhausted resources, though physical rest certainly serves those purposes. We rest fundamentally on acknowledging our profound human limitations and on trusting utterly in God's perfect sufficiency. The seventh day stands forever as a perpetual reminder, echoing through every week of human history, that we are decidedly not the center of the universe; God is. Our frantic efforts, our constant striving, our endless productivity are not what hold reality together. God's sovereign power sustains all things by the word of His power, whether we work or whether we rest, whether we are productive or whether we cease from our labors entirely.

The Foundation of Everything

"In the beginning, God created the heavens and the earth."

I return to where we started because everything stands or falls here. If Genesis 1:1 is true, then we live in a created universe with inherent meaning and purpose. If it is false, then nothing else in Scripture matters because Scripture's credibility crumbles when its opening statement fails.

The implications cascade in every direction.

If God created all things, then He owns all things completely, absolutely, without reservation or qualification. We are not owners of anything in this world; we are stewards, trustees, managers of another's property. This understanding fundamentally reshapes how we view everything we touch, everything we possess, everything we claim as "ours." We have no absolute right to our possessions, no inherent claim to our time, no autonomous authority over our bodies, no ultimate ownership of our lives. Everything from the breath in our lungs to the thoughts in our minds, from the clothes on our backs to the relationships that give life its richness, belongs to God. He is the owner. We are the managers. And like any faithful manager in relation to his master, we will give an account for how we manage, how we steward, how we handle everything He graciously entrusts to our temporary care. This is not a burden but a liberation. We are freed from the crushing weight of ownership and granted instead the privileged responsibility of faithful stewardship under the watchful, loving eye of the rightful Owner of all things.

If God created all things, then He defines all things. We do not determine truth. We discover it. We did not invent morality. We received it. We do not construct meaning. We find it in the purpose for which God made us.

If God created all things, then He sustains all things. The universe does not run on autopilot. Natural laws are descriptions of God's regular way of upholding creation, not autonomous forces independent of Him. Every breath we take, every heartbeat, every thought, every moment of existence depends on His continuing creative power.

If God created all things, then He has authority over all things. No sphere of life lies outside His jurisdiction. Not politics, not economics, not art, not science, not sexuality, not family, not work. He is Lord of all because He is the Creator of all.

This is why the opening chapters of Genesis matter so desperately. They establish the foundation for everything else. Remove this foundation, and the entire biblical worldview collapses. Grant this foundation, and everything else falls into place.

I have watched this play out over decades of ministry. Those who hold firmly to creation as taught in Genesis navigate life's challenges with stability. They know who they are: image-bearers of God. They know why they exist: to glorify God and enjoy Him forever. They know where meaning comes from: not from within themselves but from their Creator. They know what will last: not the temporary pleasures of this passing world but the eternal purposes of God.

Those who abandon or compromise on creation drift. They grasp for identity in shifting cultural categories. They chase meaning in accomplishments that rust and decay. They ground morality in a consensus that changes with every generation. They face suffering with no explanation and death with no hope beyond wishful thinking.

The stakes could not be higher. This is not an academic debate for scholars to argue in journals while the rest of us get on with practical matters. This is the difference between building on rock and building on sand. This is the difference between standing firm when storms come and being swept away.

The Call to Worship

Genesis 1 is not merely a statement of fact, though it is certainly that. It is a call to worship. When we grasp that the God who spoke galaxies into existence cares about us individually, when we understand that the infinite Creator became incarnate to redeem us, when we recognize that the One who holds all things together by His powerful Word, uses that same power to preserve us for eternity, how can we respond with anything less than awe?

The Psalms model the proper response: "The heavens declare the glory of God, and the sky above proclaims his handiwork" (Psalm 19:1). Creation itself is a continuous testimony to the Creator's power and wisdom. Every sunset blazes with His glory. Every mountain range testifies to His strength. Every intricate biological system reveals His wisdom. Every star-filled night sky whispers of His infinitude.

Paul teaches us with a sobering clarity that creation's testimony leaves all people without excuse before their Maker: "For his invisible attributes, namely, his eternal power and divine nature, have been clearly perceived, ever since the creation of the world, in the things that have been made. So they are without excuse" (Romans 1:20). The apostle's words carry the weight of divine judgment. We do not need special revelation to know that God exists, and that He is powerful and wise beyond human comprehension. Creation itself declares this truth with unceasing eloquence.

The evidence surrounds us. It confronts us. It pursues us. From the microscopic precision of DNA to the incomprehensible expanse of the cosmos, from the perfectly balanced forces that hold atoms together to the exquisite design of the human eye, creation testifies to its Creator. No one can honestly claim ignorance. The witness is universal, constant, and undeniable.

But creation alone does not reveal the gospel. It shows God's power but not His mercy. It displays His wisdom but not His love. It demonstrates His authority but not His grace. For that, we need Scripture. We need the full revelation that begins with "In the beginning, God created" and culminates with "It is finished" and "He is risen" and "I am making all things new."

This is why Genesis 1 matters so much. It opens the door to everything else. It establishes the stage on which the drama of redemption unfolds. It introduces us to the God who will not abandon His creation to sin and death but will enter it Himself to accomplish what we could not.

When I stand before a congregation or classroom and declare, "In the beginning, God created the heavens and the earth," I am not simply teaching ancient history. I am proclaiming the foundation of reality. I am calling people to recognize their Creator, to acknowledge their dependence, to embrace their purpose, and to worship the One who made them.

This is where faith begins. Not with vague spiritual feelings or personal experiences or moral improvement. With God. The eternal, sovereign, all-powerful Creator, who spoke and worlds came to be, who speaks still through His Word, and who will speak the final word when He makes all things new.

Everything else builds on this foundation. Everything else flows from this source. Everything else finds its meaning in this fundamental truth.

In the beginning, God.

Chapter Two

The Goodness of Creation and the Nature of Reality

The refrain echoes through Genesis 1 like the steady beat of a drum: "And God saw that it was good." Five times this declaration punctuates the creation account. Then, after the creation of humanity in God's image, the verdict intensifies: "And God saw everything that he had made, and behold, it was very good" (Genesis 1:31).

These simple words carry profound weight. They establish a truth that strikes at the heart of countless heresies, both ancient and modern. They answer questions that have plagued humanity since the Fall. They shape how we view our bodies, our work, our relationships, and the physical world we inhabit.

When I first began teaching the opening chapters of Genesis in my seminary classroom, I made what I thought was a reasonable assumption. I believed that students who had committed years of their lives to theological education would readily grasp this foundational point. Creation is good. God made it, looked at it, and declared it so. What could be simpler? What could be more straightforward than accepting the clear verdict of Scripture's opening chapter?

But I discovered something that both surprised and troubled me. Centuries of bad theology, layer upon layer of unbiblical thinking, had done their insidious work. Students arrived in my classroom carrying intellectual and spiritual baggage they did not even know they possessed. These were sincere believers, many preparing for pastoral ministry, yet they carried assumptions that contradicted the very text we were studying.

They spoke casually of the spiritual realm as inherently superior to the physical, as though matter itself were somehow second class in God's economy. They described salvation primarily as escaping the material world rather than participating in its ultimate redemption and restoration. They viewed their own bodies with a vague suspicion, sometimes even with barely concealed contempt, as though the flesh were an enemy to be subdued rather than a gift to be stewarded. They had absorbed, often completely unconsciously, ideas and attitudes that would have been far more at home in an ancient Gnostic gathering than in a Christian church founded on the incarnation of the Son of God.

This matters more than we might think. How we understand creation's goodness shapes everything from our approach to sexuality and marriage to our engagement with culture and our stewardship of the environment. It determines whether we view the physical world as a temporary prison to escape or a good gift to steward. It influences how we think about pleasure, work, rest, and the relationship between body and soul.

The Bible's verdict on this matter is wonderfully clear and unequivocal, leaving no room for the dualistic thinking that has crept into so much Christian thought. God made the physical world, all of it, in every detail and dimension. He personally fashioned the mountains and valleys, the seas and skies, and the intricate designs of flora and fauna. And when He surveyed what His hands had made, He pronounced it good, truly, authentically, profoundly good. Not merely acceptable as a temporary measure, not grudgingly tolerated as a necessary evil, not viewed with resigned disappointment as something that fell short of His original vision. Good. Genuinely, absolutely, unreservedly good.

And that divine declaration changes everything about how we should view the material world and our place within it.

The Meaning of Good

What does it mean when God declares His creation good? The Hebrew word for good (*tov*) carries rich connotations. It speaks of functionality, beauty, completeness, and moral uprightness. When God looked at what He had made and called it good, He was not grading on a curve or expressing mild approval. He was declaring that creation perfectly fulfilled His design and reflected His character.

Consider the first day. "And God said, 'Let there be light,' and there was light. And God saw that the light was good" (Genesis 1:3-4). Light functioned exactly as God intended. It illuminated. It made sight possible. It separated day from night. It was both useful and beautiful, practical and glorious. Nothing about it fell short of God's purpose.

The pattern continues through each day of creation. The expanse separating waters from waters: good. The dry land and vegetation: good. The sun, moon, and stars governing day and night and marking seasons: good. The sea creatures and birds: good. The land animals: good. Each element of creation fulfilled its purpose, displayed God's wisdom, and reflected His glory.

This was not goodness in some abstract, theoretical sense. The ancient Israelites who first heard these words understood *tov* in concrete, tangible terms. A good tree produced fruit. A good field yielded crops. A good tool accomplished its task. Goodness meant functioning according to design, fulfilling purpose, contributing to flourishing.

When God pronounced creation good, He declared that the physical world was neither an accident nor an illusion nor a necessary evil. It was His intentional handiwork, designed to function in harmony, to sustain life, and to display His glory. The mountains did not exist despite God's will but because of it. The oceans were not cosmic mistakes but divine masterpieces. Even in the smallest details; the pattern on a butterfly's wing or the structure of a snowflake, reflected the Creator's attention and care.

Then came the apex of creation. "So God created man in his own image, in the image of God he created him; male and female he created them" (Genesis 1:27). And the verdict: "Very good." Not just good but very good. Humanity, embodied as male and female and formed as physical beings with flesh, blood, bones, and breath, represented the pinnacle and crowning achievement of God's creative work. We are not spirits temporarily housed in bodies. Not souls unfortunate enough to be trapped in material containers. But fully integrated beings, designed from the beginning to exist as both physical and spiritual creatures united in perfect harmony.

This matters profoundly. Our bodies are not accidents. They are not prisons for our souls. They are not inferior to our spirits.

God made us as embodied creatures and declared that design very good. The physical nature of human existence was part of God's perfect plan from the beginning.

Against Ancient Heresies

The church has faced this battle before. In the early centuries, Gnostic teachers infiltrated Christian communities with a seductive lie. They taught that the material world was inherently evil, created by a lesser deity or even a malevolent one. True salvation, they claimed, meant escaping the physical realm and ascending to a purely spiritual existence. The body was a prison. Physical pleasure was suspect. Marriage and procreation perpetuated the tragedy of souls trapped in flesh.

The apostles confronted this heresy head-on. John opened his gospel with a direct assault on Gnostic dualism: "In the beginning was the Word, and the Word was with God, and the Word was God. He was in the beginning with God. All things were made through him, and without him was not any thing made that was made" (John 1:1-3). Then came the knockout blow: "And the Word became flesh and dwelt among us" (John 1:14).

The eternal Son of God did not merely take on the appearance of human flesh as a temporary disguise. No, He genuinely, truly, completely took on human flesh in all its reality. This wasn't some divine illusion or phantom body, as the Gnostic heretics desperately wanted to believe. He became fully, authentically incarnate, God in the flesh, the Word made tangible, touchable, real.

Consider what this meant. The Second Person of the Trinity experienced genuine hunger that gnawed at His stomach. He knew real thirst that parched His throat. He felt the bone-deep weariness that comes from long hours of walking dusty roads and teaching crowds that pressed in from every side. These were not performances or pretenses. They were authentic experiences of human embodiment.

He ate actual fish, its texture real on His tongue. He drank wine that warmed His throat. He felt the sting of pain when thorns pierced His brow and nails tore through His wrists and feet. He bled, not some ethereal substance, but genuine human blood that flowed from wounds and pooled on the ground beneath the cross. Every physical experience was real, was authentic, was fully human.

And in choosing to enter into human flesh this way, not reluctantly, not as a necessary evil, but purposefully and willingly, He affirmed the essential goodness of physical creation in the most dramatic, unassailable way possible. The incarnation itself became God's declaration that bodies matter, that physical existence is not something to escape but something worth redeeming.

Paul took up the same fight. When false teachers in Colossae promoted ascetic practices rooted in suspicion of the physical, Paul responded with theological precision: "For by him all things were created, in heaven and on earth, visible and invisible, whether thrones or dominions or rulers or authorities, all things were created through him and for him" (Colossians 1:16). Christ created the physical world. How then could it be evil?

Paul pressed further. These false teachers forbade marriage and demanded abstinence from certain foods. His response cut to the heart: "For everything created by God is good, and nothing is to be rejected if it is received with thanksgiving, for it is made holy by the word of God and prayer" (1 Timothy 4:4-5). He took them right back to Genesis 1. God created. God declared it good. Therefore, we receive it with gratitude, not suspicion.

The early church fathers continued this vital battle across multiple generations, refusing to surrender ground on this foundational truth. They understood that the stakes were nothing less than the integrity of the gospel itself. Irenaeus, writing in the second century against the Gnostic teachings that threatened to tear the church apart from within, insisted with an unwavering conviction that the same God who created the world also redeemed it. He saw clearly what the Gnostics denied: that creation and redemption are not opposing movements of different gods, but complementary works of the one true God who makes all things new. The Creator does not abandon His creation; He enters it, suffers for it, and ultimately restores it to its intended glory.

Tertullian took up the defense of the resurrection of the body itself against those who claimed that only the soul would be saved, that our physical forms were mere temporary prisons from which we would one day be liberated. He argued with characteristic force that such teaching gutted Christianity of its distinctive hope. The Christian gospel does not promise escape from embodiment but transformation of it. We do not hope for release from our bodies but for their resurrection and glorification.

Athanasius, in his profound theological writings, argued that the incarnation itself demonstrated God's unshakable commitment to redeeming the whole person, body and soul together, not soul alone. When the Word became flesh, God showed us that redemption is not extraction but transformation, not abandonment but renewal. The Son of God did not merely appear to have a body; He truly took on human nature in its fullness, sanctifying it by His presence and redeeming it by His sacrifice.

These were not abstract theological debates. They had immediate practical consequences. If the body is evil, why not abuse it with either extreme asceticism or unbridled license? If the physical world is evil, why steward it responsibly? If only the soul matters, why does injustice against bodies concern us? If escape from the material is the goal, why work to redeem culture or care for creation?

The church fathers understood that Genesis 1 answered these questions definitively. God made the physical world. He pronounced it good. He will redeem it, not destroy it. Our hope is not disembodied existence in a spiritual realm but resurrection to new physical life in a renewed creation.

Modern Gnosticism

The ancient heresy never truly died. It simply changed clothes, learned new vocabulary, and found a comfortable home in corners of the modern church where its presence often goes unrecognized. Walk into many evangelical churches today, churches that would vehemently deny any connection to ancient heresies, and you will hear unmistakable echoes of Gnostic dualism dressed in perfectly respectable Christian language, baptized with biblical terminology, yet fundamentally at odds with the worldview of Genesis 1.

Listen carefully to how we talk about salvation in our worship songs, our evangelistic appeals, our funeral services. How often do we reduce the fullness of redemption to "going to heaven when we die," as if the ultimate goal were escaping this fallen earth rather than eagerly anticipating its glorious renewal? How frequently do we speak of the "spiritual" as inherently superior to the "physical," creating a hierarchical dualism that Scripture never establishes and that Genesis 1 explicitly contradicts? How casually do we dismiss entire spheres of human activity, business, art, politics, agriculture, technology, as merely "secular" rather than recognizing with joy and conviction that all of life, every dimension of human existence, belongs to God and matters to Him?

I have heard well-meaning pastors, men I respect, brothers in Christ who love the Lord and His people, stand in their pulpits and tell their congregations with complete sincerity that "only souls matter" or that Christian concern for earthly justice and social issues somehow distracts from what they call "gospel priorities," as if the gospel didn't speak to every dimension of human existence. I have watched churches carefully cultivate what they call "spiritual disciplines," prayer, Bible study, Scripture memory, fasting, while simultaneously viewing the ordinary work of their members as something merely to be endured Monday through Friday, a necessary burden to bear until Sunday arrives again, rather than recognizing that work itself can and should be offered to God as an act of worship, as much a part of our calling as any church activity. I have seen believers, often those most zealous about spiritual matters, treat their own bodies with shocking neglect or even contempt, viewing them as mere vehicles for their souls, temporary housing to be discarded at death, rather than recognizing them as integral parts of who they are, fearfully and wonderfully made, destined not for destruction but for resurrection and eternal glory in the new creation.

This thinking contradicts Genesis 1 at every turn. If God declared the physical world good, how dare we call it inferior? If He made us as embodied creatures, who are we to despise our bodies? If He gave us work to do in His creation, stewarding and cultivating it, why do we view such work as less important than narrowly defined "ministry"?

The consequences extend beyond theology into practice. Christians influenced by this implicit Gnosticism often withdraw from cultural engagement, viewing art, politics, science, and business as worldly pursuits unworthy of serious Christian attention. They focus exclusively on evangelism and personal piety while ceding entire spheres of life to secular control. They fail to see that God cares about how we build cities, create beauty, pursue justice, and steward resources.

Others swing to the opposite extreme. Rejecting the physical world as hopelessly corrupt, they embrace a license to abuse it. If the body does not matter, why discipline appetites? If creation will burn anyway, why care for the environment? If only the soul counts, why does physical suffering concern us? This libertine version of Gnosticism produces different symptoms but stems from the same diseased root: failure to embrace creation's goodness.

The biblical alternative rejects both errors. Creation is good, though fallen. Our bodies matter, though mortal. Work in God's world carries significance, though it takes place in a world marred by sin. We are neither to worship creation nor despise it, neither to indulge the flesh without restraint nor to treat it as inherently evil.

The Goodness of Embodied Existence

Genesis teaches us that we are not souls trapped in bodies but embodied souls or ensouled bodies. The distinction matters. God did not create a soul named Adam and then regrettably house it in flesh. He formed man from the dust of the ground and breathed into his nostrils the breath of life, and man became a living creature (Genesis 2:7). Body and spirit together constitute the human personhood.

This unity shapes how we understand ourselves. When my body hurts, I hurt. When my body experiences physical pleasure, I experience it. My thoughts are mediated through a brain. My emotions involve biochemistry. My spiritual life is connected to my physical state. Trying to separate body from soul like pulling apart Siamese twins misses the point of how God designed us.

The resurrection proves this beyond doubt. Christ did not rise as a disembodied spirit. The tomb was empty. The body that died on the cross rose on the third day, transformed but still physical. He invited Thomas to touch His wounds. He ate fish with the disciples. He was not a ghost, but a resurrected man with a glorified body.

Paul makes the implications clear: "But our citizenship is in heaven, and from it we await a Savior, the Lord Jesus Christ, who will transform our lowly body to be like his glorious body, by the power that enables him even to subject all things to himself" (Philippians 3:20-21). Our hope is not in escaping our bodies but in their transformation. We do not look forward to disembodied existence but to resurrection life in a renewed creation.

This truth fundamentally transforms how we view our physical selves and our embodied existence in this world. Our bodies are not obstacles to godliness, hindrances to spiritual growth, or barriers we must overcome to reach God. Instead, they are instruments of worship, tools given by our Creator for His glory and our good. Paul states this with remarkable clarity: "I appeal to you therefore, brothers, by the mercies of God, to present your bodies as a living sacrifice, holy and acceptable to God, which is your spiritual worship" (Romans 12:1).

Notice the profound connection Paul draws here: presenting our bodies (these physical, tangible, flesh-and-blood realities) constitutes spiritual worship. The two dimensions are not opposed to each other, standing in tension or competition, but united in God's design. What we do with our bodies is inherently spiritual. Our physical actions express spiritual realities. The false dichotomy between body and spirit collapses under the weight of Scripture's integrated vision of human personhood.

What we do with our bodies matters. Sexual purity matters because our bodies belong to God. Stewardship of health matters because we are caretakers, not owners. Rest matters because God designed rhythms into creation. Physical pleasure, rightly ordered, matters because God created us to enjoy His good gifts.

I remember counseling a young woman who struggled with an eating disorder. She spoke of her body with contempt, viewing it as an enemy to be controlled and punished. As we worked through Scripture together, Genesis 1 kept surfacing. God made you as an embodied creature. He declared the design very good. Your body is not your enemy. It is part of who you are, and God loves the whole you, not just the parts you deem spiritual.

The transformation came slowly. She had to unlearn years of disordered thinking, much of it absorbed from a church culture that treated the body with suspicion. But as she grasped creation's goodness, something shifted. She began to see eating not as a necessary evil but as receiving God's provision with gratitude. She started to appreciate her body's strength and capability rather than fixating only on its appearance. She learned to present her body to God as an act of worship.

This is not a peripheral issue. It touches on how we approach sexuality, marriage, singleness, parenting, aging, disability, and death. If our bodies are good gifts from a good Creator, we neither worship them nor despise them. We steward them. We honor them. We use them in service to God and neighbor.

The Goodness of the Physical World

The affirmation of creation's goodness extends beyond our own bodies to the entire physical world. When God looked at the seas teeming with life, the skies filled with birds; the land covered with vegetation and animals; He declared it all good. Not merely useful. Not simply functional. Good in itself, reflecting His glory and is worthy of our attention.

This contradicts the utilitarian view that sees creation only as a resource to exploit. It also contradicts the romanticized view that elevates nature to an object of worship. The biblical position holds creation in proper tension: it is neither divine nor disposable. It is God's handiwork, made to reflect His glory and entrusted to our care.

The dominion mandate establishes our role: "And God blessed them. And God said to them, 'Be fruitful and multiply and fill the earth and subdue it, and have dominion over the fish of the sea and over the birds of the heavens and over every living thing that moves on the earth'" (Genesis 1:28). We are neither creation's slaves nor its tyrants but its stewards.

Dominion does not mean domination. The Hebrew word for dominion (*radah*) carries connotations of responsible rule, the kind exercised by a wise king who serves his people rather than exploiting them. We are to care for creation as God's representatives, managing it according to His purposes, cultivating its potential while preserving its goodness.

I learned this from an older farmer when I was in my teens, though he never framed it theologically. He farmed land in Indiana, and he took stewardship seriously. He rotated crops to preserve soil health. He maintained fence lines and waterways. He left buffer zones for wildlife. When I asked him why he went to such effort, he shrugged. "It's not mine," he said. "I'm just taking care of it for a while."

That simple statement captured a profound truth. We are caretakers, not owners. The earth is the Lord's and everything in it (Psalm 24:1). We answer to Him for how we manage what He has entrusted to us. This shapes everything from agricultural practices to urban planning, from resource extraction to waste disposal.

But stewardship is not the whole story. God also gave us His creation to enjoy. "And God said, 'Behold, I have given you every plant yielding seed that is on the face of all the earth, and every tree with seed in its fruit. You shall have them for food'" (Genesis 1:29). He provided food that nourishes but also delights. Apples taste sweet. Wine gladdens hearts. The variety of flavors and textures and aromas reflects a Creator who cares about pleasure, not just survival.

The same principle extends to beauty. God did not create a merely functional world. He made it glorious. Mountains pierce the sky with majesty. Oceans roll with power and rhythm. Forests display intricate complexity. Sunsets paint the sky with colors we can barely name. None of this was strictly necessary for human survival. It reveals a Creator who delights in beauty and invites us to share that delight.

This transforms how we engage with creation. We are meant to work in it, yes, cultivating and subduing. But also to enjoy it, receiving its gifts with gratitude. To study it, discovering the wisdom embedded in its patterns. To create from it, using its resources to make music and art and architecture. To rest in it, finding renewal in its rhythms and beauty.

When I stand on a mountain ridge and look across a valley stretching to the horizon, I am not merely observing geological formations. I am encountering the handiwork of God, and the proper response is worship. When I taste food prepared with skill and care, I am not merely consuming calories. I am receiving God's provision, and gratitude wells up naturally. When I watch the intricate dance of a bee pollinating flowers, I am not merely witnessing biology. I see divine wisdom on display.

This vision of creation's goodness calls us to reject both exploitation and idolatry. We do not ravage the earth for short-term gain, ignoring the long-term consequences. Neither do we elevate creation above the Creator, treating nature as sacred in itself rather than sacred because it reflects its Maker.

The Goodness of Work

Genesis 1 establishes work as part of God's good design, not a consequence of the Fall. Before sin entered the world, Adam received a commission: "The Lord God took the man and put him in the garden of Eden to work it and keep it" (Genesis 2:15). Work was part of life in paradise.

This contradicts the notion that work is purely a curse or that we should seek to minimize it as much as possible. God worked in creation. He worked six days and rested on the seventh, establishing a pattern for human life. We are made in His image, and part of that image-bearing involves creative, productive activity.

The curse did not introduce work but frustrated it. "Cursed is the ground because of you; in pain you shall eat of it all the days of your life; thorns and thistles it shall bring forth for you" (Genesis 3:17-18). Work became toilsome. It now involves frustration, failure, and futility. But work itself remained good, part of how we fulfill our purpose as image-bearers.

This theological truth transforms how we approach our daily vocations in the most fundamental way. Whether we spend our days farming the land or teaching in classrooms, building houses or writing complex code, caring for children in their formative years or managing businesses with all their complexities, we are engaged in work that genuinely matters to God. God does not measure the value of our labor by worldly standards of status or compensation. Not all work requires equal amounts of skill or training, and not all vocations carry equal weight in terms of their impact on eternity or their visibility in the public square. But all honest work; work done with integrity, diligence, and skill, contributes something meaningful to human flourishing and can legitimately be offered to God as an act of worship.

The apostle Paul makes this connection explicit and powerful in his letter to the Colossians: "Whatever you do, work heartily, as for the Lord and not for men, knowing that from the Lord you will receive the inheritance as your reward. You are serving the Lord Christ" (Colossians 3:23-24). Read these words carefully. Paul says, "whatever you do" not "whatever spiritual work you do" or "whatever ministry task you perform," but simply "whatever you do." The scope is universal, encompassing every legitimate human endeavor. The janitor who scrubs toilets at the end of a long night shift can perform that humble task as a genuine act of worship to the God who made him. The mechanic who repairs engines with skill and honesty serves God just as truly as the preacher who expounds Scripture. The teacher who patiently instructs students, explaining difficult concepts again and again, exercises a calling every bit as holy as any ordained ministry.

This does not mean all jobs are equally good or that we should never consider career changes. Some work truly is more significant than others. Some vocations offer greater opportunities to serve others and glorify God. Some employment situations are exploitative or degrading. But the fundamental goodness of work itself remains.

I spent years preaching and teaching at a seminary, preparing students for pastoral ministry. Important work, certainly. But I never forgot that members of my family who ranched, my dad serving in the Army, and my mother working in a factory, also mattered to God. The kingdom needs pastors, but it also needs ranchers and military personnel and factory workers. It needs people who design buildings and repair roads and cook meals and drive trucks. All of it, done well and offered to God, contributes to human flourishing and reflects the image of a working Creator.

The Reformation recovered this vision. Luther wrote about the doctrine of vocation, insisting that the milkmaid could glorify God as much as the monk. Calvin emphasized that all legitimate work served God's purposes. The Puritans taught that excellence in one's calling honored the Creator. They rejected the medieval hierarchy that elevated religious vocations over secular ones, recognizing that Scripture establishes no such distinction.

We need to recover this vision today. Too many Christians view their weekday work as merely a means to earn money for supporting "real ministry." They endure their jobs rather than embracing them as callings. They draw sharp lines between sacred and secular, failing to see that all of life belongs to God.

When we grasp that God pronounced His creation good, that He placed humanity in a garden to work it, that He Himself worked in creating and sustaining the world, our perspective shifts. Work is not a necessary evil. It is part of God's good design. The frustrations we experience come from the Fall, not from work itself. And one day, in the new creation, we will work again without those frustrations, exercising our gifts in perfect harmony with God's purposes.

The Goodness of Pleasure

If creation is good, then the pleasures it offers are also good when received rightly. This truth stands in tension with both hedonism and asceticism. Hedonism pursues pleasure as the ultimate good, making it an idol. Asceticism rejects pleasure as inherently suspect, treating God's gifts with contempt. Scripture charts a course between these errors.

God gave us taste buds that distinguish flavors. He created food of remarkable variety. He established marriage and declared sexual intimacy within that covenant to be good. He made us capable of appreciating beauty, enjoying music, delighting in friendship. None of this was strictly necessary for survival. It reveals a generous Creator who cares about our joy.

The Psalms celebrate this generosity: "You cause the grass to grow for the livestock and plants for man to cultivate, that he may bring forth food from the earth and wine to gladden the heart of man, oil to make his face shine and bread to strengthen man's heart" (Psalm 104:14-15). Notice the progression. Food does more than sustain life. Wine gladdens hearts. Oil makes faces shine. God provides not just for our needs but for our delight.

Ecclesiastes, often misread as pessimistic, actually affirms the goodness of enjoying God's gifts: "Behold, what I have seen to be good and fitting is to eat and drink and find enjoyment in all the toil with which one toils under the sun the few days of his life that God has given him, for this is his lot" (Ecclesiastes 5:18). The Preacher does not denounce pleasure but locates it properly as a gift from God to be received with gratitude.

Paul addresses this directly when confronting false teachers who forbade marriage and demanded abstinence from certain foods: "For everything created by God is good, and nothing is to be rejected if it is received with thanksgiving, for it is made holy by the word of God and prayer" (1 Timothy 4:4-5). The key phrase: "if it is received with thanksgiving." Pleasure becomes sin when we pursue it as an end in itself, when we take without giving thanks, when we indulge without restraint.

This framework helps navigate difficult questions. Is it wrong to enjoy good food? Of course not, provided we do not make gluttony our god. Is it wrong to appreciate fine wine? Not according to Scripture, though drunkenness is sin and some must abstain entirely for reasons of conscience or weakness. Is it wrong to delight in sexual intimacy with one's spouse? Absolutely not. The entire Song of Solomon celebrates such delight.

The guardrails that Scripture establishes for the proper enjoyment of pleasure are both clear and necessary. First and foremost, we receive pleasure as a gift from God's gracious hand, not as a right we can demand or an entitlement we deserve. The moment we begin to view pleasure as something owed to us, we have already stepped onto dangerous ground. Every good thing we enjoy comes undeserved from the Father of lights. "Every good gift and every perfect gift is from above, coming down from the Father of lights, with whom there is no variation or shadow due to change." (James 1:17).

Second, we pursue pleasure only within the boundaries that God Himself has established in His Word. These boundaries are not arbitrary restrictions imposed by a cosmic killjoy but wise limits set by a loving Father who knows what will truly satisfy and what will ultimately destroy. The same God who created wine also forbade drunkenness. The same God who designed sexual intimacy also reserved it for the covenant of marriage. His commands are not meant to rob us of joy but to protect the very pleasure He intends for us to experience.

Third, we must hold all earthly pleasures with open hands, never allowing any of them to become ultimate in our affections. The moment any created thing becomes more important to us than the Creator, we have crossed the line into idolatry. We enjoy, but we do not cling. We delight, but we do not depend. We receive gladly, but we would surrender willingly if God asked it of us.

Fourth, and perhaps most importantly, we thank the Giver continually, recognizing that every good and perfect gift comes down from above. Gratitude is the antidote to entitlement, the guard against presumption, and the pathway to proper enjoyment. When we pause to thank God for the pleasures He provides, we acknowledge their source and remember that they are gifts of grace, not commodities we purchase with our own goodness or achievements.

I have watched Christians make themselves miserable with needless restrictions, treating every pleasure with suspicion.

They cannot enjoy a good meal without guilt. They view laughter as frivolous. They approach marriage with duty but not delight. They have imbibed a false spirituality that equates godliness with joylessness.

This is not biblical Christianity. Jesus attended wedding feasts and was accused of being a glutton and a drunkard because He ate and drank with sinners. He turned water into wine, and not cheap wine but the good stuff. He enjoyed friendships and shared meals. He wept and laughed and felt the full range of human emotions. And He did it all without sin.

The problem is not pleasure but disordered pleasure. When we pursue it outside God's boundaries, it becomes sin. When we make it ultimate, it becomes idolatry. When we indulge without restraint, it becomes destructive. But when we receive it as a gift from our Creator, enjoying it within proper limits while thanking Him for His generosity, pleasure becomes an act of worship.

Creation's Witness to the Gospel

The goodness of creation is not merely a doctrine to affirm but a truth that shapes how we understand the gospel itself. Redemption is not escape from the physical world but its restoration. Salvation is not extraction of souls from matter but the renewal of all things.

Paul's vision in Romans 8 captures this: "For the creation waits with eager longing for the revealing of the sons of God. For the creation was subjected to futility, not willingly, but because of him who subjected it, in hope that the creation itself will be set free from its bondage to corruption and obtain the freedom of the glory of the children of God" (Romans 8:19-21).

The entire created order groans under the unbearable weight of the curse that humanity's rebellion brought into the world. The futility and corruption we observe on every side, the devastating natural disasters that leave destruction in their wake, the relentless diseases that ravage our bodies, the inexorable decay that touches everything from our physical frames to the structures we build; these are emphatically not part of God's original design for His world. They are instead the tragic and unavoidable consequences of humanity's fall into sin, evidence of a world marred and wounded by our rebellion against our Creator. Yet even in the midst of this cosmic groaning, hope remains alive and unshakeable. The very same creation that was subjected to futility against its will, bound to serve purposes contrary to its original design, will one day be gloriously set free from its bondage to corruption. The redemption that Christ accomplished through His death and resurrection extends far beyond individual human souls, it reaches to the entire cosmos, encompassing all that God originally declared "very good."

This means the goal of the gospel is not abandoning earth for heaven but heaven coming to earth. John's vision confirms this: "Then I saw a new heaven and a new earth, for the first heaven and the first earth had passed away, and the sea was no more. And I saw the holy city, new Jerusalem, coming down out of heaven from God, prepared as a bride adorned for her husband" (Revelation 21:1-2).

Notice the direction of movement. The city comes down from heaven to earth. God's dwelling place is with man. The new creation does not replace the old in the sense of total discontinuity but renews it, purging it of sin and corruption while preserving continuity with what God originally made.

This matters in how we live now. If our hope were escaping Earth, we might view our present work as pointless. Why care for creation if it will burn? Why pursue justice if this world is temporary? Why develop culture if only souls matter?

But if our hope is the renewal of all things, everything changes. The work we do now, the culture we build, the beauty we create, the justice we pursue, all of it can have lasting significance. Not because of our efforts to save the world; Christ alone does that; but because the new creation will be a restoration and consummation of this one, not its replacement.

Paul hints at this: "Therefore, my beloved brothers, be steadfast, immovable, always abounding in the work of the Lord, knowing that in the Lord your labor is not in vain" (1 Corinthians 15:58). He wrote this immediately after teaching about the resurrection. Our work is not in vain. It has purpose and meaning because we serve a God who redeems and restores, not merely destroys and replaces.

I saw this truth dawn on a student who had grown up with a rapture theology that emphasized escaping earth. He had viewed his work as a civil engineer as merely a paycheck, something to endure while waiting for the real life to begin. As we studied the Scripture's teaching on new creation, something shifted in his perspective. He began to see his work designing infrastructure as contributing to human flourishing, as stewarding creation, as reflecting God's image. His job did not change, but his understanding of its significance did.

This is what Genesis 1 gives us. A vision of a good creation made by a good God, marred by sin but destined for renewal. A framework for understanding our bodies, our work, our pleasures, and our purpose. A foundation for engaging the world as stewards rather than escapists, as cultivators rather than consumers, as image-bearers who reflect a Creator who called His work very good.

Living in Light of Creation's Goodness

How then do we live? If we truly believe that God made the physical world and declared it good, what difference does it make?

First, we receive creation with gratitude, cultivating hearts that recognize the divine fingerprints on everything we touch, taste, and experience. Every meal becomes an opportunity for thanksgiving, a moment to pause before a plate of food and remember that the God who feeds the sparrows has provided for our needs. Every sunset, painting the sky in colors no human artist could reproduce, becomes an invitation to worship the one who commanded light to shine out of darkness. Every good gift we enjoy, from the embrace of a friend to the satisfaction of meaningful work to the simple pleasure of clean water or shelter: becomes a reminder of the Giver, whose character is woven into His creation.

We do not take creation for granted, treating it as though these blessings somehow emerged from random processes or our own cleverness. Nor do we treat it with contempt, as though the physical world were inherently corrupt or unworthy of our appreciation. Instead, we receive it all as from the hand of a generous Father who provides abundantly for our needs and our joy, who delights to give good gifts to His children, whose care extends to every detail of our existence. This posture of gratitude transforms the ordinary into the sacred, the routine into the remarkable, the mundane into the meaningful.

Second, we steward creation responsibly, treating every aspect of the physical world entrusted to us as a sacred charge rather than an exploitable resource. This stewardship begins with the most intimate creation we've been given, our own bodies. We care for these fearfully and wonderfully made temples, recognizing them not as our own possession to abuse or neglect, but as gifts from God, designed for His glory and our flourishing. We nourish them, rest them, and use them in service to others, refusing both the idolatry that makes the body everything and the gnosticism that treats it as nothing.

Beyond our bodies, we manage the resources God has placed in our hands with wisdom that looks beyond our own immediate comfort or convenience. We think generationally, considering not merely what serves us today but what will bless our children and their children after them. We use what we have, not with the wastefulness that assumes abundance will never end, nor with the anxiety that hoards as though God has stopped being faithful, but with the careful consideration of those who recognize that every resource is a trust from the Lord of all creation.

We engage our vocations, whether we labor with our hands or our minds, whether we work in offices or factories, hospitals or homes; as callings from God rather than mere employment. Whatever we do, we work heartily, as for the Lord and not for men, knowing that from the Lord we will receive the inheritance as our reward. Our daily labor, mundane as it may seem, becomes an offering of worship when done for the glory of God and the good of our neighbor. We create beauty and pursue excellence in all our endeavors, reflecting the image of a Creator who looked upon His finished work and declared it not merely adequate but very good; a God who did all things well and calls us to do likewise.

Third, we enjoy creation freely and without reservation. Within the boundaries God establishes for our flourishing, boundaries that are never arbitrary restrictions but loving provisions, we delight in His good gifts without the guilt that masquerades as piety or the shame that confuses suspicion with sanctity. We eat good food with genuine thanksgiving, recognizing that every meal is a gift from the One who gives us all things richly to enjoy, who provides us with daily bread and satisfies our hunger with good things. We appreciate beauty with childlike wonder, allowing ourselves to be moved by a sunset's colors, a symphony's harmonies, a landscape's grandeur, a poem's precision, knowing that all true beauty points beyond itself to the source of all loveliness. We pursue legitimate pleasures with unencumbered joy, understanding that God is not a cosmic killjoy but a generous Father who loads us with benefits and crowns our year with His bounty. We refuse to let false spirituality, that grim counterfeit that mistakes joylessness for holiness and treats God's good gifts with suspicion rather than gratitude, rob us of the very things God intends for our good and His glory. We reject the notion that somehow denying ourselves the proper enjoyment of creation makes us more spiritual, remembering instead that it is the goodness of God that leads us to repentance, and that every good gift and every perfect gift comes down from the Father of lights.

Fourth, we hold creation with open hands rather than clenched fists, maintaining that delicate balance between proper enjoyment and inappropriate attachment. We never allow God's good gifts to become our functional gods, those replacement deities that promise what only the Creator can deliver. We refuse to let the blessings eclipse the Blesser or permit the gifts to obscure the Giver. We enjoy creation's pleasures without idolizing them, recognizing that the moment our hearts begin to need what they should merely appreciate, we have crossed from gratitude into bondage. We use the world's resources and delights without being enslaved by them, maintaining our freedom as children of God rather than becoming servants of things that cannot satisfy the deepest longings of the human heart. We appreciate beauty, comfort, pleasure, and provision without worshiping them, keeping our wonder directed toward the One from whom all good things flow rather than allowing our affections to terminate on the gifts themselves. We remember constantly, for we need this reminder daily, perhaps hourly, that the greatest gift is not creation itself, magnificent though it is, but the Creator who spoke it into being. The supreme blessing is not the provisions He supplies but the relationship with the One who blesses, not the benefits He bestows but knowing Him who is the source of every benefit. This is the wisdom that keeps joy from curdling into addiction, that preserves gratitude from souring into greed, that maintains the proper order of loves that Augustine wrote about with such clarity.

Fifth, we long with an aching, persistent hope for creation's ultimate renewal and restoration. We recognize with clear eyes and sobered hearts that what we see now all around us is simultaneously glorious and fallen, achingly beautiful yet heartbreakingly broken. The same world that displays God's fingerprints in every sunset and snowflake also bears the scars of sin in every cemetery and cancer ward. We see both realities with unflinching honesty, neither denying creation's persistent beauty nor minimizing its deep brokenness. We groan with creation itself, as Paul describes in Romans 8, waiting eagerly and expectantly for the redemption of our bodies and the restoration of all things to their intended glory. This groaning is not despair but anticipation, not resignation but hope straining forward toward certain consummation. We work toward that coming renewal in whatever ways we can, large and small, knowing with unshakeable confidence that our labor in the Lord is never in vain, that every act of faithful stewardship and redemptive cultivation participates in some mysterious way in God's ultimate purposes for His world. We plant gardens and clean rivers, create beauty and pursue justice, care for bodies and renew communities, all as signposts pointing toward the day when God makes all things new.

This is the vision Genesis 1 sets before us. A good creation made by a good God, given to image-bearers who are called to steward it, enjoy it, and long for its final restoration. Not an escape from the physical but its redemption. Not the rejection of matter but its renewal. Not the abandonment of this world but its transformation into a dwelling place for God Himself.

And it all begins with those simple, profound words: "And God saw that it was good."

Very good.

Chapter Three

The Image of God: Human Dignity and Design

I still remember the moment it hit me, really hit me, during my first deployment. We had been in country for three weeks, living in conditions that stripped away every pretense of civilization. Mud, blood, fear, exhaustion. The kind of grinding reality that reduces human existence to its most basic elements. And then I saw it: a young Marine, probably nineteen years old, sharing his last protein bar with a local child whose hollow eyes spoke of hunger I had never known growing up in America. The Marine didn't speak Arabic. The child didn't speak English. But something passed between them in that moment, something that transcended language and culture and the chaos of war.

I thought about that moment years later, sitting in a seminary classroom, when a student asked me why human dignity matters if we are just highly evolved animals. The question annoyed me at first, seemed almost willfully obtuse. But then I realized he had never seen what I had seen. He had never watched a man lay down his life for his friends. He had never witnessed the stubborn persistence of human compassion in contexts where pure evolutionary self-interest would dictate abandonment and flight. He had never encountered that mysterious something that sets humanity apart from every other creature God made.

Genesis 1:26-27 provides the answer: "Then God said, 'Let us make man in our image, after our likeness. And let them have dominion over the fish of the sea and over the birds of the heavens and over the livestock and over all the earth and over every creeping thing that creeps on the earth.' So God created man in his own image, in the image of God he created him; male and female he created them."

These verses contain depths that theologians have explored for millennia without exhausting. They answer the most fundamental questions of human existence: Who are we? Why are we here? What makes us different? What is our purpose? The answers provided in these two verses undergird every doctrine of human dignity, every system of justice, every ethical framework that takes human life seriously. Strip away the image of God, and you strip away the very foundation of human worth. Remove this truth from the public consciousness, and you unleash consequences that every age that has forgotten it has discovered to its horror.

What the Image Is Not

Before we can properly understand what it means to bear God's image, we must clear away some persistent misconceptions that cloud our thinking and lead us into error. These false understandings, some ancient and some modern, some crude and some sophisticated, all miss the mark in ways that matter deeply for how we live and think.

First, the image of God is not a physical resemblance. God is spirit, as Jesus makes clear in John 4:24: "God is spirit, and those who worship him must worship in spirit and truth." He does not have a body composed of matter and occupying space. When Scripture speaks of God's eyes or hands or face, it employs anthropomorphic language to make transcendent realities comprehensible to finite minds. The fact that we have bodies while God does not mean that whatever imaging God entails, it cannot primarily be about physical form. This matters enormously when we consider questions of disability, disfigurement, aging, and death. A person in a coma bears God's image no less than an Olympic athlete. A child with severe physical disabilities images God just as truly as the most beautiful supermodel. The paralyzed veteran carries the divine image as fully as the Marine in peak physical condition. Physical capacity or appearance cannot be the essence of what makes us image-bearers, though our bodies matter in ways we will explore.

Second, the image is not simply rationality or intelligence, though these certainly participate in what it means to be human. This is a view that goes back to some of the church fathers and has enjoyed considerable popularity through the centuries. The idea seems plausible at first glance. Humans reason, and animals do not, at least not in the same way. We engage in abstract thought, contemplate philosophy, construct arguments, and pursue science. Surely this is what sets us apart and constitutes the image. But this view stumbles when confronted with concrete realities. What about a person with severe cognitive disabilities? What about the infant? What about the elderly person suffering from advanced dementia? Do they bear God's image to a lesser degree? Does their human dignity diminish in proportion to their intellectual capacity? Any view that makes the image of God dependent on intellectual function leads inevitably to horrifying conclusions that the church has rightly rejected. A simpler, more human child with Down syndrome bears the divine image just as fully as the most brilliant philosopher. To suggest otherwise is not merely a theological error but a monstrous assault on human dignity.

Third, the image is not earned through moral achievement or spiritual growth, nor can it be lost or diminished through sin and failure. We do not become image-bearers by practicing virtue, pursuing holiness, or accumulating spiritual disciplines. Neither do we lose or damage the image through wickedness, rebellion, or degradation. This matters profoundly in our therapeutic age that constantly measures worth by performance and achievement, that assigns value based on productivity and moral conduct, that ranks human beings on sliding scales of dignity according to their contributions to society or their adherence to ethical standards.

Consider the implications: The serial killer on death row, awaiting execution for unspeakable crimes, bears God's image no less than the missionary who has devoted fifty years to serving the poor in some distant corner of the world. The prostitute trapped in addiction, selling her body in dark corners of the city, images God just as truly as the pastor who has walked faithfully with Christ for decades, preaching the gospel and shepherding God's flock with integrity. The corrupt politician who has betrayed the public trust for personal gain bears the divine image just as fully as the philanthropist who has given away millions to feed the hungry and house the homeless.

This is a hard truth, one that grates against our intuitive sense of justice, our deeply ingrained feeling that surely the righteous deserve more dignity than the wicked, that surely moral character ought to make some difference in how we assess human worth. Our instincts rebel against the notion that the virtuous and the vicious stand on equal ground in this one fundamental respect. Yet Scripture knows nothing of gradations of image-bearing based on moral performance or spiritual maturity. The image of God establishes an intrinsic worth that no amount of sin can erase and no amount of righteousness can augment. It is not a quality we possess in varying degrees but a status we hold absolutely.

We bear the image because God made us that way, not because we earned it, not because we deserve it, not because we've achieved some threshold of moral or spiritual development. We retain the image even in our fallenness, even in our rebellion, even in our most degraded state when we have descended to depths of wickedness that shock the conscience and horrify the imagination. This is precisely why murder deserves capital punishment, as Genesis 9:6 makes unmistakably clear: "Whoever sheds the blood of man, by man shall his blood be shed, for God made man in his own image." The prohibition against murder and the severe penalty prescribed for it rest entirely on the reality that even the murder victim's life possesses infinite worth because it bears God's image, not because of what that person achieved, not because of their moral character, not because of their contribution to society, but simply because they were human, made in the image of their Creator.

The Relational Dimension

Notice the language Genesis 1:26 employs: "Let us make man in our image, after our likeness." The plural pronouns arrest our attention and have generated considerable theological discussion. Some have seen here a hint of the Trinity, a suggestion that the one God exists eternally as a communion of persons, Father, Son, and Holy Spirit. Others have proposed that God addresses His heavenly court, speaking to the angels who surround His throne. Still others suggest the plural expresses divine deliberation, God speaking to Himself about this momentous creative act.

Without entering too deeply into this debate, which has occupied better theologians than I am, we can observe something significant. However we understand the plural, it suggests that God Himself exists in relationship. The God who makes us for relationship is Himself relational in His very being. And this matters for understanding what it means to bear His image.

Genesis 1:27 reinforces this relational dimension: "So God created man in his own image, in the image of God he created him; male and female he created them." The text moves seamlessly from singular to plural, from "him" to "them." This is not careless grammar but profound theology. Humanity as image-bearer is not first and foremost individual but corporate, not solitary but communal. We bear the image not in isolation but in relationship.

This is why Genesis 2 elaborates on what Genesis 1 declares. After creating Adam, God pronounces something "not good" for the first time in creation: "It is not good that the man should be alone" (Genesis 2:18). The solution is not simply a helper but a complement, someone who corresponds to him, someone who is "bone of my bones and flesh of my flesh" (Genesis 2:23). The creation of male and female as distinct yet united, different yet complementary, establishes the fundamental pattern of human relationality.

I have watched my wife battle cancer. I have held her hand through chemotherapy sessions that left her exhausted and sick. I have prayed for her through dark nights when the fear threatened to overwhelm us both. And I can testify that in those moments, we were not two isolated individuals who happened to be in proximity. We were one flesh, bearing each other's burdens, sharing each other's sorrows, finding strength in a union that marriage created but that points to something deeper about how God designed humanity.

The relational dimension of the image extends beyond marriage. It encompasses all human connection, all genuine community, all the ways we live in relationship rather than isolation. When Scripture speaks of the church as the body of Christ with many members, when it commands us to love one another and bear one another's burdens, when it presents heaven as a great multitude that no one can number from every nation and tribe and people and language, it builds on this foundational truth: we are made for relationship because we are made in the image of a relational God.

This has profound implications for how we think about personhood and community. The radical individualism of Western culture, which treats persons as autonomous units pursuing self-defined purposes, contradicts the biblical vision of humanity. We are not meant to be alone. We are not designed for isolation. We are not complete in ourselves. The person who says, "I don't need anyone" is not expressing strength but denying their own created nature. The vision of the self-made individual who owes nothing to anyone and needs no one is not biblical anthropology but anti-biblical fantasy.

Dominion and Stewardship

The creation mandate includes a commission: "And let them have dominion over the fish of the sea and over the birds of the heavens and over the livestock and over all the earth and over every creeping thing that creeps on the earth" (Genesis 1:26). This dominion is reiterated in verse 28: "And God blessed them. And God said to them, 'Be fruitful and multiply and fill the earth and subdue it, and have dominion over the fish of the sea and over the birds of the heavens and over every living thing that moves on the earth.'"

These verses have been profoundly misunderstood and tragically misused throughout history to justify environmental destruction, reckless exploitation, and the systematic abuse of the natural world entrusted to our care. Critics of Christianity, both within academia and the broader culture, have not hesitated to blame biblical religion for the ecological crisis facing our planet, arguing with considerable passion that the dominion mandate gave humanity an unchecked license to rape and pillage creation without any meaningful restraint or accountability. They point to centuries of environmental degradation and claim that Genesis bears responsibility for it all. Even some Christians, who should know better, have treated the earth as essentially disposable, viewing it as nothing more than a temporary platform for human activity, a stage that will eventually burn in the final conflagration anyway, so why invest energy in careful stewardship of something destined for destruction? This attitude, sadly, has found expression both in careless individual practices and in broader cultural indifference to creation care.

But this distorted interpretation fundamentally misrepresents what dominion actually means in the Genesis narrative.

The dominion that humanity receives is delegated authority under God's sovereign oversight, not absolute ownership that answers to no higher power. We rule creation as God's appointed vice-regents, His chosen representatives on earth who are accountable to Him for how we exercise the authority He has entrusted to us, not as autonomous sovereigns who can do whatever we please without consequence or accountability. Our dominion over creation is explicitly meant to reflect and mirror God's own rule, which is consistently characterized throughout Scripture by wisdom, attentive care, generous provision, and the sustaining power that holds all things together. Just as God rules creation by continually upholding it through His Word and ordering it purposefully toward the ends He has established, so humanity is called to exercise dominion by thoughtfully cultivating creation's potential and faithfully directing it toward the flourishing that brings glory to its Creator.

Genesis 2:15 clarifies the nature of this dominion: "The Lord God took the man and put him in the garden of Eden to work it and keep it." The Hebrew words translated "work" and "keep" convey cultivation and protection. Adam is not placed in the garden to exploit it but to develop its potential and guard it from harm. His dominion is gardening, the careful tending that brings creation to fuller expression of its God-given capacities.

I learned something about dominion during my years of teaching. A good teacher exercises authority over a classroom, but that authority serves the students' growth and development. A teacher who uses authority to crush students, to humiliate them, to make them feel small, has perverted the very nature of teaching authority. But a teacher who guides, challenges, cultivates potential, protects from harm, and delights in students' flourishing exercises authority the way God intended. The authority exists for the sake of those under it.

This is the pattern for human dominion over creation. We exercise authority over the earth and its creatures not as tyrants but as servants, wielding power for their good and God's glory, not merely for our selfish consumption or short-sighted convenience. We develop the creation's resources with wisdom and forethought rather than squandering them wastefully in our generation. We protect vulnerable species and preserve biodiversity rather than carelessly driving God's creatures to extinction through greed or negligence. We cultivate beauty, order, and harmony as well as mere productivity and profit. We think not only of present convenience or immediate financial gain but consider how our choices will affect our children and our children's children. We receive creation as a sacred trust to be faithfully stewarded with care and passed on in better condition than we found it, not as a possession to be consumed without restraint or responsibility.

This vision of dominion is neither ruthless exploitation nor misguided idolatry. It is not the rapacious strip-mining mentality that tears resources violently from the earth without a moment's thought for the consequences tomorrow will bring. Neither is it the fashionable neo-pagan worship of nature that elevates creation above humanity and treats all human activity as inherently destructive, as if our very presence corrupts what would otherwise remain pristine. It is instead the biblical middle way that carefully affirms both creation's inherent goodness as God's handiwork and humanity's unique, divinely ordained calling to rule creation under God's sovereign authority for creation's flourishing and God's eternal glory. We are neither parasites upon the earth nor mere animals within it, but vice-regents appointed by the Creator Himself to tend His cosmic garden with the same careful attention He demonstrates toward all His works.

Creativity and Culture-Making

Part of bearing God's image involves creativity, the remarkable capacity to bring into existence that which did not previously exist. God is the supreme Creator who spoke the cosmos into existence, whose powerful word called forth light from darkness, order from chaos, beauty from emptiness. When He makes humanity in His image, He creates creatures who themselves create, who share in this divine characteristic of bringing forth the new, the beautiful, the useful, the meaningful. We do not create *ex nihilo*, out of nothing, as God does in His absolute sovereignty and unlimited power. We cannot simply speak and watch mountains rise at our command or galaxies burst forth at our word. We always work with materials and possibilities God has already provided, with the clay He formed, the wood He grew, the metals He embedded in the earth, the sounds He wove into the fabric of reality, the colors He painted across creation. But within those limits, and they are genuine limits we must humbly acknowledge, we genuinely create new things that did not exist before, bringing forth innovations and expressions that add to the richness of human experience and the glory of God's world.

This remarkable capacity for creativity manifests in countless ways across every culture and every generation of human history. We compose music that stirs the soul and paint pictures that capture beauty the eye alone cannot fully comprehend. We write novels that illuminate the human condition and perform plays that dramatize eternal truths about virtue and vice, love and loss, redemption and ruin. We design buildings that provide shelter while inspiring wonder and engineer machines that multiply human capacity and extend our reach. We develop recipes that transform simple ingredients into experiences of delight and craft furniture that combines utility with elegance. We formulate theories that explain the patterns woven into creation and conduct experiments that unveil the hidden mechanisms by which God sustains the universe. All of this is fundamentally human activity that flows naturally and inevitably from our nature as image-bearers of the Creator, expressions of the divine imprint that marks us as unlike any other creature God has made.

Genesis 4 presents Cain's descendants developing civilization. Jabal becomes the father of those who dwell in tents and have livestock. Jubal is the father of all those who play the lyre and pipe. Tubal-cain forges instruments of bronze and iron. Even in a line descended from the first murderer, even in a family under judgment, the image of God persists in cultural development and technological advancement. Humanity cannot help but create because we bear the image of the Creator.

This has enormous implications for how we think about work, art, science, and culture. All honest labor that produces genuine goods participates in the creation mandate. The farmer cultivating crops; the engineer designing bridges; the musician composing symphonies; the teacher shaping minds; the chef preparing meals; the programmer writing code; all of these image God's creative activity in their respective spheres. There is no sacred-secular divide that makes ministry work inherently more valuable than other vocations. The missionary translator and the software developer both fulfill the cultural mandate in their distinct callings.

I have known Marines who could strip and reassemble a rifle blindfolded. I have known mechanics who could diagnose an engine problem by sound alone. I have known cooks who could feed two hundred men with limited ingredients and equipment. These skills, developed through practice and experience, reflect the image of God no less than the theological treatises I helped students write. God is glorified when His image-bearers exercise the capacities He built into them, whether in combat, in kitchens, in classrooms, or in churches.

This means we need not be suspicious of culture or creativity. We need not treat art as dangerous or science as threatening. We need not see human achievement as competition with God's glory. Rightly understood and rightly ordered, human creativity enhances God's glory by displaying the capacities He endowed His image-bearers with. When we marvel at a Gothic cathedral, when we stand in awe before a masterpiece of painting, when we benefit from medical advances or technological innovations, we are witnessing what creatures made in God's image can accomplish when they exercise their creative capacities.

Of course, we must acknowledge a sobering reality: sin distorts, corrupts, and twists human creativity in profound and devastating ways. The same ingenuity that develops vaccines to save millions also engineers weapons capable of unimaginable destruction. The same aesthetic sensibility that produces breathtaking poetry and soul-stirring music also creates pornography that degrades the image of God in both its subjects and consumers. The same technological prowess that brings clean water to villages and enables global communication also generates environmental catastrophes that mar God's creation. The same architectural genius that builds cathedrals pointing heavenward also constructs monuments to human pride and temples to false gods.

This paradox reveals a fundamental truth about our condition: the image of God in humanity remains real and recognizable, yet it is undeniably fallen, marred by sin's corrupting influence. It persists across cultures and throughout history, evident in every human achievement and creative endeavor, yet it is simultaneously perverted, bent toward ends that dishonor rather than glorify our Creator. We retain the God-given capacity to imagine, to innovate, to build and create, but we often, perhaps more often than not—direct these capacities toward destructive rather than constructive ends, toward self-glorification rather than God's glory, toward temporal pleasures rather than eternal purposes.

This is precisely why redemption matters so profoundly, why the gospel is not merely about individual souls escaping hell but about Christ restoring all things. The Redeemer does not abolish human creativity as though it were inherently evil; rather; He redirects it toward its proper end. He does not destroy our cultural capacities as corrupted beyond repair; instead; He sanctifies them, cleansing and consecrating them for holy purposes. He does not eliminate our work as though labor itself were the curse; rather; He reorients it, pointing it once again toward the purposes for which God originally designed it, the cultivation and care of His creation, the flourishing of human communities, and ultimately the display of His manifold wisdom and glory.

Moral Capacity and Responsibility

Bearing God's image includes moral awareness and accountability. Unlike animals, which act according to instinct and conditioning, humans possess a conscience, that inner witness that commends what is right and condemns what is wrong.

We are moral agents, capable of distinguishing good from evil, responsible for our choices, accountable for our actions.

This moral dimension of the image appears even before the fall. God gives Adam a command: "You may surely eat of every tree of the garden, but of the tree of the knowledge of good and evil you shall not eat, for in the day that you eat of it you shall surely die" (Genesis 2:16-17). The prohibition assumes Adam's capacity to understand moral instruction, to choose obedience or disobedience, and to bear responsibility for his decision. God does not command the animals in this way because they lack the moral capacity to respond.

This moral dimension of the image persists even after the fall. Romans 2:14-15 describes how Gentiles who do not have the law still show that the work of the law is written on their hearts, their conscience bearing witness and their conflicting thoughts accusing or even excusing them. Every human being, regardless of whether they know Scripture or acknowledge God, possesses this basic moral awareness. They may suppress it, distort it, rationalize away its demands, but they cannot entirely eliminate it.

I have watched hardened criminals struggle with guilt over crimes committed decades earlier. I have seen soldiers haunted by actions taken in the fog of war. I have counseled men who insisted they felt no remorse but whose sleepless nights and self-destructive behaviors testified to a conscience they claimed not to possess. The moral dimension of the image is stubborn and persistent. We can deny it but not destroy it, ignore it but not erase it.

This moral capacity grounds human responsibility and makes justice possible. We hold people accountable for their actions because they possess the capacity to choose. We distinguish between accidents and crimes because intent matters for beings with moral agency. We establish laws and courts and punishments because humans are responsible agents who can and must answer for what they do.

This has profound implications for how we think about justice and mercy, punishment and rehabilitation, law and grace. A purely deterministic view of human behavior that treats persons as products of genetics and environment eliminates moral responsibility. If people cannot help what they do, if their actions are merely the inevitable results of factors beyond their control, then punishment makes no sense, and neither does praise. We would no more hold a person accountable for murder than we would punish a rock for falling on someone's head.

But this is not the biblical vision of humanity. We are moral agents, created with the capacity to choose, endowed with a conscience, responsible for our decisions. This does not mean we have libertarian free will in the philosophical sense. Reformed theology rightly insists that sin has so comprehensively corrupted human nature that, apart from divine grace, we inevitably and freely choose what our fallen nature inclines us toward, and that inclination is always, without exception, away from God and his righteous standards. This is what theologians mean when they speak of total depravity: not that we are as evil as we could possibly be, but that sin has affected every part of our being, mind, will, affections, conscience. The corruption runs deep, touching everything we think, desire, and do.

Yet even in this fallen state, even with natures twisted by rebellion and hearts bent away from their Creator, humanity retains sufficient moral capacity to be held fully accountable for sin. This is crucial. We are not mere puppets jerked about by forces beyond our control, nor are we animals acting purely on instinct without moral consciousness. We choose what we desire, yes—our choices flow from our desires, from the inclinations of our hearts. But we are genuinely responsible both for the choice itself and for the desire that gave birth to it. The alcoholic who takes another drink chooses to do so, and bears responsibility for that choice, even though his desire for the drink has become a powerful force in his life. The adulterer who betrays his marriage vows chooses to commit adultery, and cannot escape accountability by pointing to the strength of his lustful desires.

The Persistence of the Image After the Fall

Genesis 3 records humanity's catastrophic rebellion against God. Adam and Eve, given every blessing and only one prohibition, chose to grasp at autonomy rather than live under God's authority. The consequences were immediate and devastating. Shame replaced innocence. Fear displaced intimacy. Blame supplanted responsibility. Death entered creation. The whole human race fell in Adam, inheriting both his guilt and his corrupted nature.

But notice what the fall did not do. It did not erase the image of God from humanity. Genesis 5:1-3 is instructive: "This is the book of the generations of Adam. When God created man, he made him in the likeness of God. Male and female he created them, and he blessed them and named them Man when they were created. When Adam had lived 130 years, he fathered a son in his own likeness, after his image, and named him Seth." Adam, after the fall, still bears God's image and passes it to Seth. The image persists even in fallen humanity.

Genesis 9:6 reinforces this point in the context of judgment after the flood: "Whoever sheds the blood of man, by man shall his blood be shed, for God made man in his own image." This command comes after the fall, after sin has thoroughly corrupted humanity, after God has judged the world with water. Yet the prohibition against murder still rests on humanity's status as image-bearers. Even fallen humans, even wicked humans, even humans deserving of judgment, still bear God's image in a way that makes their lives sacred.

James 3:9 captures this same enduring reality in a New Testament context, and it does so in a way that should arrest our attention every time we consider speaking ill of another person: "With it we bless our Lord and Father, and with it we curse people who are made in the likeness of God." Notice carefully what James is addressing here. He is not restricting his observation to pre-fall humanity living in Edenic innocence, nor is he speaking exclusively about regenerate believers who have been renewed in Christ. Rather, James is talking about people in general, humans as such, regardless of their spiritual condition or moral standing. He is describing the fundamental reality of what it means to be human in this fallen world.

And observe the foundation upon which James rests his prohibition against cursing others; he grounds it firmly in their continuing status as beings made in the likeness of God. The wickedness of cursing another person, James argues, lies not primarily in the harm it causes to their reputation or the discord it creates in relationships, though both of these are certainly significant. Rather, the fundamental evil of cursing someone rests in the fact that we are directing our malice toward an image-bearer of the Almighty. To curse a human being is, in a very real sense, to assault the image of the One in whose likeness they were created.

What does this mean? The image of God in humanity is defaced but not erased, damaged but not destroyed, corrupted but not eliminated. We are like a masterpiece painting that has been vandalized, slashed, and covered with graffiti. The original image remains recognizable but marred. We retain capacities for reason, relationship, creativity, and morality, but all of these are twisted by sin. We still bear the image, but in a distorted form that requires redemption to restore.

This persistence of the image after the fall has enormous practical implications. It means that every human being possesses inherent dignity regardless of their spiritual state, moral condition, intellectual capacity, or social status. The atheist who blasphemes God bears His image. The criminal who violates His law displays His likeness. The infant who cannot reason or the elderly person who has lost cognitive function still image the Creator. The disabled person, the sick person, the poor person, the marginalized person, all bear the image of God and therefore possess infinite worth.

This is why the church has historically opposed abortion and euthanasia, slavery and racism, genocide and ethnic cleansing. These practices treat image-bearers as disposable commodities, as problems to be solved, as obstacles to be eliminated. They assault human dignity at its foundation by denying the image of God in those deemed inconvenient, inferior, or unwanted.

This is also why the church must speak clearly and compassionately about the modern assault on human embodiment through transgender ideology and the horrifying medical interventions that accompany it. The image of God includes our creation as male and female. Genesis 1:27 could not be clearer: "So God created man in his own image, in the image of God he created him; male and female he created them." Our embodiment as male or female is not incidental to our humanity. It is not a cosmic accident to be corrected or a biological starting point to be transcended. It is part of the divine design, woven into the very fabric of what it means to bear God's image.

When our culture tells confused adolescents that they can be born in the wrong body, when physicians prescribe puberty blockers to halt normal development, when surgeons remove healthy breasts from teenage girls or castrate young men in the name of gender affirmation, they are not offering compassionate care. They are mutilating image-bearers of God. They are treating the body as raw material to be manipulated according to disordered desires rather than as a sacred trust to be received with gratitude and stewarded with care.

The body is not a prison from which we need liberation. It is a gift from our Creator, fearfully and wonderfully made, as Psalm 139:14 declares: "I praise you, for I am fearfully and wonderfully made. Wonderful are your works; my soul knows it very well." To treat it as malleable matter to be reshaped according to internal feelings is to deny both creation and resurrection. God made us embodied creatures. Christ took on a body in the incarnation and rose bodily from the grave. Our hope is bodily resurrection, not escape from physicality into some disembodied spiritual existence.

When we remove healthy organs, when we flood developing bodies with cross-sex hormones, when we create surgical approximations of opposite-sex anatomy, we are not healing the person. We are disfiguring an image-bearer to accommodate a broken mind. We are sacrificing the body on the altar of psychological confusion. We are telling desperate people that the solution to their distress lies in permanent physical alteration rather than in the renewal of the mind that Paul commands in Romans 12:2.

This is not compassion but cruelty dressed in therapeutic language. True compassion would tell the truth, even when the truth cuts against the cultural consensus. True love would point confused people toward their Creator's design rather than affirming their departure from it. True care would seek the healing of disordered desires and confused thinking rather than the surgical alteration of healthy bodies.

The church must recover the courage to say clearly what Scripture teaches: God made us male and female, and this is very good. Our sexed bodies are not mistakes to be corrected but gifts to be embraced. The dysphoria that leads people to reject their embodiment is real and often agonizing, but the solution is not surgical mutilation. It is the same solution offered to all who struggle with the disorder sin has introduced into creation: repentance, faith, and the patient work of sanctification as the Spirit progressively conforms us to Christ.

I remember counseling a young woman who had procured an abortion. She came to me years later, wracked with guilt, convinced she was beyond forgiveness. She had believed the lie that what she carried was just tissue, just a clump of cells, just a choice she was entitled to make. But her conscience knew better. Her nightmares and her grief testified to what she had done: she had destroyed an image-bearer, a person made in God's likeness, a life with infinite worth. My task was not to minimize her sin but to proclaim the greater reality of Christ's sufficient sacrifice for even that sin. But I could never have offered her true comfort by pretending what she had destroyed was not fully human.

Christ as the True Image

The Old Testament presents humanity as image-bearers but leaves us with questions. What does the image look like when it is not defaced by sin? How is humanity supposed to function when the image operates as God intended? What is the goal toward which the image points?

The New Testament answers these questions by presenting Christ as the image of God in a way that surpasses how Adam bore the image. Colossians 1:15 declares that Christ "is the image of the invisible God, the firstborn of all creation." 2 Corinthians 4:4 speaks of "the light of the gospel of the glory of Christ, who is the image of God." Hebrews 1:3 describes the Son as "the radiance of the glory of God and the exact imprint of his nature."

Christ is the image of God perfectly, fully, without distortion or defect. In Him we see what God is like because He is God incarnate. In Him we also see what humanity is supposed to be, what the image looks like when sin has not marred it. Jesus is the true Adam, the true image-bearer, the one who succeeds where the first man failed.

Romans 5:12-21 presents the parallel and contrast between Adam and Christ. Adam's disobedience brought sin and death. Christ's obedience brought righteousness and life. Adam's failure plunged humanity into condemnation. Christ's faithfulness secured justification for all who believe. The contrast could not be sharper, nor the stakes higher.

But there is more. The New Testament teaches that those united to Christ are being conformed to His image. Romans 8:29 states that God predestined those He foreknew "to be conformed to the image of his Son, in order that he might be the firstborn among many brothers." 2 Corinthians 3:18 declares that believers "are being transformed into the same image from one degree of glory to another." Colossians 3:10

speaks of putting on the new self, "which is being renewed in knowledge after the image of its creator."

This is the goal of salvation: not merely forgiveness of sins, though that is essential; not merely escape from hell, though that is wonderful; but transformation into the likeness of Christ. God is restoring His image in humanity, repairing what sin damaged, renewing what the fall corrupted. This process begins at conversion and continues through sanctification until it reaches completion at glorification.

I have watched this transformation occur in people's lives. The angry, bitter man who gradually becomes patient and kind. The selfish woman who develops a sacrificial love for others. The fearful person who grows in courage and faith. The proud individual who learns humility. These changes are not superficial modifications but deep transformations that reflect the image of God being restored by the Spirit's work.

This means that the gospel is not just about individual salvation but cosmic restoration. Christ came not only to save souls but to restore humanity to its intended glory as God's image-bearers. He is the firstborn among many brothers, the pioneer of a new humanity that will finally display God's image without the distortion sin introduced. Every person united to Christ by faith is being remade in His likeness, becoming more truly human as they become more like the one true human who is also fully God.

Implications for Human Dignity

All of this theological reflection has intensely practical implications for how we treat other people and advocate for justice in a world that constantly assaults human dignity.

First, the image of God demands that we treat every person with respect and honor regardless of their condition, character, or capacity. We cannot categorize people into those who matter and those who do not, those who deserve dignity and those who do not, those whose lives are worth protecting and those whose lives are disposable. Every human being from conception to natural death, in every state of health or disability, at every level of intellectual capacity or moral development, bears the image of God and therefore possesses infinite worth.

This conviction shaped my pastoral ministry. I visited nursing homes where elderly saints with dementia could no longer recognize their families. I counseled families facing decisions about severely disabled children. I walked with couples through miscarriages that others dismissed as merely unfortunate medical events. And in every case, I insisted that we were dealing with persons, with image-bearers, with those whom God made and values and loves. The world might categorize them as burdens or problems or inconveniences. But the church must see them as God sees them: image-bearers worthy of honor.

Second, the image of God prohibits all forms of racism, ethnic prejudice, and discrimination based on external characteristics. Acts 17:26 declares that God "made from one man every nation of mankind to live on all the face of the earth." We are one human family, all descended from Adam, all bearing the same image regardless of skin color, ethnic origin, or cultural background. The divisions we construct between peoples, the hierarchies we establish, the prejudices we harbor, all contradict the fundamental unity of humanity under God.

I served alongside Marines from every conceivable background. Black, white, Hispanic, Asian. Rich kids from the suburbs and poor kids from the inner cities. Northerners and

Southerners. College graduates and high school dropouts. And I learned what really matters when bullets fly: not where someone came from but whether they would stand with you when everything fell apart. The superficial differences that obsess civilian society mattered not at all when lives depended on unity and trust.

The church should lead the way in demonstrating this truth. We should be the community where ethnic and cultural divisions find their proper resolution in Christ, where Jew and Gentile become one new man, where there is neither slave nor free, where people from every nation and tribe and language gather around one Lord, one faith, one baptism. When the church reflects the world's divisions rather than transcending them, when we segregate along racial or economic lines, when we allow prejudice to persist unchallenged, we deny the image of God in our brothers and sisters.

Third, the image of God requires that we protect the vulnerable and advocate for justice on behalf of those who cannot defend themselves. The unborn child in the womb bears God's image just as fully as the nine-month-old infant, which means abortion is not healthcare but homicide. The elderly person facing pressure to end their life through assisted suicide bears God's image just as truly as the young athlete, which means we must resist the culture of death that treats suffering as meaningless and life as disposable. The disabled person bears God's image no less than the able-bodied, which means we must ensure they receive the care and respect they deserve rather than treating them as burdens to be eliminated.

Proverbs 31:8-9 commands: "Open your mouth for the mute, for the rights of all who are destitute. Open your mouth, judge righteously, defend the rights of the poor and needy." This is not optional for those who take the image of God seriously.

We must speak for those who cannot speak for themselves. We must defend those who cannot defend themselves. We must ensure that society's most vulnerable receive protection rather than exploitation.

Fourth, the image of God shapes how we think about and practice human sexuality. Genesis 1:27 establishes that God created humanity as male and female, a binary distinction that is foundational rather than incidental. The two sexes are different but complementary, distinct but united, diverse but designed for each other. This sexual differentiation is part of what it means to be human and to bear God's image.

Genesis 2 elaborates on this by presenting marriage as the union of a man and a woman becoming one flesh. This is not merely a social convention or cultural construct but a creation ordinance, something built into the fabric of reality by God's design. Marriage images something about God and His relationship to His people. Ephesians 5:25-27 makes this explicit by presenting marriage as a picture of Christ and the church: "Husbands, love your wives, as Christ loved the church and gave himself up for her, that he might sanctify her, having cleansed her by the washing of water with the word, so that he might present the church to himself in splendor, without spot or wrinkle or any such thing, that she might be holy and without blemish."

This means that the current confusion about sex and gender represents not progress toward a more enlightened future but regression toward primordial chaos, not liberation from oppressive structures but bondage to destructive lies, not enlightenment breaking free from ancient superstitions but darkness masquerading as light. When contemporary society insists with increasing fervor and intolerance that biological sex is fundamentally irrelevant to human identity or infinitely malleable according to individual feelings and preferences, when it categorically denies the significance and meaning of the male-female binary that God wove into the fabric of creation itself, when it actively promotes and celebrates sexual relationships and expressions that stand in direct contradiction to God's revealed design for human flourishing, it is engaged in nothing less than an assault on the image of God by systematically denying and deconstructing the created order that reflects His character and purposes.

The implications and consequences of this coordinated assault extend far beyond political debates, legislative battles, or cultural skirmishes that dominate headlines and social media feeds. What we are witnessing in our generation is nothing less than a deliberate, systematic attempt to fundamentally redefine what it means to be human; to sever humanity from the very Creator who carefully and lovingly designed us, who spoke us into existence, who declared His image-bearing creatures "very good." This represents an effort to unmoor human identity from the bedrock of divine revelation and anchor it instead in the shifting sands of subjective experience and autonomous self-determination.

This is emphatically not a minor theological dispute confined to academic journals and seminary classrooms, not a peripheral concern that thoughtful Christians can safely relegate to the margins of their faith, not a secondary issue on which well-meaning believers can reasonably disagree while maintaining unity on supposedly more important doctrines. Rather, this strikes directly at the very heart of the doctrine of creation itself, at the foundational truth that God made us in His image, male and female, for His glory and purposes. It assaults the image of God stamped indelibly on every single human being from the moment of conception, that divine imprint that cannot be erased by cultural trends, redefined by academic theories, or overridden by personal feelings, no matter how sincerely felt or passionately expressed. True compassion does not tell people what they want to hear but what they need to hear, even when the truth is difficult.

Living as Image-Bearers in a Broken World

How then should we live in light of this tremendous truth that we bear the image of God? How does this doctrine shape daily life in a world that ignores or denies it?

First, we live with gratitude for the dignity God has conferred on us. We are not cosmic accidents or evolutionary flukes. We are not meaningless specks in an indifferent universe. We are not sophisticated animals or complex machines. We are image-bearers, creatures made by God to reflect His character and rule His creation. This is our identity, our calling, our dignity. When we feel insignificant or worthless, when the world treats us as disposable or unimportant, we remember whose image we bear and stand in the confidence of our God-given worth.

Second, we live with humility appropriate to creatures. We bear God's image, but we are not God. We are finite, limited, dependent. We exist by His will and for His glory, not our own. The modern project of human autonomy, the dream of defining ourselves and determining our own purposes, contradicts our created nature. We find true freedom not in asserting independence from God but in embracing dependence on Him, not in claiming autonomy but in accepting our place as creatures made to worship and obey our Creator.

Third, we live with love for all who bear God's image alongside us. We cannot love God while despising His image-bearers. We cannot claim to honor the Creator while dishonoring those He made in His likeness. 1 John 4:20 makes this devastatingly clear: "If anyone says, 'I love God,' and hates his brother, he is a liar; for he who does not love his brother whom he has seen cannot love God whom he has not seen." Our treatment of other people reveals what we really believe about the image of God.

Fourth, we live with hope that God is restoring His image in us. We are not stuck in our current condition. We are not condemned to remain as we are. God is at work transforming us into the likeness of Christ, renewing the image that sin defaced, restoring capacities that the fall damaged. Every act of obedience, every victory over sin, every growth in grace represents progress toward the goal of bearing Christ's image fully.

This is the glorious truth Genesis 1:26-27 establishes and the whole Bible develops: we are made in God's image, fallen but not beyond redemption, damaged but capable of restoration, corrupted but destined for renewal in Christ. This is who we are. This is what we were made for. This is the hope that sustains us even in a world that denies these truths.

And it all flows from those magnificent words: "Let us make man in our image, after our likeness."

Chapter Four

Male and Female He Created Them: God's Design for Humanity

The Bible wastes no time establishing one of the most foundational and, in our current cultural moment, most controversial truths about human existence. Genesis 1:27 declares with crystal clarity: "So God created man in his own image, in the image of God he created him; male and female he created them." Notice the structure of this verse. It establishes the image of God, then immediately specifies that this image exists in two distinct but complementary forms. Male and female. Not as interchangeable categories. Not as socially constructed roles. Not as fluid identities subject to individual choice. Male and female as God's deliberate, purposeful, good design for humanity.

This is not peripheral in the biblical account of creation. This is not a minor detail that Genesis happened to mention in passing. This is central to what it means to be human. God could have created humanity as androgynous beings, as self-reproducing individuals, as genderless entities. He chose not to. He chose deliberately to create us male and female, with distinct characteristics, complementary roles, and unique capacities. This choice was not arbitrary. It was intentional. It reveals something profound about God's purposes for humanity and His design for human flourishing.

I understand that to many modern readers, this sounds restrictive, oppressive, even hateful. We live in an age that insists the highest good is radical autonomy, the ultimate freedom is to define ourselves however we choose, and the greatest evil is to suggest that there might be divinely established boundaries around identity or sexuality. To speak of God's design for male and female sounds to contemporary ears like claiming God has trapped people in categories they never chose, imposed identities that might not fit their felt experience, created rigid boxes that crush individual expression and authentic selfhood.

But this gets it exactly backward. God's design is not a prison. God's boundaries are not oppressive. God's categories are not destructive. They are the path to genuine flourishing, the framework for authentic identity, the context in which we discover what it truly means to be human. A fish does not find freedom by leaving the water. A bird does not discover its true potential by denying it has wings. And humans do not flourish by rejecting the sexual differentiation God built into creation from the beginning.

The Biblical Foundation for Complementarity

Let me be clear from the outset about what Scripture teaches. The scriptural perspective on man and woman does not align with contemporary egalitarianism, which reduces masculine and feminine distinctions to purely physiological variations without bearing on functions, duties, or relational dynamics. Neither is it what critics often caricature as patriarchal tyranny, where men rule arbitrarily and women exist in subjugation. Rather, Scripture presents what theologians have termed complementarity, the profound biblical truth that men and women stand absolutely equal in dignity, value, and worth as bearers of God's image, yet are purposefully and beautifully distinct in their created roles, divinely appointed responsibilities, and fundamental design according to God's wise and intentional ordering of creation from the very beginning.

This profound truth of complementarity appears immediately and unmistakably in Genesis 2, which provides a much more detailed, intimate account of how God deliberately and purposefully created humanity in its fullness. Genesis 2:18 records God's remarkable declaration: "It is not good that the man should be alone; I will make him a helper fit for him." Notice several absolutely crucial details embedded in this seemingly simple statement that revolutionize our understanding of sexual differentiation and relational design.

First, and perhaps most striking, this marks the very first time in the entire creation account that God calls something "not good." Everything else in creation, light and darkness, sky and sea, vegetation and animals, sun and moon; God surveyed and pronounced good. Indeed, after completing His creative work, Genesis 1:31 tells us God saw everything He had made and declared it "very good." But here, something different emerges. Adam alone, man in isolation, man without woman, was explicitly "not good." This single phrase carries profound theological weight and tells us something absolutely vital about the nature of humanity and the divine design for human flourishing.

Male and female together, not male alone or female alone, not one sex elevated above the other or one sex existing independently of the other, reflect the fullness and completeness of God's image stamped upon humanity. The solitary man, however perfect and sinless in his unfallen state, was incomplete. God Himself declared this incompleteness, this fundamental insufficiency that required divine remedy through the creation of woman.

Second, we must examine carefully how God created woman as a "helper" for man, a designation rich with a theological significance that modern readers frequently misunderstand or distort. Contemporary ears often stumble over this word, our cultural sensibilities immediately assuming it implies inferiority, subordination, or some lesser status in the created order. But this interpretation betrays a fundamental ignorance of the Hebrew language and a tragic misreading of Scripture's intent.

The word translated "helper" in our English Bibles is the Hebrew word *ezer*, and understanding this term properly revolutionizes our comprehension of the man-woman relationship. This is not a trivial linguistic detail but a matter of profound theological importance. The word *ezer* appears frequently throughout the Old Testament, and remarkably, it is used most often to describe God Himself as Israel's helper in their desperate times of need. Consider the beautiful words of

Psalm 121:1-2, which ask the fundamental question of human existence: "I lift up my eyes to the hills. From where does my help come? My help comes from the LORD, who made heaven and earth." The same word. The identical Hebrew term. God is Israel's *ezer*, their strong helper, their mighty deliverer, their source of strength in weakness. Woman is man's *ezer*, his strong helper, bringing capabilities and strengths that he desperately needs but does not possess in himself.

Far from suggesting weakness or inferiority, the term *ezer* conveys strength, vital support, and complementary capacity that makes survival and flourishing possible. It speaks of someone who provides what is critically lacking, who brings essential resources to desperate need, who completes what is dangerously incomplete. This is the biblical vision of woman's role: not subordinate or inferior, but absolutely essential, bringing strength where there is weakness, wisdom where there is folly, perspective where there is blindness.

Third, she is a helper "fit for him" a translation that barely captures the profound meaning embedded in the original Hebrew phrase *kenegdo*. The term literally means "corresponding to him," "matching him," or, more precisely, "as opposite to him." Think of puzzle pieces that lock together precisely because they are different, not despite their differences. Think of two hands, mirror images of each other, able to work together in ways identical hands never could. This is the picture Scripture paints of the relationship between man and woman in God's original design.

She is emphatically not identical to him, not a duplicate, not a copy, not merely another version of the same thing. Instead, she corresponds to him in the deepest sense. She completes what remains dangerously incomplete when he stands alone. She provides what he fundamentally lacks, not through any deficiency in God's creation of him, but by divine design that intended human flourishing to require this sacred partnership. She brings capacities that complement his own, not lesser capacities, but different ones. She offers perspectives that his vantage point can never achieve in isolation. She possesses strengths that answer his weaknesses, even as his strengths answer hers. Together, they form something far greater than the sum of their individual parts.

This is the biblical vision in all its beauty and complexity: not sameness, but complementarity. Not interchangeability, as though either could fulfill the other's role without significant loss. Not competition for superiority or dominance, but cooperation; profound, intimate, essential cooperation in fulfilling the purposes that God established before the foundation of the world. They need each other. This mutual dependence is not a flaw to be overcome but a feature to be celebrated, a reflection of the relational nature of the Triune God in whose image they are both created.

Genesis 2:21-23 unfolds the remarkable account of how God fashioned woman from material taken from Adam's very side, not from the dust of the ground as He had formed Adam, but from living flesh already animated by the breath of God. The text describes God causing a deep sleep to fall upon Adam, then taking one of his ribs and closing up the flesh in its place. From this rib, this portion of Adam himself, God built the woman and brought her to the man. The Hebrew word translated "built" (*banah*) is the same word used for constructing a house or temple, suggesting careful, purposeful craftsmanship in her creation.

When Adam awakens and sees her for the first time, this creature who is like him yet wonderfully unlike him, he does not respond with clinical observation or detached analysis.

Instead, he bursts spontaneously into poetry, the first recorded human speech in all of Scripture taking the form of joyful verse: "This at last is bone of my bones and flesh of my flesh; she shall be called Woman, because she was taken out of Man." The exclamation "at last" suggests Adam had been searching, longing, waiting for this completion. Of all the creatures he had named, none had proven suitable as a helper corresponding to him. But now finally here stands one who answers his deepest need.

The Hebrew language reveals an exquisite wordplay that simply cannot be captured fully in English translation. The word for man is *ish*. The word for woman is *ishshah*. The similarity between these terms is deliberate and profound. They share the same root, echo each other phonetically, and demonstrate their fundamental connection. Similar yet distinct. Unmistakably related yet beautifully different. This is unity expressed in diversity, sameness revealed through difference, perfect equality maintained alongside clear distinction.

The Purpose of Sexual Differentiation

Why did God create humanity this way? Why male and female rather than some other arrangement? Scripture points to several profound purposes woven into creation's fabric.

First, sexual differentiation reveals something about God Himself. Genesis 1:27 links the image of God directly to male and female: "So God created man in his own image, in the image of God he created him; male and female he created them." The plurality within the Godhead, the eternal relationship of love between Father, Son, and Holy Spirit, finds an echo in the relationship between man and woman. Not that God has gender in the way humans do. God transcends our categories. But the relational dynamic within the Trinity, the unity in diversity, the mutual love and honor, the distinct roles within perfect equality, all this finds reflection in the complementary relationship between male and female.

This is precisely why marriage between one man and one woman carries such profound theological weight throughout the entire sweep of Scripture, from Genesis to Revelation. It is not merely a social arrangement that evolved through human custom, not simply a civil contract negotiated between parties, not just a convenient institution for organizing society or regulating property rights. Marriage is something far more profound, far more weighty, far more central to God's purposes in creation. It is a living, breathing picture of divine realities that transcend time and culture. It is a window into the very heart of God's eternal purposes.

Ephesians 5:31-32 makes this connection breathtakingly explicit, pulling back the curtain on marriage's deepest meaning: "Therefore a man shall leave his father and mother and hold fast to his wife, and the two shall become one flesh. This mystery is profound, and I am saying that it refers to Christ and the church." The apostle Paul, writing under the Holy Spirit's inspiration, reveals that every marriage between a man and woman serves as an earthly portrait, however imperfect, of the relationship between Christ and His beloved bride, the church. The husband's self-sacrificing love images Christ's love for His people. The wife's glad submission images the church's response to her Lord. The one-flesh union images the mystical union between Christ and those He redeemed.

This is precisely why Scripture consistently upholds and celebrates marriage exclusively as the lifelong, covenant union of one man and one woman, without a single exception across both testaments, without wavering from culture to culture, without bending to accommodate the prevailing winds of human opinion in any era where God's people lived. From Genesis to Revelation, through patriarchal societies and monarchical kingdoms, through exile and restoration, through the giving of the Law and the coming of grace, through every shift in human civilization and every evolution in cultural norms, God's definition of marriage remains unwavering: one man, one woman, for life.

This consistency is not accidental. It is not the product of a limited ancient imagination or cultural blindness. It is the inevitable consequence of marriage's fundamental purpose as a divinely ordained picture of Christ and His church. Any other configuration, however our modern culture might celebrate it, however our courts might legitimize it, however our neighbors might normalize it, however our own hearts might sympathize with it, fails to mirror the particular heavenly truth that marriage was created to display from the beginning of creation. A man with multiple wives cannot picture Christ's exclusive devotion to one bride. Two men or two women together cannot picture the complementary union of Christ and the church, the sacrificial bridegroom and the responsive bride. A temporary arrangement cannot picture Christ's eternal commitment to His people, His promise never to leave or forsake them. Only the permanent, exclusive, complementary union of one man and one woman can bear the weight of this sacred symbolism, can serve as the earthly billboard pointing to heavenly realities.

Second, sexual differentiation serves the essential, God-ordained purpose of procreation, the bringing forth of new life. When we turn to Genesis 1:28, we encounter God's very first command to humanity, spoken over Adam and Eve in the garden: "Be fruitful and multiply and fill the earth and subdue it." This was not a suggestion or a mere option among many lifestyle choices. It was a divine mandate, a foundational purpose woven into the fabric of human existence from the very beginning.

Children require both a male and a female for their natural conception. This biological reality is not some incidental detail in God's design, not a mere accident of evolutionary development that we're now free to work around or dismiss as we see fit. It is absolutely central to understanding why God created us as He did. The complementary union of male and female in the covenant of marriage provides the God-ordained context for bringing new image-bearers into the world, for extending the reach of God's image across the whole of creation, for continuing the human story across generations yet unborn. Each child conceived within marriage represents another reflection of the divine image, another soul created for relationship with God, another participant in the ongoing drama of redemption history.

Modern reproductive technology can circumvent this biological reality to some degree, allowing conception to occur without the intimate sexual union of husband and wife, allowing individuals to have genetic children entirely apart from the covenant bonds of marriage. Various assisted reproductive techniques can separate procreation from the marital embrace, can introduce third parties into the creation of new life, and can reduce the profound mystery of conception to a clinical procedure performed in sterile laboratories rather than in the intimacy of the marriage bed. But we must ask ourselves a crucial question: Does the mere existence of such technologies somehow overturn or nullify God's fundamental design for human sexuality and procreation? Does our technological capability to work around God's created order mean we should do so? Does the fact that we can achieve certain ends through artificial means transform those means into God's intended pattern?

The answer, I would argue, is no. The existence of such technologies does not overturn God's design for marriage and procreation any more than the existence of infant formula somehow overturns the clear biological design of a mother's breasts for nursing her child. Formula can nourish an infant; there's no denying that medical reality. In cases of necessity, it serves a legitimate purpose. But its existence and usefulness in certain circumstances doesn't change the fact that God designed the female body to produce milk specifically for feeding children, that nursing establishes bonds between mother and child that go beyond mere nutrition, that this is the natural, created pattern for infant feeding. The natural pattern, the created order as God established it in the beginning, remains the standard by which we must evaluate our choices, our technologies, our attempts to achieve desired outcomes through means that bypass or work around what God has ordained.

Third, sexual differentiation creates the context for complementary roles in marriage, family, and church; roles that flow naturally from the biological and psychological distinctiveness God has woven into male and female from the beginning. This is the point where modern sensibilities don't merely brush against Scripture's teaching but actively bristle, where the offense becomes most acute, where even many within the church begin to shift uncomfortably and look for interpretive escape routes. We live in a culture thoroughly saturated with the conviction that equality necessarily requires interchangeability, that any distinction whatsoever in roles must imply a hierarchy of value, that complementarity is merely sophisticated coded language designed to obscure and perpetuate oppression. The very notion that men and women might be designed by God for different yet complementary functions strikes contemporary ears as inherently suspect, a remnant of patriarchal thinking that enlightened people should have left behind generations ago.

But Scripture, faithful to the creation pattern established in Genesis, presents a radically different vision, one that affirms both the equal dignity of male and female as image-bearers while simultaneously embracing the reality that equality of worth does not necessitate sameness of function. The Bible refuses to collapse these categories or to assume that different roles somehow communicate different value in God's eyes.

Ephesians 5:22-33 lays out this complementarian pattern with breathtaking clarity and undeniable force: "Wives, submit to your own husbands, as to the Lord. For the husband is the head of the wife even as Christ is the head of the church, his body, and is himself its Savior. Now as the church submits to Christ, so also wives should submit in everything to their husbands. Husbands, love your wives, as Christ loved the church and gave himself up for her."

This passage, perhaps more than any other in the New Testament, offends modern egalitarian assumptions at almost every point, violating nearly every article of faith in our contemporary catechism of gender relations. Submission, the very word lands like a verbal assault on contemporary sensibilities. Headship, a concept that sounds not merely archaic and out of touch at best, but actively dangerous and fundamentally oppressive at worst. The passage makes no apologies, offers no qualifying footnotes to soften its edges, provides no escape clause for those who find its teaching uncomfortable or culturally inconvenient.

But look closer, far closer, at what Scripture actually teaches here. The husband's headship is explicitly, unmistakably modeled on Christ's headship over the church. And how does Christ exercise His headship? By dying for the church. By sacrificing Himself utterly and completely. By giving up absolutely everything, including His comfort, His rights, and His very life, for her good. This is not tyranny dressed up in religious language. This is not domination disguised as spiritual authority. This is self-sacrificial love in its purest, most demanding form. The husband is called to love his wife precisely the way Christ loved the church, which means he is called to die for her if necessary, to put her interests consistently ahead of his own comfort and preferences, to give of himself without reservation or calculation for her flourishing and wellbeing. This is headship understood as service rather than dominance, authority conceived as responsibility rather than privilege, leadership expressed as sacrificial love rather than self-serving control. The pattern could not be clearer or more challenging to our natural instincts for self-preservation and self-advancement.

The wife's submission, likewise, is utterly revolutionary when properly understood, when we strip away the cultural caricatures and the painful distortions that have marred God's beautiful design throughout history. She is called to submit as the church submits to Christ, and this qualification, this crucial parallel, transforms everything about how we understand what submission truly means in the context of biblical marriage. She is not submitting to a tyrant who demands his own way regardless of the cost to her wellbeing. She is not submitting to an oppressor who uses his position to diminish, control, or manipulate her for his own selfish ends. She is not subjecting herself to someone who views her as inferior, as less valuable, as somehow less fully made in the image of God. Rather, she is submitting to one who is called to love her as Christ loved the church, to one who has vowed before God and witnesses to die for her if necessary, to one who is commanded by Scripture itself to seek her good consistently and sacrificially above his own comfort, convenience, or preferences.

Her submission, when we see it clearly through the lens of Scripture rather than through the distorting lens of cultural abuse and misapplication, is not weakness masquerading as virtue but rather strength expressed through voluntary trust. It is not subjugation that crushes her spirit and diminishes her personhood but rather a confident entrusting of herself to someone who has committed himself to her flourishing. It is not a diminishment of her gifts, her calling, her full humanity, but rather the flourishing that comes from embracing the complementary role God designed specifically for her, the role that allows her unique gifts and strengths to shine most brightly within the partnership of biblical marriage.

I know this sounds impossibly countercultural, perhaps even shocking to modern ears. I know many will dismiss it immediately as outdated patriarchy, as oppressive traditionalism dressed up in spiritual language, as harmful teaching that has kept women in bondage for centuries and needs to be discarded along with other relics of less enlightened ages. I understand the objections. I've heard them countless times from students, from critics, from well-meaning believers who cannot reconcile what Scripture teaches with what our culture insists must be true about gender, equality, and human flourishing.

But I have watched this pattern work in countless marriages over my time of pastoral ministry, including my own marriage to my beloved wife. I have seen wives not merely survive but genuinely flourish under loving, Christ-centered headship that protects rather than dominates, serves rather than controls, sacrifices rather than demands. I have seen husbands who initially resisted the weight of sacrificial leadership grow into men who love their wives with a tenderness and commitment that mirrors Christ's love for the church. I have watched children thrive in homes where biblical complementarity shapes not just the marriage relationship but the entire texture of family life, where they see lived out before them daily what it means to love sacrificially, to submit joyfully, to honor the distinct callings God has placed on men and women.

And on the other side of the ledger, I have witnessed the wreckage, the pain, the confusion, and the spiritual devastation that results when couples reject God's design as revealed in Scripture and try instead to build a marriage on autonomous, egalitarian foundations that deny or diminish the very real distinctions God built into creation from the beginning.

The Beauty of Biblical Manhood

What does it mean to be a man according to Scripture? This question has never been more urgent or more confused. Our culture offers contradictory messages. Traditional masculinity is toxic, we are told, marked by aggression, dominance, emotional repression, and the abuse of power. Men should become more like women, we hear, more nurturing, more emotional, more collaborative, less competitive. At the same time, pornography and popular culture present a hypersexualized vision of manhood centered on sexual conquest, physical strength, and domination. Young men are left bewildered, uncertain what healthy masculinity looks like, paralyzed between competing visions that all fail to capture biblical manhood.

Scripture presents a vision of manhood that is neither brutish dominance nor feminized passivity, but something altogether different, something our confused age can scarcely comprehend. Biblical manhood is sacrificial strength. It is servant leadership modeled after Christ himself. It is a courageous responsibility that runs toward danger rather than shrinking from it. It is gentle firmness that speaks truth without harshness yet holds the line without compromise. It combines qualities our culture insists are contradictory, even incompatible: strength and tenderness working together in harmony, courage and compassion flowing from the same heart, authority exercised through service rather than exploitation, confidence grounded in humility before God. This is the pattern of masculinity God designed from the beginning, the kind of manhood that reflects the character of Christ himself, who led by laying down his life, who commanded by serving, who exercised authority by becoming obedient unto death.

Consider how Genesis 2 describes Adam's role in the created order. God placed him in the garden of Eden specifically "to work it and keep it" (Genesis 2:15). The Hebrew word translated "keep" in this passage is *shamar*, a term that carries far deeper significance than we might initially recognize. It means to guard, to protect, to watch over with vigilant care, to stand as a sentinel against any threat that might approach. Adam was not merely a gardener tending plants and pulling weeds. He was a guardian, a watchman stationed at the gates of paradise itself. God entrusted the garden, this sacred space where heaven and earth met, to his care and gave him the weighty responsibility to protect it from any intrusion or corruption. When the serpent invaded Eden with his subtle lies and twisted half-truths, Adam failed in his God-given responsibility in a catastrophic way. He stood by passively, silently, while the serpent deceived his wife, offering no protection, no warning, no intervention. He abdicated his role as protector at the very moment protection was most desperately needed. He failed to guard what God had entrusted to him, and the consequences of that failure echo through every generation since.

This fundamental pattern of protective, responsible leadership, this calling to stand as a guardian and provider, appears consistently throughout Scripture's comprehensive description of what constitutes godly manhood. Men are called, without qualification or equivocation, to provide materially and practically for their families. The apostle Paul states this obligation with startling severity in his first letter to Timothy: "But if anyone does not provide for his relatives, and especially for members of his household, he has denied the faith and is worse than an unbeliever" (1 Timothy 5:8). Notice the weight of Paul's language here. He doesn't merely say such a man has failed in his duty or fallen short of an ideal. He says this man has denied the faith itself, renounced what he professes to believe. He has become worse than an unbeliever, more culpable than those who make no claim to follow Christ, because he knows what God requires yet refuses to fulfill it.

But the calling extends far beyond mere material provision, important as that is. Men are called to protect their families from physical danger, yes, but also from spiritual deception, from corrupting influences, from false teaching that would lead them astray. They are called to lead their families intentionally and consistently in the paths of righteousness, to take full responsibility for the spiritual direction and health of their households. This is the pattern God established in Eden, the pattern Adam abandoned to humanity's ruin, and the pattern Scripture consistently upholds throughout its pages.

This does not mean women are passive, uninvolved, or merely decorative in God's design. Far from it. The woman celebrated in Proverbs 31, that noble woman whose worth is far above jewels, engages vigorously in business transactions, purchases fields with shrewd judgment, plants vineyards with her own hands, manages complex household affairs with wisdom and efficiency, extends her hands to care for the poor and needy, and speaks with wisdom that commands respect. She is anything but passive. She exercises agency, makes decisions that affect her household's prosperity, and demonstrates competence that would put many men to shame. Her husband trusts her completely, and she brings him good all the days of his life.

But notice the overall pattern of Scripture, the consistent thread that runs through both Old and New Testament teaching. Despite the active, engaged, competent role women play in God's design, the primary responsibility, not the exclusive responsibility, but the primary accountability, for provision, protection, and spiritual leadership in both home and church rests on the shoulders of men. This is the pattern God established, the order He wove into creation itself, and the responsibility from which men cannot abdicate without abandoning their God-given calling.

In the church, Scripture restricts the office of elder, the position of spiritual oversight and authoritative teaching, to qualified men. This is not a suggestion or a cultural preference that we might adjust based on changing times. It is a clear biblical mandate. 1 Timothy 2:12 states plainly, without ambiguity or qualification: "I do not permit a woman to teach or to exercise authority over a man; rather, she is to remain quiet." The language is direct and uncompromising. Paul doesn't soften it with cultural explanations or apologetic qualifications. He simply states what God has ordained for the ordering of His church.

Furthermore, both 1 Timothy 3:1-7 and Titus 1:5-9 provide detailed lists of qualifications for those who would serve as elders in Christ's church. Read these passages carefully, and you'll notice that they consistently use masculine pronouns throughout, not as a grammatical accident or a limitation of ancient languages, but as a deliberate reflection of God's design. These qualifications include specific requirements that clearly assume the elder is male, such as being "the husband of one wife." This is not accidental language. This is intentional divine instruction about who bears the responsibility for spiritual leadership in the gathered assembly of God's people.

These restrictions do not reflect a cultural accommodation of ancient patriarchy, as if Paul were simply mirroring the prejudices and limitations of his time. They are not temporary measures designed to avoid scandal in a first-century Roman world that wasn't ready for radical egalitarianism. No, these restrictions reflect something far deeper and more permanent: creation order itself. God's design from the very beginning, before sin corrupted human relationships and distorted our understanding of authority and submission.

Paul makes this crystal clear in 1 Timothy 2:13-14, where he deliberately grounds his prohibition on women teaching or exercising authority over men not in the customs of Ephesus or the social structures of the Roman Empire, but in the very fabric of creation: "For Adam was formed first, then Eve; and Adam was not deceived, but the woman was deceived and became a transgressor." Notice where Paul directs our attention. He appeals directly to Genesis, to the fundamental order of creation and the tragic nature of the fall. He reaches back past all human culture, past all social development, past all historical circumstances, to the garden itself, to those first moments when God shaped humanity and established the pattern for how men and women would relate to one another in His purposes.

This is not culturally conditioned application that we are now free to discard in our supposedly more enlightened times, as if Paul were merely a man of his age whose instructions we can lovingly set aside now that we know better. This is divine design rooted in creation itself, as permanent and unchanging as the God who ordained it..

This offends modern sensibilities to the very core. I understand that. I know the objections that rise immediately in many hearts, especially in our egalitarian age that views any distinction as discrimination. Women are just as intelligent as men, often more so. They are just as spiritual, just as gifted in discernment and insight, just as capable of study and communication. Some of the finest theological minds I have known belonged to women. Some of the most profound insights into Scripture I have encountered came from godly women whose grasp of biblical truth humbled me. So why, then, would a loving and just God restrict the roles of teaching and exercising authority in the gathered church to men?

The answer is crucial; Not because women are inferior in any way. Not because women lack the necessary gifts, abilities, or spiritual maturity. Not because God values women less or considers them less capable of handling truth. But because God, in His wisdom, designed distinct and complementary roles for men and women from the very beginning, those God-ordained distinctions extend purposefully into the life and structure of His church. God calls men specifically to bear the weight of responsibility for leadership, authoritative teaching, and governance in the church, not because women cannot do these things (clearly many could do them well), but because this pattern deliberately reflects the created order established in Eden and images profound divine realities about Christ and His church that transcend our cultural moment.

The Beauty of Biblical Womanhood

What does it mean to be a woman according to Scripture? Here again, our culture offers competing and contradictory messages. Women should compete with men on identical terms, breaking into every male-dominated field, proving they can do anything men can do. Women should embrace their sexuality, using it for personal empowerment and pleasure without constraint. Women should reject traditional roles like wife and mother as limiting and oppressive. At the same time, culture celebrates motherhood when convenient, praises feminine beauty when marketable, and claims to champion women's rights while often reducing women to sexual objects.

Scripture presents a radically different vision, one that cuts against both the reductionist caricatures of our secular age and the well-meaning but misguided attempts to defend womanhood by making women honorary men. Biblical womanhood is not defined by competition with men or by imitation of masculine patterns of strength, leadership, or achievement. It is not about proving that women can do everything men can do, as though feminine worth depends on matching masculine performance in identical tasks. Rather, it is about embracing with joy and confidence the distinct design, the unique gifts, the particular calling that God Himself has given to women as women, a calling that is neither inferior to nor interchangeable with that of men, but complementary, necessary, and beautiful in its own right.

Genesis 2:18 describes a woman with a phrase that deserves our careful attention: "a helper fit for him." We have already examined how the word "helper" in this passage implies strength rather than weakness, capability rather than subordination. Throughout Scripture, God Himself is most often called our helper, hardly a position of inferiority or servitude. Woman brings to the human partnership capacities, perspectives, and strengths that man genuinely lacks. She completes and fulfills what remains fundamentally incomplete in man alone, just as he provides what she needs in the complementary design of creation. This is her foundational calling, her God-given identity: to be a strong helper, a capable and competent ally, an absolutely indispensable partner in fulfilling the vast purposes God has ordained for humanity from the foundation of the world. This is not a calling of lesser dignity or diminished worth, but one of essential significance in God's good design for His image-bearers.

The specific shape this calling takes varies significantly based on a woman's particular circumstances, unique gifts, and individual calling from God. For some women, this calling to be a helper primarily and beautifully finds expression in the vocations of marriage and motherhood, roles that Scripture never treats as inferior or limiting, but rather celebrates as profound and dignified. Proverbs 31:10-31 offers an extended celebration of the wife of noble character, a woman who manages her household with extraordinary skill, wisdom, and entrepreneurial energy. This is no picture of narrow domesticity or passive subservience, but rather a portrait of a capable woman exercising genuine authority within her sphere, making significant decisions, engaging in commerce, teaching with wisdom, and bringing honor to her husband and household through her industry and competence. Similarly, Titus 2:4-5 instructs older women to train younger women "to love their husbands and children, to be self-controlled, pure, working at home, kind, and submissive to their own husbands, that the word of God may not be reviled." These are not arbitrary cultural preferences or outdated social conventions, but vital aspects of Christian witness that reflect God's design for the family.

Notice carefully that Paul explicitly grounds this instruction in theology and gospel witness, not merely in culture or pragmatism. These patterns exist not because first-century Mediterranean society expected them, but because they honor God's Word and protect the reputation of the gospel itself. When women embrace these roles with joy and excellence, they prevent the gospel from being blasphemed or dismissed by a watching world. They demonstrate that following Christ produces beautiful, flourishing lives that stand in stark contrast to the brokenness of fallen relationships. This teaching is not about attempting to return to an idealized 1950s American domesticity or enforcing Victorian-era gender norms that often reflected cultural preferences more than biblical truth. Rather, this is about faithfully honoring patterns rooted deeply in God's original creation design and consistently upheld throughout the entire canon of Scripture, patterns that reflect God's wisdom for human flourishing across every culture and every generation.

For other women, the calling to be a helper takes different forms. Deborah served as a judge in Israel (Judges 4-5). Priscilla taught Apollos, instructing him in the way of God more accurately (Acts 18:26). Phoebe served as a deacon in the church at Cenchreae (Romans 16:1). Women exercise the gifts of hospitality, mercy, service, prophecy, and teaching in appropriate contexts. The church desperately needs gifted women who use their abilities for God's glory.

But Scripture does maintain clear and unmistakable boundaries around certain offices and functions within the covenant community. Women are not called to exercise governing authority over men in the gathered assembly of God's people. Women are not called to serve as elders, shepherding and ruling the flock as under-shepherds of Christ. This biblical limitation is not oppression masquerading as theology, nor is it the residue of ancient patriarchal prejudice that the enlightened modern church should finally outgrow. This is God's carefully designed order for His church, reflecting both creation patterns and redemptive purposes that transcend culture and time.

And women who embrace this design with faith and joy, who flourish within these graciously established boundaries rather than chafing against them as restrictive constraints, discover through lived experience that God's ways truly are good. They find that His commandments are not burdensome but life-giving, not limiting but liberating, not diminishing but enriching. They experience the deep satisfaction that comes from aligning themselves with their Creator's intention rather than striving against it in pursuit of autonomy that promises freedom but delivers only confusion and emptiness.

The Tragedy of Rejecting God's Design

Our culture has largely rejected these biblical patterns. We have embraced radical egalitarianism that denies any meaningful distinction between male and female beyond basic biology. We have accepted a gender ideology that claims maleness and femaleness are social constructs, that biological sex is separate from gender identity, that individuals can identify as the opposite sex or as neither sex or as both sexes simultaneously.

The consequences have been devastating. Confusion about sexual identity now begins in childhood, with children being encouraged to question whether they are really boys or girls. Schools hide social transitions from parents. Doctors prescribe puberty blockers to children barely into adolescence. Teenagers undergo irreversible surgeries to align their bodies with their gender identity. And anyone who questions this madness is labeled a bigot, a transphobe, a threat to vulnerable people.

But this is not compassion; it is cruelty of the highest order, wrapped in therapeutic language and progressive rhetoric. This is telling confused, hurting people, people made in God's image who deserve truth spoken in love, that the path to wholeness, peace, and self-acceptance lies in the very opposite direction from where healing actually resides. We tell them their path forward requires rejecting the design their Creator stamped into their very chromosomes, pursuing an impossible transformation that science cannot truly achieve no matter how many surgeries are performed or hormones administered, warring against the reality of their own bodies as if those bodies were enemies to be conquered rather than aspects of their personhood to be accepted and integrated into a whole identity.

The tragic outcome reveals the lie. The suicide rates among those who identify as transgender remain devastatingly, heartbreakingly high, even after transition, even after the promised relief that medical intervention was supposed to bring. The numbers don't improve the way activists promised they would.

The regret rates are rising with alarming speed as a growing number of detransitioners find the courage to speak out publicly about the irreversible harm done to their bodies, the years stolen from their lives, the lies they were told by adults who should have protected them. The long-term health consequences of cross-sex hormones and radical surgeries are becoming increasingly apparent to anyone willing to look honestly at the evidence: sterility, sexual dysfunction, bone density loss, cardiovascular problems, and a host of complications that compound over time.

God's design is good, unshakably, eternally, beautifully good. Maleness and femaleness are not arbitrary social constructs we can conveniently reject when they become culturally unpopular or personally challenging. They are not categories we can redefine according to our feelings, desires, or contemporary ideologies. They are woven into the very fabric of creation from the beginning, stamped into humanity at the moment God spoke us into existence. Genesis 1:27 establishes this foundational truth with clarity that should leave no room for doubt or debate: "So God created man in his own image, in the image of God he created him; male and female he created them." This divine design, this binary reality established before the fall corrupted our world, is not oppressive despite what our culture screams with increasing volume and vehemence. This is reality, the way things actually are, the way God intended them to be, the truth that remains true regardless of whether we acknowledge it or rail against it. And we do not help people, not truly, not in any lasting or meaningful way, by encouraging them to deny reality, to wage war against the bodies God gave them, to chase an illusion of transformation that can never deliver what it promises. We help them by pointing them to the God who made them with intentionality and purpose, who loves them with a love that transcends their confusion and brokenness, who offers genuine forgiveness for sin and supernatural power to live according to His design rather than according to the shifting standards of a fallen culture.

Marriage likewise suffers profoundly under our culture's wholesale rejection of biblical complementarity, and the devastating consequences ripple far beyond individual couples into the very fabric of society itself. Divorce rates remain stubbornly, tragically high, even among those who claim the name of Christ, testifying to our failure to live according to God's design for this sacred institution. Marriages today often function as mere partnerships of convenience, contractual arrangements between autonomous individuals who maintain separate bank accounts, separate goals, separate lives, rather than the covenantal unions of self-giving love that Scripture describes and God intended them to be. Husbands abdicate the leadership role that God assigned them, either because they don't understand what biblical headship actually means or because they lack the courage to embrace it in a culture that mocks and vilifies male authority at every turn. Wives bombarded with messages that submission equals weakness, that yielding to their husband's leadership somehow diminishes their worth or value, reject the very role that God designed to bring flourishing and beauty to the marriage relationship. And the children; oh, the children suffer most of all, don't they? They grow up in homes without clear, consistent, biblical models of manhood and womanhood, without seeing what godly masculinity actually looks like in practice, without witnessing biblical femininity lived out with joy and strength. The confusion, the distortion, the brokenness doesn't stop with one generation; it spreads relentlessly across generations, each one drifting further from God's design, further from the truth that could set them free.

The church, the very body of Christ that should stand as an unwavering pillar and buttress of truth in a confused and darkening world, has too often capitulated shamefully to cultural pressure on these very issues, compromising the clear teaching of Scripture for the sake of cultural relevance and societal acceptance. Egalitarian theology, which flattens God's good design for complementary roles and rejects the biblical pattern of male leadership in the church, has made significant and troubling inroads into evangelical churches across the spectrum, churches that once held firmly to the authority of Scripture but now bend like reeds in the cultural wind. Women now serve as senior pastors and teaching elders in congregations that claim biblical authority, despite Scripture's clear, unmistakable restrictions on women serving in the office of elder or teaching with authority over men in the gathered assembly of God's people. Even many complementarian churches, those that officially affirm biblical roles for men and women, those that include complementarian language in their statements of faith, sometimes give mere lip service to these biblical principles while functionally operating on essentially egalitarian principles in practice, creating a disconnect between stated doctrine and actual practice that confuses everyone involved. The authority of Scripture itself gets systematically undermined, its foundation eroded piece by piece, when we pick and choose which commands to obey based on their cultural acceptability rather than on divine authority, when we let the surrounding culture determine which biblical truths we'll embrace and which we'll quietly set aside as outdated or culturally conditioned.

Living According to God's Design

How then should we live in light of God's design for male and female? How do these truths shape daily life in a culture that rejects them?

First, we embrace our God-given sexual identity with gratitude. If God made you male, embrace manhood. Develop the qualities of biblical masculinity. Grow in strength and courage. Take responsibility. Lead with sacrificial love. Protect those God has entrusted to your care. If God made you female, embrace womanhood. Develop the qualities of biblical femininity. Use your gifts to help and support others. Embrace the distinct calling God has given you. Flourish within the good boundaries He has established.

This does not mean conforming to every cultural stereotype of masculinity or femininity. Not all men are physically strong or athletically gifted. Not all women are nurturing or domestic. God creates tremendous variety within the categories of male and female. But the categories themselves are fixed. They are good. They are purposeful.

Second, we honor these distinctions in marriage and family. Husbands, love your wives as Christ loved the church. Lead with gentleness and wisdom. Provide for your families. Protect your families. Take spiritual responsibility for your households. Wives, respect your husbands. Submit to their leadership. Support them in their calling. Use your gifts to build strong homes where children flourish and the gospel is lived out daily.

Single men and single women honor these patterns too. Singleness is not a failure or second-class status. Paul himself was single and considered it a gift. But even in singleness, we live out biblical manhood or womanhood, using our gifts according to God's design, honoring the boundaries Scripture establishes.

Third, we uphold these truths in the church. We restrict the office of elder to qualified men. We celebrate the gifts of women and create abundant opportunities for them to serve, teach other women, minister to children, and use their gifts in appropriate contexts. We reject egalitarian theology that undermines Scripture's authority. We refuse to capitulate to cultural pressure to ordain women as pastors or elders, no matter how unpopular this stance becomes.

Fourth, we speak the truth in love to a confused culture. We do not compromise biblical truth to gain cultural acceptance. We do not soften Scripture's teaching to avoid being labeled bigots or transphobes. But neither do we speak truth without love, compassion, or understanding. We recognize that many people genuinely struggle with gender dysphoria, with confusion about identity, with attractions and desires that conflict with biblical teaching. We extend compassion while upholding the truth. We offer hope in the gospel, which has the power to transform desires, renew minds, and enable obedience even when it is costly.

This is difficult. It requires courage. It invites opposition. But it is necessary. Too much is at stake. God's design for humanity hangs in the balance. The authority of Scripture stands or falls here. The welfare of confused, hurting people depends on whether we speak truth or affirm lies.

The Hope of Redemption

Here is the glorious reality that must shape everything we say about gender, sexuality, and God's design for male and female:

we are all broken. We all fall short of God's design. We all struggle with sin that distorts our sexuality, our relationships, our very identity as male and female image-bearers.

Some struggle with same-sex attraction. Some struggle with gender confusion. Some struggle with pornography addiction. Some struggle with adultery or fornication. Some struggle with pride, domineering leadership, or passive abdication of responsibility. Some struggle with rebellion against God's design, with bitterness about the roles He has assigned, with envy of the opposite sex.

All of us struggle with something. The fall corrupted every aspect of human existence, including our sexuality and our relationships. We do not perfectly embody biblical manhood or womanhood. We fail. We fall. We sin.

But here is where the gospel blazes with hope that cannot be extinguished. Christ came into this broken world specifically to redeem fallen image-bearers, to restore what sin has so deeply corrupted, to renew and rebuild what the fall damaged beyond any human capacity to repair. The apostle Paul, writing to the troubled church at Corinth, declared this transformative truth: "Therefore, if anyone is in Christ, he is a new creation. The old has passed away; behold, the new has come" (2 Corinthians 5:17).

This sweeping promise encompasses everything about us, including our sexuality, including our understanding of ourselves, including our identity as male and female image-bearers of God. The redemptive work of Christ reaches into every corner of human existence that the fall corrupted. Nothing lies beyond His power to renew. Christ is not merely adjusting or improving us; He is making all things new, and that comprehensive work of recreation most certainly includes us, our bodies, our desires, our identities, our relationships, everything we are as gendered beings created in His image.

This transformative promise of new creation does not translate into instantaneous perfection, as if the moment we place our faith in Christ every struggle with identity or sexuality evaporates like morning mist under the risen sun. The theological reality is more nuanced, more patient, more gracious than such an understanding would allow. Sanctification, the process by which God progressively conforms us to the image of His Son, unfolds over time, sometimes over many years, sometimes over the entirety of our earthly pilgrimage. Spiritual growth, genuine transformation of heart and mind, requires time, requires perseverance, requires the slow, often painful work of the Spirit reshaping us from the inside out.

I have seen believers who wrestle with same-sex attraction for decades, faithful brothers and sisters who choose celibacy and obedience to Scripture's clear teaching even as the attraction itself persists, sometimes with undiminished intensity. I spoke with pastors who counseled men and women who experience profound gender dysphoria, who battle daily against the feeling that their body does not match their internal sense of self, yet who refuse to pursue transition because they trust God's design more than their own perception. I have sat with countless Christians who struggle against the chains of pornography addiction, fighting month after month, year after year for purity, stumbling and rising again, repenting and pressing forward in the power of the Spirit.

The Christian life, as Scripture repeatedly makes clear, is warfare, active, costly, demanding warfare against the world, the flesh, and the devil. It is not passive rest, not effortless victory, not immunity from temptation or struggle.

But the Spirit gives power to resist sin, to mortify the deeds of the flesh, to walk in obedience even when desires pull us elsewhere, even when the battle seems overwhelming. This is the promise that sustains us in the trenches of spiritual warfare. Romans 8:13 promises: "For if you live according to the flesh you will die, but if by the Spirit you put to death the deeds of the body, you will live." Notice the conditional nature of this promise, the necessity of active participation in the Spirit's work. Notice the ongoing nature of mortification—putting to death, not having already put to death. This is present-tense warfare, a daily battle, continual reliance on the Spirit's power rather than our own strength.

We are not left to fight in our own strength. We are not abandoned to face these struggles alone, left to generate victory through willpower or determination or sheer effort. God provides everything necessary for life and godliness through His divine power and the knowledge of Him who called us to His own glory and excellence. The Spirit who raised Christ from the dead dwells in us, and that same resurrection power is available for our sanctification, for our daily battle against sin, for our pursuit of holiness in every area of life.

And ultimately, our hope rests not in perfect conformity to biblical gender roles in this life, but in the resurrection. When Christ returns and raises us from the dead, He will complete the work of redemption He began. He will give us resurrection bodies perfectly suited to our created design. He will remove every trace of sin's corruption. He will restore the image of God in us fully and finally. We will be perfectly, gloriously, joyfully male or female in the new creation, bearing God's image without the distortions sin introduced.

This hope sustains us when obedience is costly, when cultural pressure is intense, when our own desires war against

God's design. We are not asked to conform to arbitrary rules for no purpose. We are invited to align ourselves with reality, to embrace the design of the God who made us and loves us, to trust that His ways truly are good even when they conflict with our feelings or our culture's wisdom.

Male and female He created them. This is not oppression. This is grace. This is God's good design for human flourishing. And those who embrace it, who trust it, who live according to it, discover what it truly means to bear the image of God.

Chapter Five

The Sabbath Pattern: Rest, Worship, and God's Rhythem

"Thus the heavens and the earth were finished, and all the host of them. And on the seventh day God finished his work that he had done, and he rested on the seventh day from all his work that he had done. So God blessed the seventh day and made it holy, because on it God rested from all his work that he had done in creation." Genesis 2:1-3.

Before sin entered the world, before the curse corrupted creation, before thorns grew and labor became toil, God established a pattern that would shape human existence forever. He worked for six days, creating everything from nothing, speaking light into darkness, separating waters from land, forming humanity from dust, declaring all things good. Then, on the seventh day, He rested.

This fact stops us when we take time to reflect on it. The God who never grows weary, who needs no sleep, who sustains the universe by the word of His power, rested. Not because He was tired. Not because creation had depleted His strength or exhausted His resources. The eternal God, infinite in power, omnipotent in all His works, chose to rest.

Why?

The answer to that question unlocks something profound about the nature of reality, about God's design for human life, about the rhythms that lead to flourishing rather than burnout, about worship and work and the proper ordering of our days. The Sabbath pattern, instituted before the Fall, written into the fabric of creation itself, reveals truths we desperately need to recover in our frantic, harried, exhausted age.

The Meaning of Divine Rest

When Scripture says God rested, it does not suggest He was tired. Isaiah 40:28 makes this clear: "Have you not known? Have you not heard? The Lord is the everlasting God, the Creator of the ends of the earth. He does not faint or grow weary; his understanding is unsearchable." God does not need rest the way His creatures need rest. He does not require sleep or recuperation. He does not experience fatigue.

So what does it mean that God rested on the seventh day?

The Hebrew word translated "rested" is *shabat*, from which we get our word "Sabbath." It means to cease, to stop, to desist from labor. God ceased from His work of creation. He stopped. Not because He had to, but because the work was complete, finished, accomplished. The seventh-day rest marks completion, declares satisfaction, announces that nothing more needs to be added.

Consider the significance. God could have continued creating. He could have made more galaxies, more worlds, more creatures. His creative power knows no limits. But He chose to stop, to declare the work finished, to pronounce it complete. The seventh-day rest testifies to the sufficiency of what God had made. Creation needed nothing more. It was good, thoroughly good, exactly as God intended it to be.

This divine rest also establishes something profoundly important: a pattern, a rhythm, a model for all human life that follows. God did not need to rest, as we have seen. His power never diminishes. His strength never fails. His energy never flags. But we do need rest. We need it desperately. And by resting Himself, by choosing to cease from His creative work even though He required no recovery or recuperation, by establishing the Sabbath principle before humanity ever knew the devastating effects of sin or experienced the soul-deep weariness that comes from living in a fallen world, God built into the very fabric of the created order itself a rhythm that acknowledges and honors our fundamental nature as creatures. Creatures who are finite rather than infinite, limited rather than limitless, utterly dependent upon Him for our strength and our sustenance and our very life itself.

The Sabbath was not an afterthought. It was not something God added later when He saw how tired Adam and Eve would become after the Fall. It was woven into creation from the beginning, part of the original design, embedded in the structure of time itself. This tells us something crucial: our need for rest, for rhythm, for limits on our labor is not a consequence of sin. It is part of what it means to be human, to be creatures made by God and for God.

The Marines taught me something about rest that I have never forgotten. During boot camp, sleep deprivation was a weapon wielded with precision. The drill instructors understood that exhaustion breaks down resistance, exposes weakness, reveals character. We learned to function on minimal sleep, to push through fatigue, to accomplish the mission regardless of how tired we felt. This training proved invaluable in combat zones, where rest was a luxury we could not always afford.

But the Marines also taught me that sustained operations require planned rest. Even the most elite units, the most dedicated warriors, cannot function indefinitely without sleep. Commanders who drove their troops without adequate rest eventually commanded ineffective units. Fatigue degrades judgment, slows reaction time, increases mistakes, and causes accidents. Rest is not weakness. It is recognition of reality, acknowledgment of human limitations, wisdom about how God designed us to function.

The Sabbath pattern acknowledges these same truths about human nature, but it goes deeper, much deeper than mere physical recuperation. The rest God commands and models is not just about recovering from exhaustion. It is about worship, about remembering who we are and whose we are, about reorienting our lives around the reality that God is God and we are not.

Creation's First Full Day

Here is a detail that startles when we notice it: Adam and Eve's first full day of existence was the Sabbath.

Think through the timeline. God created humanity on the sixth day. He made Adam from the dust, breathed life into him, placed him in the garden, brought the animals for naming, created Eve from Adam's side, and joined them together in the first marriage. All this happened on day six. Then, day seven arrived, and God rested.

This means Adam and Eve's first full day of life was a day of rest. They had not yet worked. They had not yet labored in the garden, had not yet begun the task of cultivating and keeping Eden. Their first experience of life was rest in God's presence, enjoyment of His completed work, fellowship with their Creator, who delighted in what He had made.

The theological significance of this truth runs so deep it reaches to the very foundations of how we understand our relationship with the living God. Humanity's relationship with the Almighty was not founded on work, not established through human labor, not earned by personal accomplishment or merit. Before Adam and Eve did anything productive, before they contributed anything of value, before they proved themselves worthy or capable through any effort of their own, they simply rested with God, enjoying His presence and the goodness of His completed creation.

Their fundamental identity as image-bearers of the Most High preceded, both chronologically and theologically, their work as stewards of the earth. Their relationship with the Creator, established by His sovereign act and gracious initiative, came before their responsibility to creation. They were loved before they labored. They were accepted before they achieved. They belonged before they performed.

This stands in stark contrast to the devastating pattern that the Fall introduced into human existence and that our fallen world continuously reinforces with relentless pressure. We naturally tend to define ourselves, our very essence, our fundamental worth, our core identity, by what we do, by what we accomplish through our efforts, by what we produce with our hands and minds. Our secular culture measures human worth almost exclusively by productivity, evaluates people based primarily on their output and efficiency, and assigns value to individuals according to their tangible contribution to society's machinery. The marketplace becomes the measuring stick for human dignity.

Even in the church, despite our theological commitments and doctrinal statements, we slip with alarming ease into performance-based thinking that mirrors the world's values more than God's grace. We subtly begin believing, though we would never openly confess it, that our standing with God somehow depends on how much we do for Him in service and ministry, how faithful we prove ourselves to be in the small and large tests of obedience, how diligently we serve in various capacities, how consistently we maintain our spiritual disciplines. The gospel of grace gets quietly displaced by a gospel of works, and we find ourselves back under a burden Christ died to remove.

But the Sabbath pattern reveals a different reality. We are human beings, not human doings. Our identity comes from who we are, not from what we accomplish. We rest in God's finished work before we engage in our assigned work. This is the gospel pattern displayed from the beginning.

After the Fall, after sin entered the world and corrupted every dimension of human existence, after death became the universal sentence and spiritual separation from God became humanity's desperate condition, this ancient pattern of rest before work continues throughout Scripture's unfolding narrative, but it takes on profound and additional layers of meaning that speak directly to our spiritual condition. The rhythm established in creation now carries gospel implications we dare not miss.

We cannot work our way to God through any amount of religious effort or moral achievement. We cannot earn His favor through our most diligent efforts at righteousness or our most impressive displays of spiritual fervor. We cannot accomplish enough good deeds to merit His acceptance, pile up enough spiritual credentials to warrant His approval, or perform sufficiently to deserve His blessing. The distance between our righteousness and God's holiness remains infinite, unbridgeable by human effort.

Instead, we must rest completely, unreservedly, without qualification, in His finished work accomplished for us in Christ. We must trust wholly in what He has done on our behalf rather than what we might do for Him. We must cease from our own labors of self-justification, stop striving to establish our own righteousness, and rely entirely, absolutely, without reservation upon His grace freely given to undeserving sinners.

Hebrews 4:9-10 makes this spiritual connection explicit and brings the Old Testament pattern into sharp gospel focus: "So then, there remains a Sabbath rest for the people of God, for whoever has entered God's rest has also rested from his works as God did from his." The writer of Hebrews is not merely drawing a loose parallel or making a vague spiritual application. He is showing us that the Sabbath, from its very inception in the garden, pointed forward prophetically to the ultimate rest we discover only in Christ Jesus our Lord. It speaks of the cessation, the complete and final stopping, of our futile attempts to earn divine favor through human effort. It means the end of our exhausting striving to achieve righteousness through our own works and moral performance. It signals the beginning of trusting wholly, completely, unreservedly in His finished and perfect work accomplished on the cross at Calvary, where He declared with His final breath, "It is finished."

This rest is not partial but complete, not temporary but eternal, not based on our continuing performance but secured by His once-for-all sacrifice.

The Fourth Commandment

When God gave the Ten Commandments at Sinai, He included the Sabbath command. Exodus 20:8-11 records His words: "Remember the Sabbath day, to keep it holy. Six days you shall labor, and do all your work, but the seventh day is a Sabbath to the Lord your God. On it you shall not do any work, you, or your son, or your daughter, your male servant, or your female servant, or your livestock, or the sojourner who is within your gates. For in six days the Lord made heaven and earth, the sea, and all that is in them, and rested on the seventh day. Therefore the Lord blessed the Sabbath day and made it holy."

Notice the rationale. God did not introduce the Sabbath at Sinai. He reminded Israel of the pattern established at creation. "Remember the Sabbath day." This command points back to Genesis, back to God's rest after completing creation, back to the rhythm built into the fabric of reality itself. The Sabbath did not begin with Moses. It began in Eden.

The command contains both a prohibition and a prescription. Negatively, do not work on the Sabbath. Positively, keep it holy. The day belongs to God in a special way. It is set apart, sanctified, different from the other six days. This is not just a day off, not merely a break from labor, not simply time for recreation or personal pursuits. This is a holy day, consecrated to the Lord, dedicated to worship and rest in His presence.

The scope of the command extends beyond the individual. It includes children, servants, and even livestock. Everyone and everything under your authority gets rest. This reveals God's compassion, His concern for the whole household, His care for those who might otherwise be exploited or driven without mercy. The Sabbath protects the vulnerable, ensures that servants cannot be worked without ceasing, and guards against the tyranny of unending labor.

Deuteronomy 5:12-15 gives another version of the fourth commandment, but with a different rationale: "Observe the Sabbath day, to keep it holy, as the Lord your God commanded you. Six days you shall labor and do all your work, but the seventh day is a Sabbath to the Lord your God. On it you shall not do any work, you or your son or your daughter or your male servant or your female servant, or your ox or your donkey or any of your livestock, or the sojourner who is within your gates, that your male servant and your female servant may rest as well as you. You shall remember that you were a slave in the land of Egypt, and the Lord your God brought you out from there with a mighty hand and an outstretched arm. Therefore the Lord your God commanded you to keep the Sabbath day."

Here the emphasis falls on redemption rather than creation. Remember that you were slaves in Egypt. Remember that you had no rest, no relief, no escape from unending toil. Remember that God delivered you, brought you out, gave you freedom. The Sabbath testifies to this deliverance, celebrates this redemption, acknowledges that you are no longer slaves but God's free people.

Both of these theological rationales carry profound significance for understanding the Sabbath's meaning and purpose.

The Sabbath simultaneously points backward to the foundation of all things in creation and forward to the ultimate consummation of God's redemptive work. It serves as a bridge spanning the entire arc of biblical history, from the garden where God first rested to the promised rest that awaits His people.

On one hand, the Sabbath continually reminds us that we are creatures, not the Creator. God fashioned us with His own hands, breathed life into us, and placed us in a world He pronounced good. We did not create ourselves, nor do we sustain ourselves by our own power. The weekly rhythm of work and rest reflects the divine pattern established at creation's dawn. It acknowledges that God built into the very fabric of human existence certain rhythms, certain patterns, certain boundaries within which we flourish and thrive. We are not machines designed for endless productivity, but human beings created in the image of a God who worked and rested.

On the other hand, the Sabbath reminds us with equal force that God has accomplished a mighty act of deliverance on our behalf. We were once enslaved, trapped in bondage with no hope of escape, laboring under cruel taskmasters who knew neither mercy nor compassion. But God heard our cries, saw our affliction, and came down to rescue us with power and glory. He brought us out of the house of slavery, liberated us from our chains, and set us free to serve Him rather than tyrants. The Sabbath rest celebrates this freedom, this redemption, this transformation from slaves to beloved children of the living God.

The Sign of the Covenant

In Exodus 31:12-17, God calls the Sabbath a sign of the covenant between Himself and Israel: "And the Lord said to Moses, 'You are to speak to the people of Israel and say, "Above all you shall keep my Sabbaths, for this is a sign between me and you throughout your generations, that you may know that I, the Lord, sanctify you. You shall keep the Sabbath, because it is holy for you. Everyone who profanes it shall be put to death. Whoever does any work on it, that soul shall be cut off from among his people. Six days shall work be done, but the seventh day is a Sabbath of solemn rest, holy to the Lord. Whoever does any work on the Sabbath day shall be put to death. Therefore the people of Israel shall keep the Sabbath, observing the Sabbath throughout their generations, as a covenant forever. It is a sign forever between me and the people of Israel that in six days the Lord made heaven and earth, and on the seventh day he rested and was refreshed."'"

The severity of the penalty for Sabbath-breaking startles modern readers. Death for working on the Sabbath seems extreme, disproportionate, harsh. But the severity reveals how seriously God takes the Sabbath, how central it is to Israel's covenant relationship with Him, how vital it is as a sign of their identity as His people.

Breaking the Sabbath was not just breaking a rule. It was rejecting the sign of the covenant, denying Israel's relationship with God, abandoning the very thing that marked them as His people. It was covenant unfaithfulness, a form of apostasy, a declaration that they would live like the nations rather than as God's chosen people.

The Sabbath distinguished Israel from the surrounding nations. While Egypt's slaves worked without rest, Israel rested one day in seven. While Canaanite laborers toiled endlessly, Israel paused to worship. While other peoples measured worth by productivity, Israel acknowledged that their value came from being God's people, not from their economic output. The Sabbath testified to a different way of life, a different set of priorities, a different understanding of human flourishing.

Jesus and the Sabbath

When we come to the Gospels, we find Jesus repeatedly confronting the Sabbath question. The religious leaders had surrounded the Sabbath command with hundreds of additional regulations, creating a fence around the law that became more burdensome than the law itself. They defined exactly how far you could walk, precisely what actions constituted work, and strictly what activities were permissible. The day of rest became a day of anxiety, where every action had to be scrutinized, every movement analyzed for potential violation.

Jesus challenged this distortion head-on, deliberately and decisively. He healed on the Sabbath, fully knowing it would provoke controversy and confrontation. He understood that restoring sight to the blind, strength to the paralyzed, and wholeness to the broken would scandalize the religious establishment, and He did it anyway. He allowed His disciples to pluck heads of grain and eat them while walking through fields on the Sabbath, then defended them boldly when the Pharisees objected with their accusations of unlawful harvesting. He rescued animals that had fallen into pits on the Sabbath, then turned to His critics with a penetrating question: would any of them leave their own ox or donkey to suffer and die in a ditch simply because it happened to be the seventh day? Would they really value their regulations above compassion, their traditions above mercy, their interpretations above the very purpose for which God instituted the Sabbath in the first place?

His most direct statement comes in Mark 2:27-28: "The Sabbath was made for man, not man for the Sabbath. So the Son of Man is lord even of the Sabbath." Notice what Jesus affirmed and what He corrected. He did not abolish the Sabbath. He did not say it no longer mattered, did not declare it obsolete, did not free people from any obligation to rest. Instead, He corrected the misunderstanding of its purpose. The Sabbath was made for humanity's benefit, not as an arbitrary burden. God gave the Sabbath as a gift, not a curse. It exists to serve human flourishing, to provide rest and worship, to create space for what matters most.

But Jesus also claimed authority over the Sabbath. As Lord of the Sabbath, He has the right to interpret it, to apply it, to show what proper Sabbath observance looks like. The Son of Man, fully God and fully human, reveals both the divine intention behind the Sabbath and the human need it addresses.

The Lord's Day

After Jesus' resurrection, the early church began to gather on the first day of the week rather than the seventh. Acts 20:7 mentions this practice: "On the first day of the week, when we were gathered together to break bread, Paul talked with them, intending to depart on the next day, and he prolonged his speech until midnight." First Corinthians 16:2 assumes regular Sunday gatherings: "On the first day of every week, each of you is to put something aside and store it up, as he may prosper, so that there will be no collecting when I come."

By the time John writes Revelation, the first day of the week has become known as "the Lord's day." Revelation 1:10 states: "I was in the Spirit on the Lord's day, and I heard behind me a loud voice like a trumpet."

Why did the church shift from the seventh day to the first day of the week for its primary gathering?

The resurrection of Jesus Christ changed absolutely everything about how we understand time, worship, and God's redemptive purposes. When Christ rose triumphantly from the dead on that first day of the week, the day after the Sabbath, He did far more than simply return to life. He inaugurated the new creation itself, fulfilling everything the original creation pointed toward. The resurrection wasn't merely a reversal of one man's death; it was the dramatic reversal of the curse that had fallen upon all humanity in the Garden of Eden. In rising from the grave, Christ decisively defeated death itself, conquered the power and penalty of sin that had held humanity captive, and opened wide the way to eternal life for all who would believe in Him.

The resurrection marks nothing less than the beginning of God's new and glorious work in human history, the definitive start of the age to come breaking powerfully and irrevocably into the present age. This wasn't merely another significant event in the ongoing story of redemption; it was the climactic moment that fundamentally altered the trajectory of all creation. In that empty tomb, God demonstrated His sovereign power over death itself and vindicated His Son's perfect sacrifice on our behalf.

This cosmic shift, this hinge point of all history, this earth-shattering moment when heaven invaded earth, deserved, indeed demanded, its own day of remembrance and celebration. The early church understood intuitively what theology would later articulate systematically: that gathering on the first day of the week was not simply a convenient scheduling change or a minor adjustment to their worship calendar. Rather, it was a profound theological statement about the new reality Christ's resurrection had inaugurated.

The Christian Sabbath, rightly understood, celebrates something far more profound than merely creation; it celebrates the glorious reality of recreation, of God's decisive work to make all things new. It commemorates not simply rest after six arduous days of human labor, but rather our joyful entrance into the eternal rest that Christ's finished work on the cross has secured for all who believe. This is no ordinary day of cessation from activity; it is a weekly reminder that we have been ushered into something eternally significant.

We gather together on Sunday, the first day of the week, because that is precisely when Jesus rose triumphantly from the dead, shattering the grave's hold on humanity. That is when the tomb was discovered empty by those first faithful witnesses, when death's seemingly insurmountable power was broken forever, decisively and irrevocably. Every Lord's Day gathering, then, becomes a miniature Easter celebration, a weekly commemoration of the victory that changed everything.

Reformed theology has consistently affirmed that the Sabbath principle continues, but the specific day has changed. The Westminster Confession of Faith states this clearly: "As it is the law of nature, that, in general, a due proportion of time be set apart for the worship of God; so, in his Word, by a positive, moral, and perpetual commandment binding all men in all ages, he hath particularly appointed one day in seven, for a Sabbath, to be kept holy unto him: which, from the beginning of the world to the resurrection of Christ, was the last day of the week; and, from the resurrection of Christ, was changed into the first day of the week, which, in Scripture, is called the Lord's Day, and is to be continued to the end of the world, as the Christian Sabbath" (WCF 21.7).

The principle remains: one day in seven set apart for worship and rest. The specific day shifted because redemption history moved forward, because Christ accomplished what the old creation could not, because we now live in light of the resurrection rather than merely the creation.

Work and Rest in Proper Balance

The Sabbath pattern reveals that both work and rest are good, both ordained by God, both necessary for human flourishing. We were not created for endless toil, but neither were we made for perpetual leisure. The rhythm is six days of work, one day of rest. Both matter. Both have their place.

During my years in pastoral ministry, I watched believers struggle at both extremes. Some became workaholics, driven by anxiety or ambition or the need to prove their worth through accomplishment. They worked seven days a week, never truly resting, never stopping long enough to worship without distraction, never acknowledging their need for Sabbath rest. Their health suffered. Their families suffered. Their souls suffered.

Others swung to the opposite extreme, treating every day like the Sabbath, avoiding work whenever possible, pursuing leisure and entertainment as life's primary goals. They missed the dignity of labor, the satisfaction of accomplishment, the purpose that comes from stewarding God's gifts through productive work. Their lives lacked direction, purpose, and the sense of contributing something meaningful.

The biblical pattern avoids both extremes. Work is good. God worked in creation, and He calls us to work as His image-bearers. But work is not ultimate. It does not define us. It serves a purpose but does not become our purpose. We work six days, then we rest, acknowledging that our identity and worth come from being God's children, not from our productivity.

This rhythm protects us from idolatry. When we refuse to rest, we functionally declare that everything depends on us, that the world cannot function without our constant activity, that we are indispensable. This is pride masquerading as diligence. It is functional atheism, living as if God cannot sustain what He created without our help.

Conversely, when we refuse to work, treating all time as leisure time, we reject our calling as image-bearers, abdicate our responsibility to steward God's creation, and live as parasites rather than contributors. This too dishonors God, who worked to create and calls us to work in cultivating what He made.

The Sabbath rhythm says: work matters, but it is not everything. Rest matters, but it is not an end in itself. Together, work and rest create the pattern that honors God and enables human flourishing.

Rest as Trust

At its deepest level, Sabbath rest is an act of trust.

When I stop working, I acknowledge that the world does not depend on me. When I set aside tasks that need doing, emails that need answering, projects that demand completion, I declare that God is sovereign, that He can manage what concerns me, that I can trust Him to handle what I must leave undone.

This proved particularly difficult during my time as a seminary professor. The work never ended. There were always more papers to grade, more lectures to prepare, more books to read. I could have worked seven days a week and still not finished everything that needed doing. The demands were endless.

Learning to rest, truly rest, required me to trust that God cared more about those students than I did, that He could work in their lives even when I was not working, that my limitations as a creature did not hinder His infinite power as Creator. It required me to believe that resting in obedience to His command was more important than accomplishing everything on my list.

This is what Sabbath rest teaches us to do every single week, week after week, year after year. We learn to stop controlling outcomes we were never meant to control in the first place. We stop striving to accomplish what only God can accomplish. We stop acting as if everything depends on our efforts, our wisdom, our strength. Instead, we rest in God's providential care, trust His faithful provision, acknowledge with both our words and our actions that He is God and we most certainly are not.

Psalm 127:1-2 captures this fundamental truth with striking clarity and power: "Unless the Lord builds the house, those who build it labor in vain. Unless the Lord watches over the city, the watchman stays awake in vain. It is in vain that you rise up early and go late to rest, eating the bread of anxious toil; for he gives to his beloved sleep."

Consider those words carefully. God gives sleep to His beloved. He provides rest not as a luxury but as a gift, not as something we earn through exhaustion but as something He freely offers. He sustains what He creates. He watches over what He establishes. He builds what will last. We do not need to labor anxiously, rising early before dawn and retiring late into the night, eating bread earned through constant worry and relentless stress.

We can work diligently for six days, pouring ourselves into the tasks He has given us, and then rest on the seventh, trusting that God will provide for our needs, that He will accomplish His eternal purposes through means we cannot always see, that our simple obedience to His established rhythm pleases Him far more than our anxious striving and frantic busyness ever could.

Worship as the Heart of Sabbath

While rest is essential to the Sabbath, worship is its heart and purpose. The day is not primarily about what we stop doing but about what we start doing. We cease from ordinary labor to engage in extraordinary worship. We stop our work to focus on God's work. We set aside our agenda to attend to His.

The Sabbath was never meant to be merely a day off, a chance to catch up on sleep or pursue hobbies or relax. These things may have their place, but they are not the purpose. The Sabbath is holy, set apart, consecrated to the Lord. It is a day for corporate worship, for gathering with God's people, for hearing His Word proclaimed, for singing His praises, for celebrating the sacraments, for prayer and fellowship.

Hebrews 10:24-25 commands: "And let us consider how to stir up one another to love and good works, not neglecting to meet together, as is the habit of some, but encouraging one another, and all the more as you see the Day drawing near."

The command assumes regular gathering, corporate assembly, meeting together for mutual encouragement and stirring up to love and good works. The writer addresses those who had begun neglecting these gatherings, treating them as optional, skipping them when inconvenient or uninteresting. He calls them back to faithfulness, to consistency, to making corporate worship the priority the Sabbath demands.

During my years as a pastor, I encountered countless Christians who treated Sunday worship as one option among many, something to fit in if the schedule allowed, something to skip when other activities conflicted. They would miss worship for youth sports, for sleeping in after a late Saturday night, for weekend trips, for any number of reasons that seemed legitimate to them but revealed misplaced priorities.

The Sabbath principle challenges this casual approach to worship. If the day belongs to the Lord, if He has set it apart for holy purposes, if corporate worship is central to what it means to keep the Sabbath, then we cannot treat gathering with God's people as optional or secondary. It must be the priority around which we arrange everything else.

This does not mean legalism, does not require rigid rules about every activity, does not demand we spend every moment of Sunday in explicitly religious exercises. But it does mean that worship comes first, that we structure the day to honor its holy character, that we prioritize gathering with believers over personal convenience or entertainment.

The Sabbath and Soul Care

The Sabbath also serves our souls in ways we desperately need in our frantic age. We live in a culture of constant stimulation, endless entertainment, and relentless demands on our attention. Technology has erased the boundaries between work and home, between weekday and weekend, between waking hours and sleeping hours. We are always on, always available, always connected.

This pace is killing us. Anxiety disorders are epidemic. Depression affects millions. Burnout plagues every profession. We are exhausted, overwhelmed, unable to stop even when we desperately need rest.

The Sabbath offers a different way. One day each week, we stop. We unplug. We cease from the constant activity that marks the other six days. We create space for silence, for reflection, for an unhurried time with God and with people we love.

This kind of rest is not laziness. It is sanity. It is recognition that we are finite creatures who need regular rhythms of rest and renewal. It is wisdom about how God designed us to function. It is obedience to the pattern He established from the beginning.

I have watched what happens when believers embrace this rhythm. They are less anxious, more peaceful, better able to handle the pressures of daily life. They have a perspective that frantic busyness destroys. They maintain relationships that constant activity undermines. They guard their souls in ways that unending activity makes impossible.

The Sabbath is not about rules. It is about rest. Not just physical rest, though that matters. But soul rest, the kind that comes from pausing long enough to remember who you are, whose you are, what ultimately matters. The kind that comes from setting aside striving and simply being in God's presence. The kind that comes from worship that is not rushed, fellowship that is not squeezed between other commitments, time with Scripture that is not limited to a few hurried minutes.

Practical Sabbath Keeping

What does Sabbath observance look like practically?

Reformed theology has always emphasized that the specific regulations given to Israel do not directly transfer to Christians. We are not under the Mosaic Law. We are not bound by the detailed requirements that governed Old Testament Sabbath keeping. The New Testament does not give us a list of permissible and forbidden Sabbath activities.

But the principle remains, and wisdom requires that we apply it thoughtfully to our lives.

First, corporate worship must be absolutely central to our Sabbath observance. The Lord's Day is first and foremost a day set apart for gathering together with God's covenant people, not as isolated individuals pursuing private spiritual experiences, but as a unified body assembled in Christ's name. We come together to hear His Word proclaimed with authority and clarity, to sing His praises with voices joined in harmony, to celebrate the sacraments that visibly remind us of invisible grace, and to enjoy fellowship with brothers and sisters who share our faith and our struggles. This gathering is not merely one option among many for those who happen to find it convenient or enjoyable. It is not something we fit in if our schedule permits or if we feel particularly motivated on a given Sunday. This is the very heart of biblical Sabbath observance, the central purpose for which God designed this day. Corporate worship is the axis around which all other Sabbath activities revolve, the foundation upon which genuine rest is built, the primary means by which we honor the One who gives us the day in the first place.

Second, we should intentionally rest from our ordinary labor, the work that defines our six days of the week. Now, this principle doesn't mean that all work ceases entirely, as if we freeze in place at midnight Saturday and cannot move until Monday morning. Some work genuinely falls into the category of what the Reformers wisely called "works of necessity and mercy," activities that simply cannot wait, duties that must be performed regardless of the day. If your child falls ill on a Sunday, you care for them. If you are a physician or nurse, you tend to the sick who need you. If you are a law enforcement officer, you protect and serve. If you are a firefighter, you respond to emergencies. Such work is not a violation of the Sabbath principle; it is an expression of love and stewardship that God Himself approves.

But setting aside these necessary exceptions, our regular employment, the work that occupies us throughout the week, the labor we are paid to perform, the ordinary tasks that fill our calendars from Monday through Saturday, should cease on the Lord's Day. We should not spend Sunday morning catching up on the office work we didn't finish during the week, responding to work emails that could wait until Monday, or preparing presentations for Tuesday's meeting. We should not fill our Sunday afternoons running errands we could have done on Saturday, shopping for items we could purchase another day, or tackling household projects that, while perhaps important, are not so urgent they cannot wait another twenty-four hours. The day is not meant to become merely an extension of the previous six, another opportunity to cross items off our endless to-do lists. It is meant to be different, set apart, a day when the regular rhythms of productive labor give way to something else entirely.

Third, we should intentionally pursue activities that refresh and restore us rather than exhaust and deplete us, that build up our souls rather than tear them down, that draw us consciously toward God rather than subtly away from Him. Exactly what this looks like in practical terms will vary considerably from person to person, family to family, season to season of life. There is no single blueprint that works for everyone, no one-size-fits-all approach to Sabbath rest.

For some, refreshment might mean a Sunday afternoon nap, that blessed gift of rest that restores weary bodies and quiets anxious minds. For others, it might be a walk through God's creation, observing the heavens that declare His glory and the firmament that shows His handiwork. For still others, it could mean extended, unhurried time with family or close friends, conversations that go deeper than the rushed exchanges of the workweek, meals shared without the pressure of the clock ticking away. Some might find renewal in reading good books that elevate the mind and stir the affections. Others might rest through music, art, or other gifts God has given for our enjoyment and His glory.

The unifying goal in all these varied expressions is rest and genuine renewal, not merely different activity that exhausts us in new ways. The Sabbath is not about frantically filling the hours with supposedly spiritual busyness. It is about stepping off the treadmill of productivity and remembering that we are more than what we accomplish.

Fourth, we should carefully guard against legalism while simultaneously resisting the pull of license. These twin dangers have plagued Sabbath observance throughout Christian history, and we must navigate between them with wisdom and grace.

Legalism transforms the Sabbath from a gift into a crushing burden. It creates elaborate rules and restrictions that God Himself never commanded, binding consciences where Scripture leaves freedom. It measures spirituality by the number of steps taken, the temperature of food eaten, the types of recreation avoided. It judges fellow believers harshly, condemning as sin what God has not condemned, turning the day meant for rest and joy into an exhausting exercise in rule-keeping. This was the error of the Pharisees, who had buried God's good gift under layers of human tradition.

License, on the other hand, swings to the opposite extreme. It treats the Sabbath as if it were completely optional, a quaint tradition perhaps, but one we have outgrown in our enlightened age. It sees the Lord's Day as just another Sunday, no different from any other day of the week, another twenty-four hours to fill as we please. It dismisses any attempt to honor the day as legalistic, treating all boundaries as burdensome restrictions rather than loving guidelines for our good.

Biblical wisdom charts a course between these twin errors. It honors the day God has set apart without becoming enslaved to man-made regulations. It preserves Christian liberty while also taking seriously God's design for how we use our time.

These are not laws. They are patterns that can be found helpful, practices that have enabled some to honor the Lord's Day in ways that benefit souls and glorify God. Other believers might apply these principles differently, and that is fine. The goal is not uniformity of practice but faithfulness to the principle God established.

The Eternal Sabbath

Ultimately, the weekly Sabbath points forward to an eternal rest. Hebrews 4:9-11 promises: "So then, there remains a Sabbath rest for the people of God, for whoever has entered God's rest has also rested from his works as God did from his. Let us therefore strive to enter that rest, so that no one may fall by the same sort of disobedience."

The final rest awaits. When Christ returns, when He makes all things new, when He ushers in the new heavens and new earth, we will enter a rest that never ends. No more toil. No more struggle. No more weariness. Only endless joy in God's presence, perfect fellowship with Him and with His people, complete satisfaction in the new creation He will establish.

This hope transforms how we think about the weekly Sabbath. It is not just a respite from work but a foretaste of eternity, a weekly reminder that this world is not all there is, a signpost pointing toward the rest that awaits those who trust in Christ.

Every Sunday, we practice for eternity. We gather as we will gather. We worship as we will worship. We rest in God's finished work as we will rest forever. The weekly rhythm prepares us for the eternal reality, trains our hearts too long for what is to come, reminds us that we are heading toward a destination, not just wandering aimlessly through time.

And this hope sustains us when Sabbath keeping is difficult, when we are tempted to work seven days, when our culture pressures us to treat Sunday like any other day. We rest because God commanded it, yes. But we also rest because it points us toward the rest that is coming, the day when all our labor will cease and our joy will be complete.

The Sabbath pattern matters because God matters, because we matter, because the rhythm He established leads to flourishing while the frantic pace our culture demands leads to destruction. It matters because worship matters, because rest matters, because we need both to be fully human, fully alive, fully who God created us to be.

Male and female He created them, and He gave them the Sabbath. Before sin entered. Before work became toil. Before rest became necessary for survival rather than simply good for flourishing. The pattern was there from the beginning, woven into the fabric of reality, as much a part of God's design as gender itself.

We ignore it at our peril. We embrace it for our blessing. The choice, as always, is ours.

Chapter Six

The Garden of Delight: God's Provision and Presence

Genesis 2:8 begins with a simple statement that carries profound implications: "And the Lord God planted a garden in Eden, in the east, and there he put the man whom he had formed." Notice the sequence. God formed man first, then planted a garden for him. This was not an accident of divine timing but a deliberate revelation of God's character. Before Adam drew his first breath, God was already preparing a place for him. Before he could work or worship or even wonder at creation's beauty, God was making provision.

This is our God, the God who reveals Himself in Scripture as the One who prepares with intentionality and provides with purposeful love. He does not create and then scramble to figure out how to care for His creation, as though He were somehow caught off guard by the needs of what His own hands have made. He does not form humanity and then wonder where to put them, searching desperately for some suitable place to house the image-bearers He has just brought into being. No, our God is the God who prepares provision before there is even a need to be met, who provides with generous abundance before there are hands to receive His gifts, who plans meticulously and tenderly for our good before we even exist to receive it, before we draw breath to thank Him for it, before we open our eyes to behold the beauty of what He has prepared.

This is the God whose very nature, whose essence, whose character eternally and unchangeably includes divine foresight, tender care, and deep paternal affection toward those He creates in His own image. The garden planted in Eden, planted by His own hand, cultivated by His own design, shaped according to His perfect wisdom, stands as an eternal testimony to His character, a permanent witness to what kind of God we serve. He is not a God who merely tolerates His creatures, enduring their presence with cosmic patience, grudgingly making room for them in His universe. He is not a deity who creates by accident and then figures out what to do with what He has made. No, He is a God who genuinely delights in preparing good things for them, who takes joy in provision, who finds pleasure in creating spaces of beauty and abundance for those who bear His image, who loves to give gifts to His children before they even know to ask.

The word "garden" itself invites us into beauty and order. This was not a wild, untamed wilderness. Neither was it the artificial sterility of modern landscaping, where everything is controlled and nothing is allowed to grow as God intended.

Eden was cultivated beauty, purposeful design, nature shaped by divine hands for human flourishing.

And God planted it. The sovereign Creator of all things, who spoke galaxies into existence with a word, took time to plant a garden. He could have simply commanded it to appear fully formed. He could have created it instantly, as He created light and darkness and the foundations of the earth. But Scripture tells us He planted it, suggesting care, attention, deliberate artistry.

This tells us something absolutely crucial about work, about creation, and about God's relationship to the physical world He made. God is not distant from matter and material. He is not some abstract philosophical concept, hovering far above the messy realities of dirt and seeds and growing things, uninvolved in the tactile particulars of creation. He gets His hands dirty, so to speak. He involves Himself personally, intimately in the specific details of creating a place for the man He formed from the dust of the ground.

This should fundamentally shape how we view our own work, our own engagement with the physical world. If God Himself is not above planting, then no honest labor is beneath our dignity. If the Creator stoops to cultivate, then cultivation itself is sanctified. The God who spoke stars into existence did not consider it beneath Him to plant a garden. Let the truth settle into your soul the next time you think your work is too mundane, too physical, too ordinary to matter.

The location matters too, and Scripture preserves it for us with careful precision. Eden, in the east. Scholars have debated the precise geography for centuries, searching ancient maps and studying the rivers named in the text, but Moses preserves enough detail to anchor this firmly in real space and time, in the actual geography of the ancient Near East. This was not mythology spun from the human imagination. Not allegory meant merely to convey spiritual truth while remaining safely detached from physical reality. This was a real place, occupying real coordinates, in a real location on the earth God created, prepared by the real God for the first real humans who would walk its paths and tend its soil.

Later, when sin entered and humanity fell, God would place cherubim with a flaming sword east of the garden to guard the way to the tree of life. East becomes the direction of exile, the reminder of what was lost. But here, before the fall, east is simply where God chose to plant His garden, the direction from which blessing came.

Abundance Beyond Measure

Genesis 2:9 describes what God planted: "And out of the ground the Lord God made to spring up every tree that is pleasant to the sight and good for food." Every tree. Not some trees. Not adequate trees. Every tree that was pleasant to the sight and good for food. God's provision was not minimal. It was not just enough to survive. It was abundance, variety, beauty combined with utility, delight mingled with nourishment.

The trees were pleasant to the sight. God cares about beauty. He did not create a garden that merely kept Adam alive. He created one that would fill his eyes with wonder, that would delight his aesthetic sensibilities, that would remind him every day that his Creator was not just powerful but also generous, not just capable but also kind.

This matters more than we often recognize. Modern evangelicalism sometimes treats physical beauty as suspect, as if caring about how things look is somehow less spiritual than caring about how things work. We have inherited a functional minimalism that sees beauty as optional at best, frivolous at worst.

But God did not share this impoverished, truncated view of beauty's place in creation. He made trees pleasant to the sight, not merely functional, not just adequate for survival, but deliberately, intentionally beautiful. He crafted flowers in remote valleys that would bloom unseen by human eyes for centuries. He painted sunsets in riots of crimson and gold over oceans where no ship would sail for millennia. He sculpted mountains whose peaks would pierce clouds in places no human foot would tread for generations. He filled the depths of the oceans with creatures of breathtaking complexity and beauty, creatures whose intricate designs would remain hidden until technology finally allowed us glimpses into those dark waters.

He is not utilitarian. He is not a cosmic efficiency expert, calculating the minimum required beauty quotient necessary to keep His creation functioning. He is an artist, lavish, generous, extravagant in His creativity. And He made us in His image, which means we inherit something of His aesthetic sensibility. He gave us eyes that can appreciate beauty, not just assess utility. He fashioned hearts that respond to loveliness with something deeper than mere appreciation of function. We are drawn to beauty because our Creator is beautiful, because He loves beauty, because He scattered it throughout His creation with the abandon of infinite wealth.

The trees were also good for food. Beauty without utility would have been cruel. Utility without beauty would have been joyless. God gave both because both matter, because humanity needs more than bread alone, because we are embodied souls who require nourishment for body and delight for spirit.

Think about what this tells us about God's heart toward His creation. He did not create Adam and Eve and tell them to figure out their own food supply. He did not make them hunt and gather and struggle for every calorie. He planted a garden full of trees, each one ready to provide, each one offering its fruit freely.

This was provision before work. Blessing before labor. Grace before obedience. Adam would work in the garden, yes. But his work would not be to earn his sustenance. It would be to steward what God had already provided, to cultivate and expand and care for what was already given as a gift.

The parallel to the gospel of grace is impossible to miss, and it strikes at the heart of how we understand our relationship with God. We do not work to earn God's favor, laboring under the crushing weight of trying to make ourselves acceptable to Him. Rather, we work because we have already received His favor, because we have been welcomed into His family, because the gift has already been given. We labor not to achieve a righteousness we could never attain through our own efforts, but because righteousness, the very righteousness of Christ Himself, has been credited to us, given to us as a free gift through faith. Our obedience, our service, our cultivation of the spiritual life all flow from grace already received, not toward grace we desperately hope might one day be ours if we try hard enough. This is the beautiful, liberating logic of the gospel that transforms everything about how we approach God and how we live in His world.

The Tree of Life

In the midst of the garden stood two trees that demand our attention: "the tree of life was in the midst of the garden, and the tree of the knowledge of good and evil." The tree of life appears first in the text, and this order matters. Before God gave any command, before He established any boundary, He placed at the very center of the garden a tree that represented ongoing, sustained life. This was not just biological existence but fullness of life, communion with God, existence as it was meant to be.

Scripture does not describe what the tree of life looked like, whether it towered above the other vegetation, whether its branches spread wide in graceful arcs, whether its leaves caught the light in some particular way. We are not told how its fruit tasted, whether sweet or complex, whether unlike anything we might imagine or somehow familiar. The text simply tells us it was there, standing in the midst of everything, at the very heart of the garden, available and accessible to the man and woman who walked there in fellowship with their Creator.

Adam and Eve could eat from it freely, without restriction or limitation. God placed no prohibition on this tree, established no boundary around it, issued no warning about its fruit. Unlike the other tree that would soon enter the narrative with its divine command attached, the tree of life stood open, inviting, a constant offer of continued blessing and sustained communion with the One who had breathed life into Adam's nostrils.

It stood there as a perpetual reminder that life itself, not merely biological existence but the fullness of what it means to truly live, is God's gift to His creatures. It testified that vitality and blessing, strength and flourishing, do not arise from within ourselves or spring from the ground beneath our feet, but flow from Him who is the fountain of all good things. That magnificent tree, placed at the center of all God had made, declared to every part of creation that He is the source of all that sustains us, the wellspring of everything that makes existence not just possible but glorious.

The tree of life bookends the entire sweep of the biblical story, standing as a profound marker at both its beginning and its end. It appears here in Genesis 2, planted by God's own hand in the garden He designed for human flourishing. It appears again in Revelation 22, standing in the midst of the new Jerusalem, that glorious city God will establish when He makes all things new at the culmination of all things, when history itself reaches its appointed consummation.

Between these two points, between the first garden and the final city, between innocence and glorification, between creation and re-creation, stretches the entire narrative arc of Scripture. The whole grand story unfolds across this span: the fall that plunged humanity into darkness, the flood that swept away the corrupted world, the patriarchs who walked by faith in God's promises, the exodus that brought liberation from bondage, the law given at Sinai that revealed both God's holiness and our failure, the prophets who spoke His word to stubborn hearts, the exile that scattered the people in judgment, the return that offered fresh hope, the incarnation when the Word became flesh, the crucifixion where sin was dealt with once and for all, the resurrection that vindicated Christ and conquered death, the birth and growth of the church through which God is gathering His people.

But the tree of life remains. What was lost in Eden will be restored in the new creation. What humanity forfeited through sin, what we threw away in our rebellion, will be regained through Christ. The tree that stood in the midst of the first garden will stand again, but now in a transformed context, not in a garden, but in a city; not for two people standing alone in their innocence, but for all the redeemed from every tribe and tongue and nation, gathered from throughout human history.

This tells us something crucial about God's purposes, something that should fundamentally shape and inform how we understand both the original creation and the ongoing work of redemption throughout all of history. He does not abandon His original design when we fail Him. He does not look at the catastrophic wreckage of human sin, the devastation we have brought upon ourselves and the world He made, and decide that the whole project was a terrible mistake, that He needs to scrap everything and start over with something completely different, some alternate plan that bears no resemblance to what He first intended. No. God redeems. God restores. God takes what was broken and shattered by our rebellion and makes it whole again, but, and here is the wonder of it, He does so in a way that transcends and surpasses the original, bringing forth something even more glorious than what stood in Eden.

He brings us back to the tree of life, full circle to where we began at the very dawn of human history, but now we approach it not in our own righteousness, not trusting in our own obedience or our own ability to maintain our standing before Him, not depending on our moral performance or spiritual achievement. We come clothed instead in the righteousness of Christ, purchased by His precious blood, made secure in His finished work on the cross. What we lost through Adam's disobedience, we regain through Christ's obedience. Where the first man failed, the Last Adam succeeded.

The tree stood in the midst of the garden, central and available, right where life was meant to be lived. Life was never meant to be scarce or hard to find, never intended to be hidden away or difficult to access. God placed it right in the middle of everything, easily accessible, constantly present, perpetually available to those who dwelt in His presence. Humanity's problem was never that life was hidden from us or that God made it difficult to obtain, never that we lacked opportunity or access. Our problem was that we rejected the life He so freely offered and reached instead for something else, something that promised more but delivered only death.

The Tree of Knowledge

The second tree presents us with more complexity: "the tree of the knowledge of good and evil."

God would soon command Adam not to eat from this tree, but for now, the text simply notes its presence. It stood in the garden alongside the tree of life, another option, another possibility.

The name itself is puzzling upon first consideration. What could possibly be wrong with knowing good and evil? Should we not understand and clearly discern the difference between right and wrong? Is not moral knowledge, the ability to distinguish righteousness from wickedness, something to actively pursue and cultivate rather than something to carefully avoid?

The Hebrew construction helps us understand what's actually at stake here. "Knowledge of good and evil" is what scholars call a merism, a particular figure of speech that uses two opposite extremes or endpoints to represent the complete whole of something. Much like when we say "young and old" to mean everyone regardless of age, or when we speak of "heaven and earth" to encompass all of creation in its entirety, "good and evil" here represents the totality and fullness of moral knowledge. It signifies a comprehensive, complete understanding of right and wrong in all their manifestations.

More significantly, it represents the authority and prerogative to define and determine for oneself what is good and what is evil, to establish the very standards by which morality itself is measured and judged.

This was not about whether Adam and Eve could distinguish between right and wrong in a basic sense. It was about who gets to make that determination. It was about authority. About autonomy. About whether humanity would accept God's definitions of good and evil or insist on establishing their own.

God alone has the wisdom, the knowledge, the perspective to rightly determine good and evil. He sees all things. He knows all ends. He understands how every choice ripples through time and affects not just the chooser but all of creation. He is perfectly good, perfectly wise, perfectly just. His determinations about right and wrong flows from His character and serves the ultimate good of His creation.

Humanity, by contrast, lacks this comprehensive knowledge. We see dimly. We understand partially. We misjudge consequences and mistake evil for good and good for evil. We need God to define morality for us because we cannot reliably define it for ourselves.

The tree of the knowledge of good and evil, then, represented a choice. Would humanity accept their creaturely status and trust God's wisdom about what is good? Or would they grasp for autonomy, for the ability to determine right and wrong independent of God's revelation?

This choice still confronts every human being. Every ethical decision, every moral question, every judgment about what is right or wrong comes down to this: Will we accept God's definition or create our own?

Our culture has eaten deeply of this tree. We have rejected God's clear teaching on sexuality, marriage, gender, the value of human life, justice, and a thousand other issues. We have decided that we know better, that our wisdom exceeds God's, that we can determine for ourselves what is good.

And the results have been catastrophic. Confusion, chaos, suffering on a massive scale, all because we keep reaching for this tree, keep insisting we have the right to define reality according to our preferences rather than according to God's design.

Rivers of Blessing

Genesis 2:10-14 interrupts the narrative to describe the river that flowed through Eden: "A river flowed out of Eden to water the garden, and there it divided and became four rivers."

The text names these rivers and describes their courses, grounding the garden again in real geography. But the theological significance matters more than the geographical precision.

Water in Scripture consistently represents life, cleansing, blessing, the presence of God. Here, water flowed from Eden to water the garden. It did not flow into Eden from somewhere else. It originated there, in the place of God's special presence, and flowed out to nourish creation.

This is the fundamental pattern of blessing throughout all of Scripture, established here at the very beginning. Blessings flow from the presence of God outward into His creation. Where God dwells, life does not merely exist but flourishes abundantly. Where His presence makes its home, blessing does not remain static but spreads and multiplies. The garden, for all its perfection and beauty, could not generate its own sustenance, could not create its own life-giving power. Instead, it received everything it needed from what flowed directly from the source of all life, from God Himself, and thrived through His gracious provision alone.

The river divided and became four. Four rivers reaching in different directions, spreading blessing beyond the garden itself. This hints at God's larger purposes, at His intention that the blessing of Eden would not remain confined to one small plot of ground but would spread throughout the earth as humanity multiplied and filled it.

Imagine if Adam and Eve had remained faithful. Imagine if they had obeyed God's command, rejected the serpent's lies, and chosen to trust their Creator. They would have multiplied. Their children would have filled the earth. And everywhere they went, they would have extended the blessing of Eden, spreading the presence of God throughout creation, transforming the whole world into a garden-temple where humanity dwelled in perfect communion with their Maker.

This was the plan. This is what should have happened. The garden was not meant to be the final state but the first state, the starting point from which redeemed humanity would exercise dominion and stewardship, bringing all of creation under the joyful rule of God.

Sin interrupted this plan but did not destroy it. Christ came to accomplish what Adam failed to do. He obeyed where Adam disobeyed. He trusted where Adam doubted. He resisted temptation where Adam yielded. And now, in Christ, the plan resumes. The blessing spreads. The gospel flows like a river from Jerusalem to the ends of the earth, and one day, the knowledge of the glory of the Lord will cover the earth as the waters cover the sea.

Work as Worship

Genesis 2:15 introduces a crucial element of human purpose: "The Lord God took the man and put him in the garden of Eden to work it and keep it."

Work entered the picture before the fall. This is vital to understand. Labor is not a consequence of sin. Toil is. The curse made work difficult, frustrating, and often fruitless. But work itself, the activity of cultivating and creating and stewarding, was part of God's good design from the beginning.

God put Adam in the garden to work it and keep it. Two verbs, two aspects of the vocation God gave humanity.

"Work it" translates the Hebrew word *abad*, which means to serve, to labor, to cultivate. Adam was to serve the garden, to help it flourish, to actively participate in its ongoing fruitfulness. This was not passive enjoyment. God did not create Adam to lounge around eating fruit and admiring the scenery. He created him with a purpose, with a job to do, with meaningful labor that contributed to the garden's beauty and productivity.

"Keep it" translates *shamar*, which means to guard, to watch over, to protect. Adam was not only to cultivate what was there but also to protect it from anything that might harm it. This suggests the presence of potential threats even before the fall, responsibilities that required vigilance and care.

These two words appear together elsewhere in Scripture in contexts related to priestly service. The Levites were commanded to serve (*abad*) in the tabernacle and guard (*shamar*) it. The same vocabulary used to describe Adam's vocation in the garden describes the priests' vocation in the temple.

This is no coincidence. Eden was meant to be a garden-temple, a place where God dwelt with His people, where heaven and earth overlapped, where humanity served as priests mediating God's presence to creation. Adam's work was inherently worshipful. He was not merely a gardener but a priest-king, exercising dominion under God's authority, caring for God's creation in God's presence.

This transforms how we think about work. We tend to divide life into sacred and secular, spiritual activities and mundane ones. We go to church on Sundays, which is spiritual. We go to work on Monday, which is secular. We pray before meals, which is sacred. We cook the meals, which is ordinary.

But Scripture knows no such division. All of life is lived before the face of God. All legitimate work is service to Him. The mechanic repairing an engine, the teacher instructing students, the mother raising children, the farmer planting crops, the artist creating beauty, all of this can be worship if done for God's glory and according to His design.

Adam worked in the garden as worship. He cultivated it because God told him to, and in doing so, he served God. He guarded it because God had placed him there for that purpose, and in protecting it, he exercised the dominion God granted.

The fall corrupted work but did not eliminate its fundamental purpose. We still work. We still cultivate and create and build and steward. And when we do these things in faith, as service to God, we echo the original vocation He gave humanity in the garden.

Provision and Trust

Genesis 2:16-17 records the first direct speech from God to man: "And the Lord God commanded the man, saying, 'You may surely eat of every tree of the garden, but of the tree of the knowledge of good and evil you shall not eat, for in the day that you eat of it you shall surely die.'"

Notice how God framed this command. He began with permission, with abundance, with all that was freely given: "You may surely eat of every tree of the garden."

Every tree. The emphasis returns. Out of all the trees God planted, each one pleasant to the sight and good for food, Adam could eat freely. The garden offered overwhelming abundance. Variety beyond measure. No scarcity. No rationing. No careful calculation of calories or nutrients. Just trees, everywhere, all available, all nourishing, all delightful.

God gave first. He provided bountifully. He established generosity as the baseline reality of human existence in His presence.

Only after emphasizing this abundance did God introduce the single restriction: "but of the tree of the knowledge of good and evil you shall not eat."

One tree. One boundary. One test of obedience and trust.

This was not oppressive. This was not God limiting human freedom out of some desire to control or dominate. This was God establishing the fundamental principle that would govern all of human existence: we are creatures, not the Creator. We live under authority, not as autonomous agents. We find freedom within boundaries, not in their absence.

The test was reasonable. Adam lost nothing by avoiding this one tree. He had access to every other tree in the garden. He could eat and be satisfied, enjoy beauty and taste countless varieties of fruit. The restriction did not diminish his life but framed it properly, reminded him daily that he was accountable to God, that his existence was not self-generated but received as a gift.

God explained the consequence: "for in the day that you eat of it you shall surely die."

This was warning, not threat. A loving father telling his child not to touch the stove because it will burn. God was not eager to punish. He was protecting Adam from disaster, making clear the stakes, ensuring that disobedience could never be excused as ignorance.

Death was foreign to Eden. Nothing had died yet. Adam had no experiential knowledge of what this meant. But God's word was clear enough. Eat, and you will die. Trust Me, or face consequences you cannot imagine and do not want to discover.

The command also established something foundational to all true religion: God's Word as authoritative over human wisdom and experience. Adam knew this particular tree was forbidden not because of any inherent quality he could discern through observation or analysis, not because the fruit appeared poisonous or the tree seemed dangerous, but solely and completely because God had said so. His obedience, therefore, would be an act of trust, of believing God's revelation even when he could not fully understand or independently verify the reasons behind it. He would honor God's word simply because it was God's word.

This pattern reverberates throughout Scripture and remains at the heart of genuine faith. God commands, and we obey, not because we always comprehend the full wisdom of His instructions, not because we can trace every logical connection between command and outcome, but because we trust His character, His unfailing love, His unwavering commitment to our ultimate good. We walk by faith, not by sight, as Paul would later write. We take God at His word even when our finite reason cannot fully grasp the infinite purposes behind His commands. This is not blind obedience to arbitrary rules but confident trust in a perfectly wise and good Father who sees what we cannot see and knows what we do not yet know.

The Gift of Companionship

Genesis 2:18 introduces a problem in paradise: "Then the Lord God said, 'It is not good that the man should be alone; I will make him a helper fit for him.'"

For the first time since creation began, something was not good. Not evil, but incomplete. Not sinful, but insufficient. God looked at Adam in the garden and declared that his solitude was not good.

This is remarkable. Adam walked with God. He enjoyed unbroken fellowship with his Creator. He lived in paradise, surrounded by beauty and abundance. He had meaningful work, clear purpose, everything needed for physical flourishing. And yet, something was missing.

God Himself declared it: "It is not good that the man should be alone."

We are made for relationships. Not just a vertical relationship with God, though that is primary. But also horizontal relationships with other human beings. We are created as social creatures, designed for connection, wired for communion with those who share our humanity.

This was true before the fall. It is not a consequence of sin or a coping mechanism for a broken world. It is part of God's good design, written into our nature from the beginning.

God's solution to this incompleteness was to create "a helper fit for him." The language has been persistently misunderstood and frequently misused throughout church history, so we need to proceed with careful attention here. The word "helper" does not mean subordinate or inferior, as if Eve were created to be Adam's servant or assistant. The Hebrew word *ezer* appears twenty-one times elsewhere in the Old Testament, and in the majority of those occurrences it refers to God Himself as humanity's helper and deliverer. It carries powerful connotations of strength, of necessary and vital aid, of someone who provides what is critically lacking, not weakness or subservience.

"Fit for him" translates a Hebrew phrase (*kenegdo*) that means something like "corresponding to him" or "suitable for him" literally "as before him" or "opposite him." Not identical to him, which would be mere duplication. Not absorbed into him, which would be the loss of distinct personhood. But corresponding, matching, complementing, completing what was incomplete. Like a key corresponding to a lock, or a hand fitting perfectly into a glove designed for it.

Adam needed someone who was fundamentally like him in nature but not identical to him in person. Someone who fully shared his humanity, bearing the same image of God, but brought something different that he lacked. Someone he could relate to as a true equal, who could partner with him as a co-regent in the work God had given, who could share the profound joys and inevitable challenges of human existence in ways that even unbroken fellowship with God could not fully provide in that particular dimension of earthly companionship.

The Naming of the Animals

Genesis 2:19-20 describes a strange interlude: "Now out of the ground the Lord God had formed every beast of the field and every bird of the heavens and brought them to the man to see what he would call them. And whatever the man called every living creature, that was its name. The man gave names to all livestock and to the birds of the heavens and to every beast of the field. But for Adam there was not found a helper fit for him."

God brought the animals to Adam to be named. This was an exercise of dominion, of exercising the authority God had granted. To name something in the ancient world was to have authority over it, to define its nature, to establish one's rule.

Adam named them all. Every beast, every bird, every creature God had made. He observed them, understood their natures, and assigned appropriate names. The task demonstrated his intelligence, his capacity for language and categorization, his fitness for the dominion God had granted.

But something else happened during this process. As Adam observed the animals, he noticed something. They came in pairs. Male and female. Each creature had a corresponding partner, one fit for it, suitable to it, matching it.

The text makes this explicit: "But for Adam there was not found a helper fit for him."

He looked and found none like himself. The animals were wonderful in their own way, part of God's good creation, proper subjects for Adam's stewardship. But none of them could be his companion. None of them shared his nature. None of them could partner with him in the unique vocation God had given humanity.

This was intentional on God's part. He could have created Eve immediately after creating Adam. But He waited. He let Adam see the need first. He allowed the awareness of solitude to grow, the recognition of what was lacking, the longing for someone who could truly be called a partner.

God does this often. He lets us feel the weight of a need before He meets it. Not because He is cruel but because the recognition of need prepares us to receive the gift with proper gratitude, to value it rightly, to understand it as grace rather than entitlement.

The Deep Sleep

Genesis 2:21-22 describes the creation of woman in vivid detail: "So the Lord God caused a deep sleep to fall upon the man, and while he slept took one of his ribs and closed up its place with flesh. And the rib that the Lord God had taken from the man he made into a woman and brought her to the man."

God put Adam into a deep sleep. He was passive in this process, unconscious, unable to contribute or control what happened. The creation of his helper was entirely God's work, entirely grace, entirely a gift.

God took one of Adam's ribs. The physical details matter. Woman was not created from the dust of the ground, though God certainly could have made her that way. She was created from Adam himself, from his own body, sharing his nature in a way no animal could.

The early church fathers, in their reflections on this remarkable passage, sometimes observed that God took the rib from Adam's side with profound significance, not from his head, lest woman should rule over man, nor from his feet, lest man should trample her underfoot, but from his side, from that protected place near his heart, that she might be loved and cherished and protected. While we must exercise proper caution not to press symbolic interpretations beyond what Scripture itself warrants, and while we recognize that the fathers sometimes engaged in allegorical readings that modern biblical scholarship approaches with greater reservation, this particular observation nevertheless captures something deeply true about the nature of the relationship God intended.

Woman was created as man's partner, his companion in the work of dominion and the calling to be fruitful and multiply. She was his equal in dignity and worth, sharing his humanity fully and completely, bearing the image of God as truly as he did. The physical origin from Adam's own body emphasized this shared nature in a way that transcended anything Adam had observed in the animal kingdom, establishing the foundation for the one-flesh unity that would define marriage from that moment forward.

God "made" the rib into a woman. The Hebrew word here is *banah*, which means to build. God built woman from the material He took from man. He crafted her with the same care and attention He gave to all His creation, shaping her for the purpose He intended, designing her with both beauty and function in mind.

Then God brought her to the man. Like a father presenting a bride. Like a generous host introducing treasured guests. God Himself performed this introduction, this presentation of the gift He had made.

The First Wedding

Genesis 2:23 records Adam's response when he first saw Eve: "Then the man said, 'This at last is bone of my bones and flesh of my flesh; she shall be called Woman, because she was taken out of Man.'"

These are the first recorded words of Adam. He had named the animals, which surely required speech, but Scripture does not preserve those names. It preserves this, his first words upon seeing the woman God created for him.

"This at last." After all the animals passed by. After the naming. After the recognition of need. After the waiting. At last, here was what he had been looking for without knowing quite what it was.

"Bone of my bones and flesh of my flesh." She shared his nature completely. Not another species, however wonderful. Not a different order of being, however beautiful. But one like him, made from him, corresponding to him perfectly.

This is poetry. The Hebrew has a rhythm and beauty that elevate it above ordinary speech. Adam was not making casual observations but expressing wonder, delight, profound recognition of a gift.

"She shall be called Woman, because she was taken out of Man." The Hebrew creates a wordplay that English cannot quite capture. *Ish* for man, *ishah* for woman. The similarity in sound emphasizes the similarity in nature. They were distinct but united, different but corresponding, two who together reflected the image of God more fully than either could alone.

Genesis 2:24 draws a conclusion that echoes through all of human history: "Therefore a man shall leave his father and his mother and hold fast to his wife, and they shall become one flesh."

This is God's design for marriage. A man leaves his family of origin. A woman does the same. They cleave to each other, forming a new family unit, a new primary loyalty that supersedes even the parent-child relationship. And they become one flesh, united physically, emotionally, spiritually, in a bond that reflects the union of Christ and His church.

Jesus would later quote this verse when confronted with questions about divorce. Paul would reference it when teaching about marriage and about Christ's relationship to the church. The words spoken here in Genesis establish a pattern that governs all of human society, that shapes how we think about covenant and commitment and the joining of lives.

Naked and Unashamed

Genesis 2:25 concludes the chapter with a detail that might seem trivial but carries profound significance: "And the man and his wife were both naked and were not ashamed."

Naked. Exposed. Vulnerable. With nothing hidden, nothing covered, nothing concealed from each other or from God.

And not ashamed. No embarrassment. No desire to hide. No sense that their bodies were shameful or that intimacy was something to be approached with guilt or fear.

This was innocence. Not ignorance, but innocence. They knew they were naked, the text makes that clear. But the knowledge carried no shame because there was nothing to be ashamed of. No sin. No guilt. No broken trust. No history of betrayal or exploitation. Just two people, known fully and loved completely, with nothing between them and nothing to hide.

This is how God designed human intimacy to function. In the context of a permanent, covenantal commitment between husband and wife, physical nakedness represents and expresses emotional and spiritual intimacy. Nothing hidden. Nothing held back. Complete trust. Complete acceptance. Complete delight in each other as God's good gifts.

Sin would change this. Genesis 3 records that immediately after eating the forbidden fruit, Adam and Eve realized they were naked and tried to cover themselves. Shame entered. Fear replaced intimacy. They hid from each other and from

God, sewing fig leaves in a futile attempt to cover what had been exposed.

But here before the fall, there was only joy. Only trust. Only the pure delight of being fully known and fully loved.

This is what God wanted for humanity. This is what He prepared. A garden of abundance. Meaningful work. Divine presence. Human companionship. Physical intimacy without shame. Every need met. Every good gift provided. Life as it was meant to be lived, in unbroken fellowship with the Creator and His creation.

Lessons for Us

What do we learn from this picture of Eden? How does understanding God's original design help us navigate our fallen world?

First, we learn that God is a generous provider. He did not create humanity and leave us to fend for ourselves. He prepared a place for us, planted a garden full of good things, made provision before we could even ask for it. This is our God, the one who gives good gifts to His children, who cares about both our spiritual needs and our physical ones, who delights in blessing those He has made.

Second, we learn that work is good. Too many Christians treat work as a necessary evil, something to be endured until we can retire or reach heaven. But work was part of God's perfect design. Adam worked in paradise. Labor is not the curse; frustrated, fruitless labor is the curse. Work itself remains a gift, an opportunity to serve God and others, to exercise the creativity and capability He built into us.

Third, we learn that we need both God and other people. Adam's fellowship with God was real and precious, but it was not sufficient for all his needs. God Himself said it was not good for man to be alone. We are made for community, for relationships, for the give and take of human connection. The person who claims to love God while isolating from other believers has missed something fundamental about how God designed us.

Fourth, we learn that physical creation is good. The garden was beautiful. The food was delicious. The intimacy was joyful. God cares about these things. He is not a god who despises matter and exalts only spirit. He made bodies. He made taste buds and nerve endings and the capacity for physical pleasure. He called it all good, and we dishonor Him when we treat the physical world as inherently inferior to the spiritual.

Fifth, we learn something crucial about God's character and His way with His creatures: boundaries are not oppressive restrictions imposed by a cosmic tyrant, but protective guardrails established by a loving Father who knows His children better than they know themselves. God gave Adam one clear command, one simple restriction, one unmistakable boundary: do not eat from the tree of the knowledge of good and evil. Just one prohibition in a garden filled with countless permissions and pleasures. This was not an arbitrary exercise of divine authority, not a test designed to trip up our first parents, not the capricious demand of a deity who delights in constraining human freedom. It was wisdom flowing from perfect knowledge and perfect love.

God sees what we cannot see. He knows the consequences that lie beyond our limited vision. He understands the destruction that awaits when we violate the design specifications He built into creation. And precisely because He loves us, loves us with a fierce, unrelenting, covenant love that will not let us go, He warns us. He establishes boundaries. He marks out the territory where we will flourish and flags the areas where we will find only ruin. When Scripture sets boundaries around human sexuality, defining marriage as the covenant union of one man and one woman, it is not because God wants to deprive us of pleasure but because He wants to preserve us for the deepest, most fulfilling intimacy possible. When the Bible warns us about the love of money and calls us to generosity and contentment, it is not because God begrudges us prosperity but because He knows how wealth can poison the soul and destroy what matters most. When God establishes commands about how we relate to one another, speaking truth, forgiving offenses, bearing burdens, showing hospitality. He is not limiting our freedom but creating the conditions where a genuine community can thrive. When He prescribes how we are to worship Him, in spirit and truth, through Christ alone, with reverence and awe, He is not demanding empty ritual but protecting us from the disaster of giving ourselves to gods who cannot save and cannot satisfy.

God's boundaries are always protective, never merely restrictive. They mark the difference between life and death, between flourishing and destruction, between walking in light and stumbling in darkness. To chafe against them is to question His goodness. To transgress them is to claim we know better than our Creator what will truly make us happy, truly set us free.

Sixth, we learn that marriage is a gift and a picture. God created Eve for Adam. He designed them to complement each other, to complete what was incomplete, to reflect together something neither could reflect alone. And their union pointed forward to the greater union between Christ and His church, the ultimate marriage that gives all earthly marriages their meaning and purpose.

Finally, we learn that what was lost can be restored. Eden is gone. We cannot return to the garden. The cherubim guard the way, and the flaming sword turns in every direction. But God has not abandoned His original design. Through Christ, He is making all things new. The tree of life will reappear again. Intimacy with God will be restored. Work will be joyful again. Relationships will be healed. Bodies will be raised. And we will dwell in a new creation that surpasses even Eden in glory.

The garden of delight reveals God's heart toward His creation. He provides. He blesses. He delights in our flourishing. And though sin has marred everything, His purposes remain unchanged. What He began in Genesis He will complete in Revelation, and those who trust in Christ will find themselves, at last, in the paradise God always intended for those He loves.

Chapter Seven

Covenant Foundations in Eden

The question has occupied Reformed theologians for centuries, generating libraries of careful scholarship and passionate debate: Did God establish a covenant with Adam in the garden before the fall? The text of Genesis 2, when read in isolation, never explicitly uses the word "covenant" in its account of creation and God's commandments to the first man. Yet when we examine the structure, the components, and the nature of God's relationship with Adam, we find the unmistakable marks of covenantal administration woven throughout the narrative. As I have taught my seminary students through the years, watching their eyes widen as these connections became clear, and as I have come to understand more deeply through my own study of Scripture under the Spirit's illumination, the garden was not merely a beautiful dwelling place, a prehistoric paradise where our first parents enjoyed pleasant surroundings. It was a covenantal sanctuary, a holy space where God established the specific terms of fellowship with humanity, defining both the blessings of obedience and the consequences of rebellion.

This is not a minor point of academic interest, the kind of question best left to dusty volumes on library shelves or debates among scholars with too much time on their hands. Far from it. Understanding the covenant of works, grasping its reality, structure, and significance, shapes how we comprehend the entire biblical storyline from Genesis to Revelation. It provides the theological framework that makes sense of redemptive history itself. This covenant explains what Adam lost in his disobedience, not merely paradise, but the very relationship with God for which humanity was created. It clarifies what Christ accomplished in His perfect obedience, not simply a moral example, but the active righteousness required to satisfy the covenant's demands. It reveals why we need a Savior in the first place and illuminates how that salvation comes to us, not through our own efforts to fulfill what Adam failed to accomplish, but through union with Christ, who succeeded where the first Adam fell. The garden, then, becomes far more than a historical location somewhere in the ancient Near East, a geographical point lost to time. It becomes the stage upon which God's covenantal faithfulness would be tested by human obedience, tragically failed through human rebellion, and ultimately vindicated through the perfect obedience of the Second Adam, Jesus Christ, who would crush the serpent's head and restore what was lost in Eden's fall.

The Covenant of Works Defined

Reformed theology has historically affirmed that God entered into a covenant of works with Adam in Eden. This covenant, though not explicitly named in Genesis 2, is evident from the structure of God's relationship with the first man. A covenant, in biblical terms, involves several elements: parties who enter into a relationship, conditions that define the relationship, promises that reward faithfulness, and consequences that follow disobedience. All these elements appear in the garden account.

The parties are crystal clear, defined without ambiguity: God as the sovereign Creator, the One who speaks worlds into existence, and Adam as the responsible creature, fashioned from dust yet bearing the divine image. God, as always, initiates the relationship. He does not wait for Adam to seek Him out or establish terms of engagement. Rather, He plants the garden with His own hands, forms the man from the ground with deliberate care, breathes into him the breath of life, places him in Eden with purpose and intention, and establishes the terms of their fellowship according to His perfect wisdom. Adam, for his part, does not negotiate these terms. He does not propose alternative arrangements or suggest modifications to the divine plan. He receives what God has ordained, what God has graciously provided, what God has sovereignly decreed.

The condition is equally clear, stated with unmistakable directness: "And the Lord God commanded the man, saying, 'You may surely eat of every tree of the garden, but of the tree of the knowledge of good and evil you shall not eat, for in the day that you eat of it you shall surely die'" (Genesis 2:16-17). Here was a test of obedience, simple yet profound, a clear command accompanied by a stated consequence that left no room for misunderstanding. Adam's continued life in the garden, his ongoing fellowship with God, his experience of unbroken blessing, his enjoyment of paradise itself, all of this depended entirely on his faithful adherence to this divine command, this one prohibition set against the backdrop of abundant permission.

The promise, though implicit rather than explicit, was life. God had given Adam life. The continuation of that life, the fullness of that life, the eternal security of that life all hinged on obedience. Later Scripture would make this principle explicit: "You shall therefore keep my statutes and my rules; if a person does them, he shall live by them: I am the Lord" (Leviticus 18:5). The principle of law-keeping as the path to life was not invented at Sinai. It was established in Eden.

The consequence was death: "for in the day that you eat of it you shall surely die." Not merely physical death, though that would certainly come in time, the slow decay of flesh that had been created for immortality. Not merely spiritual separation, though that rupture would be immediate and catastrophic, a chasm opening between the holy God and His image-bearer the very moment rebellion entered the human heart. But death in all its terrible, comprehensive forms, the complete undoing of the life God had breathed into Adam, the severing of the fellowship for which humanity was designed, the introduction of corruption and decay into a world that God Himself had pronounced good, very good. Death would touch everything: body and soul, relationships and creation, present experience and future hope.

This structure, we must recognize, is fundamentally and thoroughly covenantal. God binds Himself, by His own sovereign choice and gracious initiative, to deal with humanity according to clearly stated terms that leave no room for confusion or doubt. He establishes the relationship on His own authority, defines the conditions by which that relationship will be maintained or broken, and commits Himself to respond faithfully according to those conditions, whether for blessing or for judgment. Adam, for his part, is bound to obey, called to active trust expressed in concrete faithfulness to the divine command. His obedience would secure continued blessing, ongoing life, unbroken fellowship with the God who walked with him in the cool of the day. His disobedience would bring the promised curse, all the dark implications of death unleashed upon a world that had known only life.

The Trees as Sacramental Signs

In every covenant, God provides visible signs that represent invisible realities. The rainbow after the flood. The circumcision of Abraham's household. The Passover lamb in Egypt. The bread and wine of the Lord's Supper. These signs do not create the covenant, but they represent it, seal it, and remind the covenant people of God's promises and their obligations. In Eden, the trees functioned as covenantal signs.

The tree of life stood at the center of the garden, a living symbol of the eternal life God offered to those who remained in fellowship with Him. Adam could eat freely from this tree. Its fruit was available; its life-giving properties accessible. As long as Adam obeyed, the tree of life was his to enjoy. It represented the promise: obey and live, not merely for a season but forever.

The tree of the knowledge of good and evil stood as a test. God could have created Adam incapable of disobedience. He could have programmed perfect obedience into human nature. But a love that cannot choose is not love at all, and obedience that is compulsory carries no moral weight. God wanted more than automatons. He wanted image-bearers who would freely choose fellowship with Him, who would willingly submit to His authority, who would trust His goodness even when tempted to grasp for autonomy.

The tree of the knowledge of good and evil made that choice possible. It stood as a visible reminder of God's command, a tangible test of Adam's faithfulness, a constant opportunity to reaffirm trust in God's wisdom. Every time Adam passed that tree without eating, he was choosing God. He was affirming that God's word was sufficient, that God's provision was enough, that God's authority was legitimate.

The tree was not evil in itself, a critical distinction we must grasp if we are to understand the nature of the test Adam faced. God made that tree, and everything God made was very good. There was nothing inherently corrupting in its bark, its leaves, its fruit. The tree itself was as much a testimony to divine craftsmanship as the cedars of Lebanon or the flowering plants that filled the garden with color and fragrance. But God had reserved it, set it apart from all the other trees, declared it off-limits to the one He had placed in the garden. The evil was not in the tree itself but in the act of disobedience that would occur if Adam reached out his hand to take what God had forbidden. The sin would lie in the rejection of God's word, in the prideful assertion that the creature knew better than the Creator, in the fundamental rebellion of choosing one's own wisdom over divine instruction.

These trees were sacramental in nature, serving a function far beyond mere botanical beauty or nutritional sustenance. They were physical objects that represented profound spiritual realities, making visible what was otherwise invisible. The tree of life pointed to eternal communion with God, to the promise of unending fellowship, to the hope of immortality secured through obedience and trust. The tree of the knowledge of good and evil pointed to the test of that communion, standing as a perpetual reminder that relationship with God was not automatic or unconditional but required faithfulness to His word. Together, these two trees framed the covenantal relationship between God and Adam, giving visible, tangible form to the invisible stakes of obedience and disobedience, life and death, blessing and curse.

The Command as Covenant Stipulation

Every covenant, by its very nature, contains stipulations, the specific terms and conditions that define and govern the relationship between the parties who enter into it. These stipulations are not arbitrary additions but essential components that give the covenant its structure and meaning. They spell out what each party commits to, what obligations bind them, what privileges extend to them, and what consequences follow from faithfulness or unfaithfulness to the covenant bond.

In the Mosaic covenant that God established with Israel at Mount Sinai, these stipulations filled entire chapters of Exodus, Leviticus, and Deuteronomy, creating an intricate framework of laws that touched every aspect of life, ceremonial, civil, and moral. The people received detailed instructions about worship and sacrifice, about justice and mercy, about cleanness and uncleanness, and about festivals and offerings. The sheer volume of these requirements testified to the comprehensive nature of God's claim on His people and the seriousness with which He addressed their covenant relationship.

In the Abrahamic covenant, which preceded Moses by centuries, the stipulations were considerably simpler, though no less profound. God required Abraham to walk before Him and be blameless, and in return promised to establish His covenant between them, to multiply Abraham's offspring, and to give them the land of promise. The requirement distilled down to a life of faith and obedience, of trusting God's promises even when circumstances seemed to contradict them.

But in the Edenic covenant, that original arrangement between God and Adam in the garden, the stipulation was simplest of all. There was no lengthy code of conduct, no elaborate system of sacrifices, no complex set of regulations to memorize and apply. The entire covenant obligation reduced to a single, clear command: do not eat from the tree of the knowledge of good and evil. One tree. One prohibition. One test of whether Adam would trust God's word above his own desires or judgment.

The command was clear. God did not speak in riddles or hide the requirement in obscure language. He told Adam plainly what he could do and what he could not do. "You may surely eat of every tree of the garden, but of the tree of the knowledge of good and evil you shall not eat" (Genesis 2:16-17). The permission was broad. The restriction was narrow. Adam had freedom to enjoy everything God had made, with one exception. One tree. One command. One test.

The clarity of this command matters. Adam could not plead ignorance. He could not claim he had misunderstood. He could not argue that God's will was unclear. God had spoken directly to him, face to face, in words that admitted no ambiguity. When disobedience came, it would not be because of confusion but because of rebellion.

The simplicity of this command also matters. God did not burden Adam with complex regulations. He did not require elaborate rituals or demanding sacrifices. He asked for one thing: trust Me enough to obey this single prohibition. If Adam could not obey one clear command when he was sinless, in a perfect environment, with every advantage and no external temptation beyond the serpent's lies, then the problem was not with the law but with the heart.

This principle would echo throughout redemptive history. "For whoever keeps the whole law but fails in one point has become guilty of all of it" (James 2:10). The issue is not the number of commands but the posture of the heart. Will we submit to God's authority or assert our own? Will we trust His wisdom or rely on our judgment? Will we obey because He is God and we are not?

The command in Eden established this principle from the beginning. Obedience to God is not negotiable. His word is not a suggestion. His authority is not conditional on our agreement. He is the Creator. We are the creatures. He commands. We obey. This is the structure of reality, and no amount of human philosophy or cultural evolution can change it.

The Penalty as Covenant Sanction

Every covenant includes sanctions, the consequences that follow either obedience or disobedience. Blessings for faithfulness. Curses for rebellion. This is not arbitrary vindictiveness on God's part. It is the natural outworking of a covenantal relationship. Those who align themselves with God's purposes experience His favor. Those who set themselves against God experience His judgment. In Eden, the sanction for disobedience was death: "for in the day that you eat of it you shall surely die" (Genesis 2:17).

This was not an empty threat. God does not bluff. He does not warn of consequences He does not intend to carry out.

When He told Adam that eating from the forbidden tree would result in death, He meant it. And when Adam disobeyed, death came. Not immediately in its physical form, though the process of physical decay began that day. But immediately in its spiritual form, as fellowship with God was broken and Adam hid from God's presence.

The penalty reveals several crucial truths about God's covenant with Adam.

First, it reveals the seriousness of obedience. God did not say, "If you eat of it, I will be disappointed." He did not say, "If you eat of it, you will miss out on some blessings." He said, "You will surely die." The stakes could not be higher. Disobedience was not a minor infraction. It was a capital offense. It was treason against the Creator, rebellion against rightful authority, the assertion of creature autonomy against divine sovereignty.

Second, it reveals the justice of God. Death was the appropriate penalty for sin. When Adam chose to disobey, he chose death. He chose to sever himself from the source of life. He chose to exchange the truth about God for a lie, to worship and serve the creature rather than the Creator. And the consequence of that choice was exactly what God had warned: death in all its forms, physical and spiritual, immediate and ultimate.

Third, it reveals the absolute necessity of a substitute. If the penalty for covenant-breaking is death, and if Adam's descendants inherit both his guilt and corruption, then everyone born into Adam's line stands under the same sentence of death. We are all covenant-breakers by nature and by choice. We are all deserving of death, not merely as an unfortunate consequence, but as the just verdict of a holy God against our rebellion. And no amount of good works, no degree of moral improvement, no religious performance or ethical striving can possibly reverse the sentence that has been pronounced. The verdict stands. The debt remains unpaid. The justice of God must be satisfied.

The only hope for fallen humanity is a substitute, someone who can bear the penalty in our place, someone who can stand where we ought to stand and receive what we deserve to receive. We need someone who can fulfill the covenant obligations we have failed to meet, someone who can render the perfect obedience we have refused to render, someone who can endure the judgment we have earned and emerge victorious on the other side. Without such a substitute, we are lost. Without someone to bridge the chasm between God's holiness and our sin, we remain under the covenant curse, condemned by the very law that was meant to lead us into life.

This is where the covenant of works points us forward, beyond the tragedy of Eden, toward the One who would succeed where Adam failed. Adam shattered the covenant and unleashed death into God's good creation. Christ fulfilled the covenant perfectly and brought forth life everlasting. "For as by the one man's disobedience the many were made sinners, so by the one man's obedience the many will be made righteous" (Romans 5:19). The parallel is exact and intentional. The penalty Adam incurred through his rebellion, Christ absorbed in his body on the cross. The perfect obedience Adam failed to render to his Creator, Christ provided without a single flaw or deviation. The life Adam forfeited in the garden through his grasping pride, Christ restored through his humble submission unto death.

The covenant of works established in Eden was never intended to be the final word in humanity's story. It was not designed to save anyone, for salvation comes through grace, not through our ability to keep God's law. Rather, it was designed to reveal our desperate need for a Savior, to expose the depth of our inability and the magnitude of our dependence on divine mercy. It was established to demonstrate with undeniable clarity that perfect obedience is required by God's holy character and that we, in our fallen condition, cannot possibly provide it. The covenant of works serves as a divine tutor, a tutor appointed to drive us to Christ with the force of holy law behind us. He alone is the One who could fulfill every demand the covenant makes upon us. He alone could bear the full weight of the covenant's curse without being crushed beneath it.

Adam as Federal Head

One of the most difficult doctrines for modern minds to accept is the concept of federal headship, the idea that Adam represented all humanity in the garden and that his failure affected not only himself but all his descendants. We live in an age of radical individualism, where each person is considered autonomous and responsible only for their own actions. The thought that we could be held accountable for someone else's sin, even our first father's, strikes many as fundamentally unjust.

Yet Scripture is clear on this point. Adam's sin was not merely his own. It was ours. His guilt was imputed to us. His corruption was transmitted to us. "Therefore, just as sin came into the world through one man, and death through sin, and so death spread to all men because all sinned" (Romans 5:12). We did not individually eat from the tree in Eden, but we fell in Adam. His disobedience became our disobedience. His death sentence became our death sentence.

This is the doctrine of original sin, and it finds its deepest roots in the covenantal structure God established from the very beginning in Eden. Adam was not merely the first human being, the initial member of our species, a solitary individual making personal choices that affected only himself. No, he was something far more significant, far more consequential. He was the representative of the entire human race, appointed by God to stand in the place of all who would come after him. When God made the covenant with Adam in that pristine garden, He was not entering into a private agreement with one man alone. He was making a covenant with humanity itself, with every person who would ever draw breath, with the entire lineage that would flow from Adam's body. When Adam obeyed or disobeyed the terms of that covenant, he was acting not only for himself, not merely as an individual making choices with personal consequences, but for all who would descend from him through the ages. His actions carried representative weight. His choices bound his posterity. His covenant standing determined ours.

This arrangement was not unfair. God had every right to structure His relationship with humanity this way. He is the Creator. He determines the terms. And He chose to deal with humanity corporately, through a representative head. This is how God works throughout Scripture. He chooses one to stand for many. Abraham represents Israel. Israel represents the nations. Christ represents His people. The principle of representation is woven into the fabric of redemptive history.

Moreover, the arrangement was actually merciful. If each person had to stand or fall individually before God, with no representative to act on their behalf, we would all fall. The only reason any of us can be saved is because God provided a new representative, a Second Adam, who could do what the first Adam failed to do. Christ's obedience is imputed to us just as Adam's disobedience was imputed to us. The same principle that brought condemnation in Adam brings justification in Christ.

I have counseled many people through the years who struggled with this doctrine. They asked me how it could be fair that they inherited Adam's guilt. My response was always the same: if you reject the imputation of Adam's sin, you must also reject the imputation of Christ's righteousness. You cannot have one without the other. They stand or fall together. Either we accept representation as a legitimate principle, in which case we can rejoice that Christ represents us, or we reject it, in which case we must stand before God on our own merits and face certain condemnation.

Adam's federal headship in the covenant of works is not a peripheral doctrine. It is foundational to understanding both our problem and our solution. We are in Adam by nature, guilty of his sin, condemned by his disobedience. But we can be in Christ by grace, credited with His righteousness, justified by His obedience. The covenant with Adam reveals our desperate need. The covenant in Christ provides our only hope.

The Garden as Temple

Recent scholarship has highlighted the temple imagery in the garden narrative, and I believe this strengthens the case for understanding Eden in covenantal terms. Throughout Scripture, God's dwelling places are covenantal spaces. The tabernacle was built according to the covenant at Sinai. The temple was dedicated under the Davidic covenant. The New Jerusalem is described as the dwelling place of God with His people in the eternal covenant secured by Christ's blood.

Eden was the first temple, the original sanctuary where God walked with humanity in the cool of the day. The parallels between the garden and later sanctuaries are striking and too numerous to be coincidental.

The garden was in the east, and the entrance to the tabernacle faced east. The cherubim who guarded the way to the tree of life in Genesis 3:24 were embroidered on the veil of the tabernacle and carved into the walls of the temple. The lampstand in the tabernacle was shaped like a tree with almond blossoms, echoing the tree of life in Eden. The river that flowed from Eden to water the garden (Genesis 2:10) finds its parallel in the river flowing from the temple in Ezekiel 47:1-12 and from the throne of God in Revelation 22:1-2.

Adam's role in the garden was priestly. God placed him there "to work it and keep it" (Genesis 2:15). The Hebrew words translated "work" and "keep" are the same words later used to describe the Levites' service in the tabernacle (Numbers 3:7-8; 8:26). Adam was not simply a gardener. He was a priest in God's sanctuary, tending the sacred space where heaven and earth met.

This temple imagery reinforces the covenantal understanding of Eden. Temples are places of covenant. They are where God reveals His glory, where He makes His dwelling, where He receives worship, where He meets with His people according to established terms. The sacrifices, rituals, and regulations that governed Israel's worship at the tabernacle and temple were all expressions of a covenant relationship.

If Eden was a temple, then Adam was a priest serving in that temple according to covenantal obligations. His obedience was not merely ethical. It was liturgical. It was the worship God required from the one appointed to serve in His presence. And when Adam failed to guard the sanctuary, when he allowed the serpent to enter and deceive, when he ate the forbidden fruit and broke the covenant command, he failed not only as a man but as a priest. He defiled the sanctuary. He profaned the holy place. He was driven from God's presence, just as unfaithful priests were later cut off from serving in the tabernacle.

The hope, of course, is that a faithful priest would come, one who would perfectly fulfill all righteousness, who would guard the sanctuary against every enemy, who would offer the perfect sacrifice and secure eternal access to God's presence. That priest is Christ, our great high priest, who has entered the true sanctuary in heaven and secured for us eternal redemption (Hebrews 9:11-12).

Life Through Obedience

The covenant of works established a clear principle: life comes through obedience. This was true in Eden, and it remains true throughout Scripture. "You shall therefore keep my statutes and my rules; if a person does them, he shall live by them: I am the Lord" (Leviticus 18:5). The principle is repeated again and again. Do this and live. Obey and be blessed. Keep the commandments and dwell in the land.

The problem, of course, is that no one after Adam has been able to obey perfectly. We are all born in sin, shaped in iniquity, inclined toward evil from our youth. We break God's commandments in thought, word, and deed. We fail to love God with all our heart, soul, mind, and strength. We fail to love our neighbors as ourselves. We all fall short of the glory of God, and the wages of our sin is death.

Does this mean the covenant of works is irrelevant, something we can safely set aside in our preaching and teaching? Some theologians have argued precisely that. They suggest that since no one can possibly be saved by works, since the whole enterprise of earning life through obedience has proven impossible for fallen humanity, the entire concept of a covenant of works is unhelpful at best and spiritually destructive at worst. Better, they insist, to focus exclusively on grace, to speak only of what God has freely accomplished for us in Christ, without confusing people or burdening their consciences with talk of Adam's catastrophic failure and our resulting condemnation in him.

But this criticism misses the point entirely, fundamentally misunderstanding the purpose and function of the covenant of works in redemptive history. The covenant of works was never designed to save anyone after the fall. It is not a competing path to salvation that stands alongside the covenant of grace. Rather, it is meant to reveal our desperate need for salvation, to expose the depth of our predicament. It shows us with crystalline clarity what God's justice requires: perfect, perpetual, personal obedience to every commandment, in thought and word and deed, from the heart. It shows us what we have utterly and irreversibly failed to provide. And most importantly, it shows us precisely why we need a Savior who can provide what we cannot, someone who can render the obedience we owe but cannot give.

Moreover, the covenant of works reveals what Christ accomplished. He did not merely die for our sins. He lived for our righteousness. He kept the law perfectly. He rendered to God the obedience that Adam failed to give. He earned the life that Adam forfeited. And now, by faith, His obedience is credited to us. His righteousness becomes ours. His life secures our life.

This is the doctrine of justification, and it makes no sense apart from the covenant of works. If there were no requirement for perfect obedience, then Christ's perfect obedience would be unnecessary. If there were no penalty for disobedience, then Christ's death would be pointless. But because the covenant of works established both the requirement and the penalty, Christ's work addresses both. He fulfilled the requirement and bore the penalty. He achieved the righteousness the law demanded and absorbed the wrath the law threatened.

Paul makes this connection explicit: "For as by the one man's disobedience the many were made sinners, so by the one man's obedience the many will be made righteous" (Romans 5:19). Adam's disobedience brought condemnation. Christ's obedience brings justification. The two are parallel. The two are covenantal. And understanding the covenant with Adam helps us understand the covenant in Christ.

I have spent years teaching seminary students and preaching about justification by faith alone. I have written extensively on the Reformed understanding of salvation by grace through faith. And I am convinced that this doctrine stands or falls with the covenant of works. If we abandon the covenant of works, we lose the framework for understanding what Christ accomplished. We reduce salvation to forgiveness of sins and miss the glorious truth that we are not merely pardoned criminals but righteous saints, clothed in the obedience of the Second Adam, accepted in God's presence because Christ has fulfilled every obligation we failed to meet.

The Promise of Confirmation

One question that has occupied Reformed theologians is what would have happened if Adam had obeyed. The covenant of works promised life for obedience and threatened death for disobedience. Adam disobeyed and brought death. But what if he had obeyed? What if he had resisted the serpent's temptation, refused to eat the forbidden fruit, and remained faithful to God's command?

The Westminster Confession of Faith suggests that Adam would have been confirmed in righteousness, moved from a state of mutable obedience to a state of immutable obedience. He would have passed the test. He would have proven his faithfulness. And God would have secured him in that faithfulness, removing the possibility of future disobedience and granting him eternal life.

This is, admittedly, speculation. Genesis does not tell us what would have happened if Adam had obeyed. It only tells us what did happen when he disobeyed. But the speculation is grounded in the nature of covenant and the character of God. God does not test His people endlessly. He tests them for a season, and when they prove faithful, He confirms them in their faithfulness and grants them the promised reward.

We see this pattern elsewhere in Scripture. Abraham was tested repeatedly, called to leave his country, to believe God's promise of a son, to offer that son as a sacrifice. But when he proved faithful, God confirmed His covenant with him, swearing by Himself that His promises would stand. Job was tested severely, losing everything, but when he remained faithful, God restored him and blessed him more than before. Jesus was tested in the wilderness for forty days, and when He proved faithful, angels came and ministered to Him.

The principle seems to be that God allows a season of testing, and faithfulness in that season leads to confirmation and reward. If Adam had obeyed, if he had resisted temptation, if he had trusted God's word over the serpent's lies, then presumably God would have confirmed him in righteousness and granted him access to the tree of life forever. He would have moved from probation to confirmation, from testing to triumph, from the possibility of falling to the security of eternal life.

This did not happen, of course. Adam failed the test. He chose disobedience. He brought death instead of life, curse instead of blessing, exile instead of confirmation. But the promise of confirmation through obedience remained, and it would be fulfilled in Christ.

Jesus succeeded where Adam failed. He obeyed perfectly. He resisted every temptation. He trusted God's Word completely. He fulfilled all righteousness. And because of His faithfulness, He was confirmed in glory, raised from the dead, exalted to God's right hand, given a name above every name. He passed the test Adam failed, and now He shares His reward with all who belong to Him.

Covenant Theology and the Unity of Scripture

Understanding the covenant of works established in Eden is not merely an academic exercise in historical theology, something to be debated in theological seminars and then filed away in dusty volumes. Rather, it is absolutely foundational and essential to grasping the deep unity of Scripture and the beautiful coherence of God's redemptive plan across all ages. Without this understanding, we miss the grand architecture that holds the entire biblical narrative together.

The Bible is not simply a random collection of disconnected stories, isolated moral lessons, and religious sayings that happened to be bound together between two covers. It is not an anthology of independent tales that share only the loosest connection to one another. Instead, it is the deliberate, purposeful, and progressive unfolding of God's covenantal purposes throughout human history, from the very moment of creation in Eden's garden to the final consummation when Christ returns and makes all things new. Every covenant builds upon what came before, pointing forward to what comes after, weaving together a single, magnificent tapestry of divine redemption.

The covenant with Adam establishes the pattern. God initiates relationship. He sets the terms. He promises blessing for obedience and threatens judgment for disobedience. He provides visible signs to represent invisible realities. And He holds His covenant partners accountable for their obligations.

This pattern repeats throughout redemptive history. The covenant with Noah. The covenant with Abraham. The covenant at Sinai. The covenant with David. Each covenant has its own particular features, its own specific promises, its own unique role in the unfolding story. But all of them share the basic structure established in Eden.

More importantly, all of them point forward to the ultimate covenant secured by Christ. The covenant of grace does not replace the covenant of works. It fulfills it. Christ does what Adam failed to do. He renders perfect obedience. He earns the promised life. And then He offers that life to all who will receive it by faith.

This is why Reformed theology speaks of two covenants: the covenant of works and the covenant of grace. The covenant of works was made with Adam and required perfect obedience for life. The covenant of grace was made in Christ and offers life as a free gift to all who believe. The first covenant reveals our problem. The second covenant provides our solution. The first covenant shows what God requires. The second covenant demonstrates what God provides.

I have devoted my life to studying and teaching Scripture, and I am more convinced than ever that covenant theology provides the framework that makes sense of the whole. From Genesis to Revelation, God is working out His covenantal purposes. He is calling a people to Himself, securing their salvation through the work of Christ, and conforming them to the image of His Son. Understanding the covenant with Adam helps us understand everything that follows.

Pastoral Application

This may all seem abstract and theoretical, far removed from the practical concerns of daily Christian life. What difference does it make whether there was a covenant in Eden? How does understanding the covenant of works help me live faithfully today?

Let me offer several practical applications from my years of pastoral ministry.

First, understanding the covenant of works helps us grasp the profound seriousness and weight of sin in all its dimensions. Sin is not merely making unfortunate mistakes or falling short of our God-given potential, as our therapeutic culture would have us believe. Sin is fundamentally covenant-breaking, a violation of the sacred relationship God established with humanity. It is deliberate rebellion against God's rightful authority over His creation and His creatures. It is the brazen assertion of creature autonomy against divine sovereignty; the creature declaring independence from the Creator who gives him every breath.

When we sin, in thought, word, or deed, we are doing precisely what Adam did in that fateful moment in the garden. We are choosing our will over God's revealed will, our supposed wisdom over God's perfect wisdom, our preferred way over God's appointed way. We are repeating Adam's catastrophic decision, replaying his tragic choice in our own hearts and lives. Each sin, no matter how small it may seem to us, echoes that primal rebellion in Eden when humanity first turned from the living God.

This understanding should humble us profoundly and drive us to genuine repentance. When I counsel believers struggling with persistent sin, I remind them that they are not merely dealing with behavioral problems or psychological issues, though these may be present. They are confronting the deep-seated rebellion that has infected the human heart since the Fall.

Second, understanding the covenant of works helps us appreciate the absolute necessity of Christ and His mediatorial work on our behalf. We need more than forgiveness for our sins, as vital as that is. We need more than divine pardon, though without it we would perish. We need positive righteousness, an actual record of perfect obedience credited to our account. We need someone to obey perfectly in our place, to fulfill completely the covenant obligations we have failed to meet, to satisfy every demand of God's holy law that we have violated. We need someone to succeed where Adam failed, to stand where we have fallen, to triumph where we have been defeated.

Christ is that someone. He is the Second Adam, the last Adam, the faithful covenant keeper who accomplished what the first Adam could not. He is the one who earned eternal life through perfect, unwavering obedience to every aspect of God's law. He is the one who not only paid the penalty for our sins through His death but also secured righteousness for us through His life. Without Christ's active obedience, His perfect fulfillment of the covenant of works throughout His earthly life, we have no hope whatsoever of acceptance with God, no standing before the throne of divine justice, no basis for fellowship with the Holy One.

Third, understanding the covenant of works helps us rest more fully in the gospel. The covenant of works shows us with unmistakable clarity that we cannot possibly save ourselves through our own efforts, no matter how sincere or sustained those efforts might be. Perfect obedience to every requirement of God's holy law is required, not partial obedience, not sincere attempts, not even ninety-nine percent compliance, but absolute, flawless, unwavering obedience from beginning to end, and we simply cannot provide it. We have failed. We continue to fail. We will always fail.

This is utterly devastating news for those who trust in their own righteousness, who believe their good deeds outweigh their bad ones, who think God grades on a curve or accepts our best efforts as good enough. For such people, the covenant of works becomes a relentless taskmaster, exposing every failure, condemning every shortcoming, proving beyond any shadow of a doubt that they fall hopelessly short of God's standard.

But it is absolutely glorious news, liberating, soul-satisfying, eternally secure news, for those who trust completely in Christ's righteousness rather than their own. We are not justified before God through our obedience but through His perfect obedience. We are not accepted into fellowship with the Father because of our performance but solely because of Christ's flawless performance on our behalf. The crushing pressure is finally off. The impossible burden is permanently lifted from our weary shoulders. Christ has accomplished it all, every requirement met, every demand satisfied, every obligation fulfilled.

Fourth, understanding the covenant of works helps us live gratefully, with hearts overflowing with thankfulness for mercies we could never earn and do not deserve. Every good thing we enjoy in this life, every breath we draw, every morsel of food that sustains us, every moment of joy we experience, every relationship that enriches our days, every sunset that captures our wonder, every small pleasure that sweetens our existence, is a gift from the hand of God, utterly undeserved and completely unearned. When we truly grasp the reality of what the covenant of works demands and how utterly we have failed to meet those demands, when we understand the depth of our rebellion and the magnitude of our shortcomings, we recognize that we have broken the covenant in countless ways, large and small. We have failed the test at every turn, falling catastrophically short of God's righteous standards. According to the terms established from the beginning, we deserve death, eternal separation from God, complete condemnation, utter rejection, endless punishment. We deserve nothing but wrath. We have earned nothing but judgment.

But God in His astounding mercy, His unfathomable grace, His incomprehensible love, has provided a way of salvation through Christ Jesus our Lord, a way we could never have devised, a rescue we could never have accomplished, a redemption that cost Him everything and costs us nothing. This breathtaking reality should fill us with gratitude that permeates every aspect of our existence, gratitude that shapes how we think, how we speak, how we relate to others, how we use our time and resources. It should move us, compel us, motivate us from the depths of our being to live lives of wholehearted worship and joyful service, not to earn God's favor, which we already possess in Christ, but in heartfelt response to the favor He has already so freely given us.

Fifth, understanding the covenant of works helps us make proper sense of suffering, not just intellectually, but existentially, in the depths of our hearts where pain cuts deepest. We live in a profoundly fallen world, a world still laboring under the heavy, crushing curse that resulted from Adam's catastrophic sin in the garden. The pain we experience daily, whether physical, emotional, or spiritual, the diseases that ravage our bodies and the bodies of those we love most dearly, the death that stalks us all relentlessly from the moment we draw our first breath, the frustration that marks even our noblest endeavors, the futility that seems to infect everything we attempt in this broken world, all of these harsh realities are direct, unavoidable consequences of covenant-breaking. They serve as constant, painful reminders that things are emphatically not as they should be, that we are still waiting with groaning hearts for the complete redemption that Christ has secured but not yet fully consummated, that this present world with all its beauty and promise is nonetheless not our final home, not our ultimate destination.

But suffering and its accompanying sorrows are also, paradoxically, divine assurances, evidence that God's justice is not merely theoretical but thoroughly real and operative in His creation, that sin carries genuine consequences that cannot be ignored or minimized, that our holy God takes rebellion with utmost seriousness and will not sweep transgression under the rug of cosmic indifference.

Sixth, and perhaps most profoundly transformative for our daily walk with God, understanding the covenant of works with clarity and precision helps us cultivate a deeper, more biblical longing for heaven, not as escapism from present difficulties, but as the joyful anticipation of our true inheritance. Eden, even in its pristine, unfallen glory, was magnificent beyond our current ability to fully comprehend or appreciate. Yet what is coming, what awaits us in the new heavens and new earth, will be immeasurably, incomparably more glorious still, glory upon glory, exceeding anything Adam and Eve knew even in their innocence.

Adam stood in the garden with an extraordinary opportunity spread before him, the real possibility of being permanently, irrevocably confirmed in righteousness through faithful obedience, of moving from mutable goodness to immutable glory. But in that critical moment of testing, when everything hung in the balance, he failed catastrophically. He chose the serpent's lie over God's truth, immediate gratification over eternal blessing, autonomy over joyful submission.

Christ, our greater and final Adam, has already been gloriously confirmed in His exaltation, vindicated by the Father, seated at the right hand of the Majesty on high. And in His unfailing covenant faithfulness, He has promised to share that consummate, infinite glory with all who belong to Him through faith. The tree of life, from which our first parents were justly barred after their rebellion, will be ours to enjoy again, freely and without fear. The unmediated presence of God, which Adam and Eve forfeited through their sin, will be ours to experience forever, face to face, without the veil that sin has placed between Creator and creature. The eternal, imperishable, glorious life that Adam tragically forfeited for himself and all his posterity will be ours eternally, secured not by our obedience but by Christ's perfect righteousness credited to our account.

I have walked with many believers through seasons of doubt and darkness. I have sat with those who questioned whether God truly loved them, whether their faith was real, whether they could ever be sure of salvation. And I have consistently pointed them to the covenant structure of Scripture. God has bound Himself by covenant to save all who trust in Christ. He has promised that Christ's righteousness will be credited to all who believe. He has sworn by Himself that His covenant will stand.

This is not an uncertain hope. This is covenant faithfulness. And it is grounded in the same principle established in Eden: God keeps His word. He does what He promises. And those who trust His promises will never be put to shame.

Chapter Eight

Marriage: The First Human Relationship

"It is not good." These words stopped me cold the first time I truly noticed them during my doctoral studies. I had read Genesis countless times, preached from it, discussed it in seminary classrooms. But this phrase, these four simple words, arrested my attention with fresh force one afternoon in my study.

Six times in Genesis 1, God surveyed His creative work and declared it good. Light, good. The firmament, good. Dry land and vegetation, good. Sun, moon, and stars, good. Sea creatures and birds, good. Land animals and mankind, very good. The refrain echoed through the creation account like a triumphant chorus, each declaration building upon the last until everything God had made received His divine stamp of approval.

Then came Genesis 2:18, and the pattern shattered. "Then the Lord God said, 'It is not good that the man should be alone; I will make him a helper fit for him.'" Not good. The only negative assessment in the entire creation narrative. The only thing in God's perfect world that required remedy. And what was this lack, this insufficiency that marred an otherwise flawless creation? Human aloneness.

This was no minor detail, no footnote in the biblical account. This was God Himself identifying a fundamental incompleteness in the human condition. Adam walked in paradise, enjoyed unbroken fellowship with his Creator, tended a garden of unimaginable beauty, and yet something essential was missing. He was alone.

I have counseled enough isolated, lonely people through the years to know that solitude can be crushing. The young Marine separated from family for the first time. The elderly widow, whose friends have all passed. The man, whose marriage dissolved, leaving him adrift. The teenager who feels misunderstood by everyone around her. Loneliness is a peculiar kind of suffering, a hollow ache that material abundance cannot fill.

But Adam's aloneness was different. He had not yet sinned. The world bore no curse. He experienced no guilt, no shame, no broken relationships. He had perfect communion with God. Yet even this was insufficient. Even in Eden, before the fall, before sin corrupted everything, God looked at solitary man and said, "Not good."

This divine assessment reveals something profound about human nature as God designed it. We were never meant for isolation. Relationality is woven into the fabric of our being. We are created in the image of a triune God who exists eternally in perfect relationship, Father, Son, and Holy Spirit in eternal communion. It should not surprise us, then, that we who bear this divine image are fundamentally relational creatures.

The solution God provided for Adam's incompleteness was not another man. It was not simply companionship in the abstract. It was a woman, a helper fit for him, someone corresponding to him yet distinct from him. God's remedy for human aloneness was marriage.

The Creation of Woman

What follows in Genesis 2:19-20 is often misunderstood. God brought the animals to Adam to be named. Some interpreters suggest this was God helping Adam realize his need for a companion, showing him that no animal could fill the void. Perhaps. But I believe something deeper was happening. Naming the animals was an exercise of dominion. God had commanded humanity to have dominion over creation, to fill the earth and subdue it. Adam's naming demonstrated his authority over the animal kingdom. He classified them, categorized them, understood their nature. The text says, "whatever the man called every living creature, that was its name." This was genuine authority being exercised, delegated by God to His image bearer.

But the passage also notes that "for Adam there was not found a helper fit for him." He surveyed the entire animal kingdom, every species God had made, and found no counterpart, no correspondent, no one like himself. The animals were under his authority, but they could not share his life, his work, his fellowship with God. They could not ease his aloneness.

Then came the divine surgery, perhaps the most intimate of all God's creative acts. "So the Lord God caused a deep sleep to fall upon the man, and while he slept took one of his ribs and closed up its place with flesh. And the rib that the Lord God had taken from the man he made into a woman and brought her to the man" (Genesis 2:21-22).

The language here is both tender and precise. God caused a deep sleep, not ordinary sleep, but something more profound, perhaps similar to the deep sleep that would later fall upon Abraham when God made His covenant with him. Under this divinely imposed slumber, God performed His creative work. He took from Adam's side a rib, and from that rib He fashioned woman.

The text is careful and deliberate in what it tells us and what it withholds. We are not given medical details, nor should we expect them. This is a theological narrative, not an anatomical description. What matters is the theological truth being conveyed: God did not create woman from the dust of the ground as He had created man. He did not speak her into existence as He had the stars and galaxies. Instead, He fashioned her from man himself, from Adam's very substance, from his flesh and bone.

This method of creation establishes something foundational about the relationship between man and woman. They share a common nature. They are of the same essence, of the same substance. Woman is not a different kind of creature altogether, but one who shares fully in human nature. Yet she is also wonderfully, deliberately different, fashioned by God's creative wisdom into someone who corresponds to man while remaining distinct from him.

The church fathers observed that God did not take woman from man's head, that she might lord over him, nor from his feet, that he might trample her, but from his side, that she might walk beside him as his equal partner. While such observations are not exegetically rigorous, they capture something true about the relationship God designed.

Woman was taken from man. She shared his nature, his substance, his essence. Yet she was also distinct, fashioned by God's creative power into something wonderfully different. Same nature, different expression. Equal dignity, complementary design.

The First Wedding

God brought the woman to the man. This detail matters. The first wedding had a divine officiant. God Himself performed the ceremony, presenting the bride to the groom. Every Christian wedding since echoes this primordial pattern. When a father walks his daughter down the aisle and places her hand in the groom's, he participates in this ancient ritual, representing God's own act of giving.

Adam's response has been called the first love poem. "This at last is bone of my bones and flesh of my flesh; she shall be called Woman, because she was taken out of Man." The Hebrew plays on words here. *Ish* and *ishah*. Man and woman. The sounds themselves declare their connection, their derivation, their unity and distinction. Adam recognized immediately what the animals could never be: someone like himself, someone from himself, someone corresponding to him perfectly.

"At last." The phrase conveys relief, satisfaction, completion. Here was the answer to his incompleteness. Here was a helper fit for him. Here was someone with whom he could share life, work, dominion, fellowship with God. Here was someone who could understand him because she shared his nature, yet complement him because she was wonderfully distinct. The poetic parallelism is striking. Bone of my bones. Flesh of my flesh. The repetition emphasizes their shared substance, their fundamental unity. When Adam looked at Eve, he saw himself reflected back, yet in glorious variation. She was his counterpart, his match, his equal yet complementary partner.

Then Moses, the author of Genesis, added commentary that has shaped human civilization ever since. "Therefore a man shall leave his father and his mother and hold fast to his wife, and they shall become one flesh." This verse establishes the permanence and exclusivity of marriage. A man leaves his family of origin and cleaves to his wife. The word translated "hold fast" or "cleave" carries connotations of permanent bonding, devoted attachment, covenant commitment. It appears elsewhere in Scripture to describe Israel's relationship with God, a relationship meant to be exclusive and enduring.

They become one flesh. Not merely one in purpose or goal, though that is included. Not merely united in their work or their home, though that matters. They become one flesh, a union so profound that two distinct persons become, in a mysterious yet real way, a single entity.

I performed many weddings during my pastoral ministry. Each time I reached this verse, I paused. The young couple before me, nervous and excited, had no idea what "one flesh" truly meant. They thought they did. They believed their love was strong enough for anything. But the mystery of marriage unfolds slowly, through years of shared life, through trials that test commitment, through joys that deepen affection, through the ordinary rhythms of daily existence.

My own marriage has taught me more theology than all my doctoral studies. Walking through cancer with my wife revealed what "one flesh" means when the flesh itself is under assault. Her pain was my pain. Her fear was my fear. Her suffering became our suffering. We were not two individuals cooperating. We were one flesh facing a common enemy.

The Foundation of Human Society

Marriage is the first institution. Before government, before commerce, before any social structure or cultural organization, God established marriage. It predates the fall. It exists in creation order, not merely as a remedy for sin but as part of God's good design for human flourishing.

This priority matters. When cultures collapse, when civilizations crumble, when every human system fails, marriage remains the bedrock of society. Strong marriages build strong families. Strong families build strong communities. Strong communities build strong nations. The health of any society can be measured by the health of its marriages.

I have watched America's view of marriage shift dramatically during my lifetime. What was once considered foundational and sacred is now treated as optional and malleable. Marriage has been redefined, reimagined, and in many cases, dismissed as an outdated institution. The consequences have been catastrophic.

Children raised without married parents. Homes fractured by divorce. Confusion about the very nature of family. Loneliness epidemic despite unprecedented connectivity. The sexual revolution promised liberation but delivered bondage. No-fault divorce promised freedom but produced generations of wounded children. Cohabitation promised all the benefits of marriage without the commitment but delivered neither stability nor satisfaction.

These are not abstract issues for me. I have counseled the casualties. The woman abandoned by her live-in boyfriend when she got pregnant. The man whose parents' divorce shattered his ability to trust. The children shuttled between houses, never quite at home anywhere. The young adults who have never seen a healthy marriage modeled and have no idea how to build one themselves.

Genesis 2 stands as both indictment and hope for our confused and broken generation. It serves as an indictment because it reveals, with devastating clarity, how far we have fallen from God's original design for marriage and human flourishing. The contrast between what God intended and what we have made of His gift could not be starker. Yet it also offers hope, genuine, biblical hope, because it shows us the unchanging pattern we were always meant to follow, the blueprint that has never been revised or rescinded, the design that still holds the answer to our deepest longings for connection and belonging.

Marriage is a creation ordinance, one of those fundamental structures God wove into the very fabric of human existence before any other divine institution was established. It belongs to all humanity, not merely to Christians or to the covenant community of believers. This is a crucial point we must grasp if we are to understand both the universality and the authority of God's design for marriage. God established marriage before He gave the law at Sinai, before He called Abraham out of Ur of the Chaldeans, before He instituted the sacrificial system, before any special revelation beyond what He inscribed in creation itself. Marriage predates every religious system, every theological framework, every cultural expression of faith.

Every culture in human history, across every continent and era, has recognized some form of marriage precisely because it is written into creation itself, stamped into the very nature of human existence like a divine watermark that cannot be erased. We may suppress this truth through ideology and willful blindness. We may deny it through legislation and academic theory. We may attempt to redefine it through social movements and court decisions. But we cannot escape it, no matter how sophisticated our arguments or how determined our rebellion. Reality has a way of asserting itself, often painfully, when we persist in living contrary to the grain of creation.

Helper and Companion

God's description of woman as "a helper fit for him" has been tragically misunderstood and often weaponized. Some have used this language to suggest women are subordinate, secondary, or inferior to men. This interpretation is not merely wrong. It contradicts the entire context of the passage. The Hebrew word translated "helper" is *ezer*. This word appears twenty-one times in the Old Testament. Twice it refers to the woman in Genesis 2. Three times it refers to nations Israel sought as military allies. The remaining sixteen times, it refers to God Himself as Israel's helper.

"There is none like God, O Jeshurun, who rides through the heavens to your help." (Deuteronomy 33:26)

"Happy are you, O Israel! Who is like you, a people saved by the Lord, the shield of your help, and the sword of your triumph!" (Deuteronomy 33:29)

"Our soul waits for the Lord; he is our help and our shield." (Psalm 33:20)

When God calls Himself our *ezer*, our helper, does this suggest He is subordinate to us? Inferior? Secondary? The suggestion is absurd. God helps us from a position of strength, not weakness. He helps because He is able, because He possesses resources we lack, because His power accomplishes what our weakness cannot.

Woman as man's *ezer* means she brings strength he does not possess, capabilities he lacks, perspectives he needs. She helps not because she is less but because she is essential. Without her, he is incomplete. Without her, the task of dominion cannot be fulfilled. Without her, he remains alone in a world God declared "not good."

The phrase "fit for him" translates a Hebrew expression that means "corresponding to him" or "like opposite him." Imagine two puzzle pieces. They are distinct shapes, different configurations. Yet they fit together perfectly because they were designed as counterparts. Neither is superior to the other. Both are necessary to complete the picture.

This is the relationship between man and woman in marriage. They correspond to each other. They complement each other. They complete each other. Not because either is deficient in personhood or dignity, but because God designed them for partnership, for collaboration, for shared dominion over creation.

I have watched this dynamic play out in countless marriages. The husband whose analytical mind needed his wife's emotional intelligence. The wife whose cautious nature needed her husband's willingness to take risks. The couple whose different gifts made them unstoppable as a team while each alone would have struggled. This is the beauty of complementarity. Not competition but completion. Not hierarchy but harmony. Not domination but dancing together in the rhythm God designed.

Complementarity and Equality

Here I must tread carefully, aware that the path ahead is strewn with landmines of misunderstanding and genuine hurt. The relationship between men and women in marriage has become a fierce battleground in our contemporary culture, and tragically, the conflict rages just as intensely within the church as it does without. Egalitarians (believe that men and women are equal in all aspects, with no gender-based restrictions on roles in church, home, or society) and complementarians (the Biblical belief that men and women are equal in essence but different in function, with God assigning different, complementary roles) square off across theological lines, debating intricate structures of authority and submission with an intensity that sometimes obscures the very Scriptures we claim to defend. Feminists and traditionalists argue passionately about roles and responsibilities, each side convinced the other has fundamentally misunderstood God's design for humanity. The conversation, which should draw us deeper into the beauty of God's creative intent, too often generates far more heat than light, more division than understanding, more wounded hearts than transformed lives.

I have sat across from too many couples whose marriages have been damaged not by Scripture itself, but by competing interpretations wielded like weapons rather than received as gifts. I have counseled women who felt diminished by teachings that seemed to make them perpetually subordinate, and men who felt trapped by expectations of dominance they never sought. The pain is real on all sides, and we dishonor both Scripture and the suffering when we treat this subject with anything less than pastoral care coupled with theological precision.

Genesis 2 presents us with what appears, at first glance, to be a profound paradox: both equality and distinction existing simultaneously in perfect harmony. We encounter both fundamental sameness in nature and purposeful difference in design. We discover both the essential unity of being and the intentional complementarity of function. The passage holds these realities in perfect tension, refusing to sacrifice one truth on the altar of the other. Any theology that emphasizes one aspect of this divine design while minimizing or ignoring the other inevitably distorts what Scripture actually teaches and undermines the beautiful complexity of God's creative intent for humanity.

Woman is made from man's very substance, taken from his side while he slept in divinely appointed unconsciousness. She shares his nature completely and utterly, bone of his bones and flesh of his flesh in the most literal sense possible. She bears God's image just as fully and magnificently as he does, without diminishment or qualification. She receives the same divine mandate to be fruitful, to multiply, to fill the earth, and to exercise dominion over all creation. She stands beside him as co-regent over everything God has made, sharing equally in the responsibility and privilege of stewardship. Nothing in the text, no word, no phrase, no grammatical construction, suggests inferiority of essence, subordination of being, or secondary status in worth. The equality is absolute and unequivocal when it comes to nature, dignity, and calling.

Yet she is also distinct in her creation, unmistakably and purposefully different in how she came into being. Created not from the dust of the ground as Adam was, but fashioned uniquely and deliberately from Adam's own flesh and bone. Called woman, *ishah,* a term that linguistically connects her to man while simultaneously distinguishing her from him. The Hebrew wordplay captures both the connection and the distinction in a way that reverberates through the entire narrative. She was designed and intended by divine wisdom to complement rather than to duplicate, to complete rather than to replicate. The differences between them are not merely incidental details we can overlook or minimize in our rush to affirm equality. They are intentional features of God's creative design, woven into the very fabric of how humanity was made. God, in His infinite power and creativity, could have easily made two identical humans, fashioning both from dust, giving both the same origin story, the same mode of creation, the same functional design. He deliberately and purposefully chose not to. He chose differentiation. He chose complementarity. He chose a design that would require both man and woman to fulfill the mandate He gave them. The distinction matters profoundly, both for our theology and for our lived experience of what it means to be human.

The fall, that cataclysmic rupture in Eden, has made this entire conversation infinitely more difficult than it ever should have been. Sin, that insidious poison that infected every dimension of human existence, corrupted and twisted the beautiful complementarity that God had so carefully and lovingly designed into the very structure of manhood and womanhood. Men, created to be loving leaders who would cherish and protect, began instead to dominate with harshness, to rule with an iron fist, to exercise authority in ways that crushed rather than cultivated. Women, fashioned to be helpers and partners who would bring strength and wisdom, began instead to manipulate from the shadows, to control through indirect means, to undermine rather than to support. What should have been a graceful, life-giving dance of mutual service and complementary strengths became something altogether different, a bitter power struggle characterized by suspicion, resentment, and competition. Marriage, that sacred institution meant to reflect the relationship between Christ and His church, became instead a battlefield marked by territory disputes and attempts to seize control, rather than the partnership of equals with different roles that God had always intended it to be.

But we must not allow the fall to dictate our understanding of God's original design. Yes, Genesis 3 describes consequences of sin that include distorted relationships between men and women. But Genesis 2 shows us what God intended, what Christ came to restore, and what the new creation will fully realize.

In my marriage, I have learned that leadership looks like sacrifice. My wife did not need a tyrant or a dictator. She needed a servant. She needed someone who would lay down his life for her, someone who would prioritize her flourishing above his own comfort, someone who would wash her feet as Christ washed the disciples' feet.

And I needed her strength. Her wisdom. Her perspective. Her gifts. My attempts to make decisions without her input invariably led to disaster. My stubborn independence left me isolated and ineffective. My pride convinced me I could manage alone, but Genesis 2 already declared that verdict: not good.

The best marriages I have witnessed were characterized not by rigid role enforcement but by graceful complementarity. Each partner brought unique strengths. Each deferred to the other's wisdom in different areas. Each served the other gladly. Neither competed for position nor authority. Both sought the other's good.

This is what Paul meant in Ephesians 5 when he grounded marriage in the relationship between Christ and the church. Christ leads by loving, by giving Himself up for His bride. The church submits by trusting, by receiving His leadership gladly because it is exercised for her benefit. Neither relationship is adversarial. Both are characterized by mutual devotion and joyful service.

One Flesh Union

The declaration that husband and wife become "one flesh" is perhaps the most mysterious and profound statement about marriage in all of Scripture. Jesus quoted it in Matthew 19 when confronting the Pharisees about divorce. Paul invoked it in 1 Corinthians 6 when warning against sexual immorality. The phrase carries weight far beyond its simple appearance.

One flesh union is first physical. Marriage includes sexual union, and sexual union is reserved for marriage. The physical joining of husband and wife is not merely biological function or a recreational activity. It is the physical expression of covenant commitment, the bodily declaration of "you are mine and I am yours."

I have had young people ask me why God cares about their sex lives. Why does it matter who sleeps with whom? Why are there rules and boundaries around something so personal and private?

Because sex is never merely personal and private. Because one flesh union creates bonds that transcend the moment. Because our bodies matter to God. Because physical intimacy outside the covenant of marriage is a lie told with our bodies, a promise we have no intention of keeping. When a man and woman join sexually outside marriage, they perform the one-flesh act without the one-flesh covenant. They enact physically what they deny practically. The body says "forever" while the heart says "for now." The disconnect creates deep psychological and spiritual damage.

Paul wrote, "Or do you not know that he who is joined to a prostitute becomes one body with her? For, as it is written, 'The two will become one flesh.'" (1 Corinthians 6:16) Sexual union creates a one-flesh reality whether we intend it or not, whether we want it or not. Our culture's casual approach to sex ignores this truth to its own destruction.

But one-flesh union transcends the physical. Husband and wife become one emotionally, sharing life's joys and sorrows. One financially, building a shared economic life. One socially, creating a new family unit. One spiritually, praying together, worshiping together, growing together in grace.

The comprehensive nature of this union explains why divorce is so devastating. You cannot tear apart one flesh without inflicting terrible wounds. You cannot separate what God has joined without violence to both parties. Divorce is not merely the end of a legal contract. It is the ripping apart of a unified whole.

I have sat with enough divorced people to know the pain runs deeper than inconvenience or disappointment. They describe feeling incomplete, as though part of themselves was amputated. Even when divorce was necessary because of abuse or abandonment, even when it brought relief from toxicity, it still left scars. This is the nature of one-flesh union. The joining creates something real that cannot be undone without cost.

Marriage and the Gospel

Jesus's first miracle occurred at a wedding. This detail is not coincidental. John records, "On the third day there was a wedding at Cana in Galilee, and the mother of Jesus was there. Jesus also was invited to the wedding with his disciples." (John 2:1-2) Jesus honored marriage by His presence, blessed it by His miracle, and revealed His glory in that context.

Throughout Scripture, marriage serves as the primary metaphor for God's relationship with His people. Israel is described as the bride of Yahweh. The church is called the bride of Christ. The consummation of redemptive history is pictured as a wedding feast, the marriage supper of the Lamb.

This is not arbitrary symbolism. Marriage was designed from the beginning to reveal spiritual truth. The covenant commitment between husband and wife reflects God's covenant commitment to His people. The exclusive devotion marriage requires mirrors the exclusive worship God demands. The intimacy and union of marriage point to the intimacy and union God desires with those He loves.

Paul made this explicit in Ephesians 5. After instructing husbands and wives about their responsibilities to each other, he wrote, "This mystery is profound, and I am saying that it refers to Christ and the church." (Ephesians 5:32) Marriage itself is a living parable, a flesh-and-blood sermon preached every day by every married couple.

This reality transforms how we understand marriage. It is not merely about our happiness, though God does intend marriage to bring joy. It is not merely about companionship, though that is central to its purpose. Marriage exists to display the gospel, to make visible the invisible reality of Christ's love for His church.

How a husband loves his wife reveals how Christ loves the church. Sacrificially. Unconditionally. Persistently. He "gave himself up for her, that he might sanctify her, having cleansed her by the washing of water with the word, so that he might present the church to himself in splendor, without spot or wrinkle or any such thing, that she might be holy and without blemish." (Ephesians 5:25-27)

Christ's love for the church is not passive or sentimental. It is active and purifying. He gave Himself up. He cleanses. He sanctifies. He prepares. Husbands are called to love this way, to pour themselves out for their wives' good, to lead them toward holiness, to serve their spiritual growth.

How a wife respects and submits to her husband reveals how the church responds to Christ. Trustingly. Gladly. Confidently. "As the church submits to Christ, so also wives should submit in everything to their husbands." (Ephesians 5:24) This is not servile obedience to a tyrant but confident trust in a servant leader, willing submission to one who has proven his devotion by his sacrifice.

The church submits to Christ not because He forces compliance but because He has earned trust. He laid down His life. He proved His love. He demonstrated His commitment. Wives are called to submit this way, to trust husbands who have shown themselves trustworthy, to follow leaders who lead like Jesus.

Every Christian marriage, then, becomes an acted parable. The world watches marriages and draws conclusions about the gospel. When they see sacrificial husbands and trusting wives, they witness a picture of Christ and the church. When they see selfish men and rebellious women, they see a distorted caricature that obscures the truth.

This is why marriage matters so much. This is why God hates divorce. This is why sexual sin is so serious. These things do not merely affect individuals. They corrupt the picture marriage was designed to paint. They distort the gospel message marriage was meant to proclaim.

Permanence and Covenant

Jesus addressed marriage and divorce in Matthew 19. The Pharisees approached Him with a test question. "Is it lawful to divorce one's wife for any cause?" Their question was not a sincere inquiry, but an attempted trap. The rabbinical schools debated the grounds for divorce. One school of rabbinical thought took a permissive position, allowing divorce for almost any reason. Another school of rabbinical thought took a restrictive view, permitting it only for sexual immorality. The Pharisees hoped Jesus would alienate one group or the other.

Jesus refused to engage on their terms. Instead, He pointed them back to Genesis. "Have you not read that he who created them from the beginning made them male and female, and said, 'Therefore a man shall leave his father and his mother and hold fast to his wife, and the two shall become one flesh'? So they are no longer two but one flesh. What therefore God has joined together, let not man separate." (Matthew 19:4-6)

Notice Jesus's argument. He did not debate Rabbinic interpretations of Deuteronomy 24. He went straight to creation. God made them male and female. God declared they would become one flesh. God joined them together. The conclusion follows inescapably: humans have no authority to separate what God has united.

The Pharisees pressed. "Why then did Moses command one to give a certificate of divorce and to send her away?" (Matthew 19:7) They thought they had Him trapped. Moses permitted divorce. Was Jesus contradicting Moses?

Jesus's response cut through their sophistry. "Because of your hardness of heart Moses allowed you to divorce your wives, but from the beginning it was not so." (Matthew 19:8)

Deuteronomy 24 was a concession, not ideal. It regulated an evil practice to limit its harm, particularly to protect vulnerable women. But it did not represent God's original design. From the beginning, marriage was meant to be permanent. One man, one woman, one flesh, one lifetime.

Then Jesus added, "And I say to you: whoever divorces his wife, except for sexual immorality, and marries another, commits adultery." (Matthew 19:9) The disciples found this teaching so difficult they concluded, "If such is the case of a man with his wife, it is better not to marry." (Matthew 19:10) They recognized immediately that Jesus's standard was far stricter than prevailing cultural norms. If marriage is truly permanent, if divorce is nearly impossible, if remarriage constitutes adultery, then marriage demands serious commitment.

Jesus did not soften His teaching to ease their concerns. Instead, He acknowledged that not everyone can accept this word. Some are called to celibacy. But for those who marry, the standard remains: covenant permanence.

I have counseled couples through marriage difficulties of every imaginable kind. Financial stress. Incompatibility. In-laws. Parenting disagreements. Loss of attraction. Emotional distance. Mental illness. Some situations were heartbreaking. The woman whose husband developed schizophrenia and became someone she no longer recognized. The man whose wife's chronic illness made physical intimacy impossible. The couples who simply grew apart over decades, sharing a house but not a life.

In every case, I pointed them back to the covenant. Marriage is not a contract contingent on continued satisfaction. It is a covenant sworn before God and witnesses. "For better or worse, for richer or poorer, in sickness and in health, till death do us part." These are not empty words but sacred vows. They mean something. They bind us. They call us to faithfulness when feelings fail.

I acknowledge that some marriages end in divorce. I acknowledge that abuse, abandonment, and adultery can make divorce necessary. Reformed theology has traditionally recognized these as legitimate grounds for divorce. Paul addressed abandonment in 1 Corinthians 7:15. Jesus acknowledged sexual immorality as grounds in Matthew 19:9. The Westminster Confession adds that "such willful desertion as can no way be remedied by the Church or civil magistrate" may also warrant divorce.

But these are exceptions, not the rule. They are tragic concessions to human sin, not ideals to be pursued. Even when divorce is legitimate, it remains a result of covenant breaking, a consequence of living in a fallen world where hardness of heart sometimes makes continuation impossible.

The gospel calls us to fight for our marriages. To forgive seventy times seven. To love when love is difficult. To serve when we want to flee. To honor covenant even when feelings fade. This is hard. I will not pretend otherwise. But it reflects the gospel. Christ did not abandon His bride when she was unfaithful. He pursued her. He died for her. He remains committed to her despite her failures.

Christian marriages should be marked by this same tenacious covenant love. Not because we are naturally faithful, but because we serve a faithful God who empowers us to love as we have been loved.

Fruitfulness and Children

"Be fruitful and multiply and fill the earth." (Genesis 1:28) God's first command to married humanity was to have children. This was not merely permission but a commission. Children are not optional extras or lifestyle accessories. They are central to God's purpose for marriage.

Our culture has largely rejected this vision. Children are seen as burdens, interruptions to career and leisure, expensive drains on resources. Couples delay childbearing indefinitely or forgo it entirely. Those who do have children often treat them as projects to be managed rather than gifts to be received.

The Bible presents a radically different perspective. "Behold, children are a heritage from the Lord, the fruit of the womb a reward. Like arrows in the hand of a warrior are the children of one's youth. Blessed is the man who fills his quiver with them! He shall not be put to shame when he speaks with his enemies in the gate." (Psalm 127:3-5)

Heritage. Reward. Blessing. These words describe children in Scripture. Not burdens or problems but gifts from God's hand. The psalmist compares children to arrows, weapons in a warrior's hand. Children extend our influence beyond our lifetime. They carry forward our values, our faith, our mission. A man with many children is not pitied but envied, not burdened but blessed.

I understand this seems countercultural. I understand economic realities make large families difficult. I understand health issues sometimes prevent conception or make pregnancy dangerous. I understand not every couple is called to have many children. But we must recover the biblical vision of children as blessing, not burden.

The contraceptive revolution divorced sex from procreation, treating fertility as a problem to be solved rather than a gift to be stewarded. This separation has had profound consequences. Sex became recreation. Children became optional. Marriage became about personal fulfillment rather than covenantal fruitfulness.

I am not arguing that all contraception is sinful. Reformed theology has generally permitted the use of contraception within marriage for legitimate reasons like spacing children or protecting a wife's health. But we must reject the cultural assumption that children are defaults to avoid rather than blessings to embrace.

Marriage is ordered toward children. This does not mean childless couples have failed or that their marriages are less valid. Some couples cannot conceive despite desperate longing. Some face health issues that make pregnancy dangerous. Some marry later in life when childbearing is no longer possible. These realities exist in a fallen world, and we must minister to the grief they cause with compassion.

But we must affirm that the norm, the pattern established at creation, the very design woven into the fabric of marriage itself, is that marriage produces children. This is the means by which we fulfill the creation mandate to fill the earth. This is the way God intended for us to build covenant families that extend His kingdom through generations. This is the primary avenue through which we pass down the faith to the next generation, discipling our own children in the ways of the Lord from their earliest days.

Our children are not obstacles to ministry, as modern thinking sometimes suggests, but rather precious opportunities for the most intimate, prolonged, and consequential discipleship we will ever undertake. They are not threats to the health and vitality of our marriages but the natural fruit of marital love and union. They are not burdens to be grudgingly borne until we can return to our "real lives," but arrows to be carefully crafted, aimed with prayer and wisdom, and eventually launched into the world to accomplish purposes we may never fully see.

Sexuality and Purity

God created sex. This fact needs repeating in a culture that treats sexuality as either a shameful secret or a public obsession. Sex is not evil. It is not dirty. It is not a necessary evil for procreation. Sex is God's good gift, designed for pleasure and procreation within the covenant of marriage.

The Song of Solomon celebrates marital sexuality with stunning explicitness. The lovers delight in each other's bodies. They express desire openly. They find joy in physical intimacy. Nothing in the text suggests embarrassment or shame. This is holy passion, sanctified pleasure, godly desire expressed properly within marriage.

Proverbs 5 instructs, "Let your fountain be blessed, and rejoice in the wife of your youth, a lovely deer, a graceful doe. Let her breasts fill you at all times with delight; be intoxicated always in her love." (Proverbs 5:18-19) This is Scripture. This is God's word to husbands. Take pleasure in your wife. Delight in her body. Be intoxicated with her love.

But the same passage warns against sexual sin. "For the lips of a forbidden woman drip honey, and her speech is smoother than oil, but in the end she is bitter as wormwood, sharp as a two-edged sword." (Proverbs 5:3-4) Sexual sin promises pleasure but delivers death. It offers freedom but brings bondage. It looks like life but leads to destruction.

Paul wrote, "Flee from sexual immorality. Every other sin a person commits is outside the body, but the sexually immoral person sins against his own body. Or do you not know that your body is a temple of the Holy Spirit within you, whom you have from God? You are not your own, for you were bought with a price. So glorify God in your body." (1 Corinthians 6:18-20)

Sexual sin is uniquely destructive because it involves the body in ways other sins do not. When we use our bodies sexually outside marriage, we desecrate the temple. We profane what is holy. We take what belongs to God and give it to another.

Our culture's sexual chaos stems directly from rejecting Genesis 2. When we sever sex from marriage, when we treat bodies as toys, when we deny the one-flesh reality of sexual union, we reap destruction. Pornography addiction. Sex trafficking. Abortion. Sexual abuse. Epidemic loneliness despite casual hookups. These are not random problems. They are direct consequences of abandoning God's design.

The solution is not prudish silence or shame-based purity culture. The solution is recovering the biblical vision of sexuality as God's good gift reserved for marriage. We need to teach our children that sex is wonderful, that bodies are good, that desire is natural, and that all of these finds its proper expression in covenant marriage.

I have counseled enough people enslaved by sexual sin to know the bondage is real. The man who cannot look at a woman without lust. The woman whose pornography addiction has destroyed her marriage. The young person whose sexual history has left deep emotional scars. These struggles are not overcome by willpower alone.

But the gospel offers hope. Christ died to free us from sin's dominion. The Spirit empowers us to walk in holiness. The church provides accountability and support. Sexual brokenness is not beyond redemption. No sin is too great for Christ's blood to cleanse. No habit is too strong for God's grace to break.

Marriage as Warfare

I must address a reality that our culture prefers to ignore and that many churches avoid discussing directly. Marriage is spiritual warfare. This is not hyperbole. This is not a metaphor stretched beyond recognition. This is sober biblical reality that demands our attention. From the very moment God instituted the covenant of marriage in the garden of Eden, Satan has worked tirelessly and strategically to destroy it, to corrupt it, and to turn God's good gift into something unrecognizable.

He corrupted marriage at its very inception when he approached Eve with his crafty questions and twisted half-truths while Adam stood passively by, failing in his God-given role as protector and spiritual leader. Think about that. The first recorded instance of spiritual warfare involved an attack on the marriage relationship. That should tell us something. He twisted and perverted God's design for marriage throughout the entire narrative of Scripture through polygamy, which brought misery to families, through adultery, that destroyed trust and broke covenant bonds, and through divorce that shattered what God intended to remain whole. He attacks marriage relentlessly, creatively, and viciously in every culture across the globe, in every generation throughout history, and in every season of life.

Why does he expend such focused energy on destroying marriages? Because marriage matters profoundly in God's economy. Because it displays the gospel of Christ and His church to a watching world. Because it builds covenant families that become the foundation of stable societies. Because it produces godly offspring who will carry the faith to the next generation. Because Satan hates with burning intensity what God loves with infinite passion, and God loves marriage deeply as His own creation and picture of divine love.

Peter warned, "Be sober-minded; be watchful. Your adversary the devil prowls around like a roaring lion, seeking someone to devour." (1 Peter 5:8) This is true of life generally, but it applies to marriage specifically. The enemy seeks to devour marriages through temptation, deception, accusation, and distraction.

Temptation comes through many forms. Sexual attraction to someone other than your spouse. Emotional affairs that seem innocent but erode covenant commitment. Pornography that replaces intimacy with fantasy. The grass-is-greener lie that says happiness lies elsewhere.

Deception whispers that covenant is optional. That your feelings matter more than your vows. That you deserve better. That God wants you to be happy above all else. These are lies straight from the pit, but they sound plausible when marriage is hard.

Accusation tells you that your spouse is the problem. That they will never change. That you cannot forgive again. That reconciliation is impossible. Satan is called the accuser for good reason. He specializes in highlighting faults and magnifying grievances.

Distractions keep couples too busy for each other. Work demands consume time that should go to marriage. Children become the exclusive focus, leaving the marriage neglected. Hobbies and friendships crowd out time together. Slowly, imperceptibly, spouses become roommates instead of lovers, business partners instead of intimate friends.

Fighting for your marriage means recognizing the real enemy. Your spouse is not the enemy. Circumstances are not the enemy. In-laws are not the enemy. Satan is the enemy, and he wants your marriage destroyed.

Paul wrote, "For we do not wrestle against flesh and blood, but against the rulers, against the authorities, against the cosmic powers over this present darkness, against the spiritual forces of evil in the heavenly places." (Ephesians 6:12) This warfare requires spiritual weapons. Prayer. Scripture. Accountability. Church community. Fasting. Worship. These are not optional add-ons but essential tools for fighting the good fight.

I have watched marriages survive seemingly impossible situations when couples fought together instead of against each other. The couple whose marriage was shattered by adultery but rebuilt through painful repentance and costly forgiveness. The wife who stood by her husband through addiction recovery when everyone told her to leave. The husband who loved his wife through a mental illness that made her barely recognizable.

These marriages survived because the couples understood they were in a fight. They put on the armor of God. They stood against the schemes of the enemy. They refused to surrender covenant to circumstances. They fought, and they won, not through their own strength but through God's sustaining grace.

The Hope of Redemption

I conclude where we must always conclude when wrestling with the profound challenges and beautiful possibilities of marriage: with hope. Yes, marriage is brutally hard in a fallen world where sin corrupts even our most sacred relationships. Yes, every single marriage without exception bears the unmistakable scars of sin, both the sins we commit against each other and the sins committed against us. Yes, we all fail daily to love with the self-sacrificing, covenant-keeping love that Christ demonstrated, and we all fail to submit with the joyful trust and reverence that the church should offer to her Bridegroom. The gap between the ideal and the reality can feel overwhelming, crushing even.

But here is the glorious truth that changes everything: our hope does not rest in our performance. It never has, and it never will. Our hope rests entirely in Christ's finished work, that completed, accomplished, victorious work He declared from the cross when He proclaimed, "It is finished."

Jesus Christ came into this broken world specifically to restore what Adam shattered in the garden. He lived the perfect life of absolute covenant faithfulness that we could never live, honoring every promise, fulfilling every obligation, loving without wavering. He died the death that our covenant-breaking deserved, absorbing in His own body the penalty for every betrayal, every harsh word, every act of selfishness, every failure to love. And He rose triumphant from the grave to inaugurate the new creation where all things, including the sacred institution of marriage, will be made completely, gloriously, eternally new.

On that day, we will experience the reality toward which all earthly marriage points. The marriage supper of the Lamb. The eternal union between Christ and His bride. The consummation of God's redemptive plan. Every earthly marriage, no matter how beautiful, is merely a shadow compared to that substance.

This does not diminish marriage's importance. It elevates it. Every time a husband loves sacrificially, he preaches the gospel. Every time a wife trusts and respects, she displays the church's response to Christ. Every time a couple works through conflict, they demonstrate covenant faithfulness. Every time they choose each other again, they point to the One who will never leave or forsake His own.

Our marriages are living testimonies. The world watches, and they draw conclusions. When they see marriages marked by joy, commitment, and sacrificial love, they see glimpses of the kingdom. When they see marriages characterized by bitterness, betrayal, and abandonment, they see confirmation of their cynicism.

We owe the watching world better. We owe them marriages that point to Christ. Not perfect marriages, for those do not exist this side of glory. But faithful marriages. Covenant-keeping marriages. Gospel-shaped marriages. Marriages that show the world what love looks like when it is grounded in something deeper than feelings, firmer than circumstances, and more enduring than death.

This is what Genesis 2 calls us to. One man. One woman. One flesh. One covenant. One lifetime. It is God's design from the beginning, Christ's restoration in the gospel, and the Spirit's empowering in the present. It is hard and beautiful, costly and worthwhile, challenging and rewarding.

It is marriage. The first human relationship. The foundation of society. The picture of the gospel. The gift we must fight to protect, celebrate with joy, and pass to the next generation.

May God grant us grace to honor it as He designed, to redeem it where it has fallen, and to display through it the glory of Christ and His church.

Chapter Nine

The Serpent's Strategy: Deception, Doubt, and Disorder

The transition from Genesis 2 to Genesis 3 is jarring. One moment we stand in paradise, watching the first couple walk together in perfect harmony with God, with each other, and with creation. The next moment, the serpent appears, and everything unravels. No warning. No explanation of where this creature came from or why it speaks. Just the abrupt introduction of evil into a world that had known nothing but goodness.

"Now the serpent was more crafty than any other beast of the field that the Lord God had made." (Genesis 3:1) That single sentence contains volumes. The serpent was crafty. The Hebrew word is *arum*, the same root used just verses earlier to describe Adam and Eve's nakedness. They were naked (*arummim*) and felt no shame. The serpent was crafty (arum). The wordplay is deliberate. Their innocence and the serpent's cunning stand in stark contrast. Where they possessed transparency and openness, the serpent brought deception and hidden agendas.

Notice also what Moses does not tell us. He does not explain the serpent's origin. He does not describe a cosmic rebellion in heaven or provide backstory about fallen angels. The focus remains laser-sharp on the human drama unfolding in the garden. Later Scripture will pull back the curtain and identify this serpent as Satan himself, that ancient dragon and accuser. But here in Genesis, the narrative concentrates on what happened, not on peripheral questions about demonic hierarchies.

This is instructive. When we face temptation, we often want to psychoanalyze the enemy, to understand his motives, to explore the metaphysics of evil. Genesis 3 redirects our attention. What matters is recognizing the tactics, resisting the lies, and standing firm in God's truth. The serpent's identity matters less than his strategy.

And what a strategy it was!

The Opening Gambit

Then in Genesis 3:1 the serpent asks Eve, "Did God actually say, 'You shall not eat of any tree of the garden'?" Five words in Hebrew. A simple question. And with it, the serpent launched an assault that would echo through every generation of human history. This was not a request for information. The serpent knew exactly what God had said. This was psychological warfare, carefully calibrated to create doubt, confusion, and eventually rebellion.

Look at the precision of this attack. The serpent did not deny God's existence. He did not argue against God's authority. He did not present himself as an alternative deity worthy of worship. Instead, he simply questioned whether God had really said what Adam and Eve thought He had said. He planted a seed of uncertainty about the clarity and reliability of God's Word.

"Did God actually say?" The implications ripple outward. Maybe you misunderstood. Perhaps you misheard. Could you have gotten it wrong? Is that really what God meant? The serpent's opening move was to make them doubt their own perception of divine revelation.

I have watched this same tactic deployed in countless contexts throughout my years in ministry. The seminary student who begins questioning whether Scripture truly teaches what the church has always believed. The young couple who wonder if God's boundaries around sexuality really apply to their unique situation. The businessman who debates whether biblical ethics genuinely govern modern commerce. Always the same approach. Not outright denial, but subtle questioning. "Did God actually say?"

The serpent also distorted God's command. God had said they could freely eat from every tree in the garden except one. The prohibition was narrow and specific. The permission was broad and generous. One tree was off-limits. Every other tree stood available for their enjoyment. The ratio was overwhelmingly in their favor.

But the serpent flipped the emphasis. "Did God actually say, 'You shall not eat of any tree of the garden'?" He made God's generosity sound like deprivation. He reframed abundance as restriction. He turned a minor limitation into a total prohibition. This is the alchemy of deception, transforming gold into lead through careful manipulation of perspective.

Watch how this works in your own temptations. The enemy never presents sin honestly. He always packages it as a liberation from arbitrary restrictions. God's wisdom becomes divine tyranny. His protection becomes imprisonment. His loving boundaries become evidence of His desire to keep us from happiness and fulfillment.

I remember counseling a man who was contemplating leaving his wife for a woman at work. He had constructed an entire theology to justify his decision. God wants me to be happy, he insisted. Surely God would not want me to stay in a marriage where I feel unfulfilled. The new relationship feels so right, so natural. Maybe God is leading me toward authentic love.

He had swallowed the serpent's lie whole. God's clear command about covenant faithfulness became negotiable. Feelings trumped revelation. Desire determined truth. And all of it began with a simple question: Did God actually say marriage is permanent?

Eve's Response

To her credit, in verse 2 Eve attempted to correct the serpent's misrepresentation. "We may eat of the fruit of the trees in the garden, but God said, 'You shall not eat of the fruit of the tree that is in the midst of the garden, neither shall you touch it, lest you die.'"

She got most of it right. She affirmed God's generosity in providing the other trees. She acknowledged the specific prohibition. She recognized the consequence. But she also made two subtle errors that revealed the serpent's question had already done its work.

First, she added to God's command. God had said nothing about touching the tree. He had only forbidden eating its fruit. Eve's addition might seem like a reasonable safety measure, a hedge around the law to prevent even coming close to transgression. But it revealed something troubling. She was now negotiating with God's Word rather than simply trusting it. She felt the need to improve upon divine instruction, to add her own protective clauses.

Second, she softened God's warning. God had said, "In the day that you eat of it you shall surely die." The Hebrew is emphatic, a doubling of the verb for emphasis. "Dying you shall die." It is the strongest possible way to express certainty. But Eve reported it as "lest you die," introducing a note of uncertainty that God's original statement did not contain.

These seem like minor adjustments. They probably felt reasonable to Eve at the moment. But they demonstrate a crucial principle: once you start questioning God's Word, you inevitably begin editing it. Addition and subtraction. Emphasis and de-emphasis. Interpretation shaped by desire rather than submission to clear revelation.

This is why the Reformation principle of sola Scriptura matters so profoundly. Scripture alone. Not Scripture plus tradition. Not Scripture filtered through experience. Not Scripture adjusted to accommodate cultural sensibilities. When we allow any other authority to stand alongside or above God's revealed Word, we open ourselves to the serpent's deception. We position ourselves as editors rather than readers, as judges rather than those judged.

I spent years in academic settings where this battle raged constantly. Scholars would propose that certain biblical texts reflected merely cultural accommodation rather than timeless truth. Others would argue that the church's understanding had evolved beyond Scripture's outdated categories. Still others would insist that personal experience provided a superior lens for interpreting challenging passages.

All of it amounted to the same thing. "Did God actually say?" The question never goes away. It simply gets repackaged for each generation, dressed in the vocabulary of academic sophistication or therapeutic insight or progressive enlightenment. But underneath the contemporary camouflage, the serpent's ancient strategy remains unchanged.

The Direct Assault

Having established doubt about what God said, the serpent moved to attack God's character. "You will not surely die. For God knows that when you eat of it your eyes will be opened, and you will be like God, knowing good and evil."

Now the gloves came off. The serpent directly contradicted God's warning. Where God had said they would die, the serpent declared they would not. This was no longer subtle questioning but flat denial. And with that denial came an alternative explanation for God's prohibition.

God was holding out on them. He was protecting His own position. He knew that eating the fruit would elevate them to His level, and He did not want the competition. The boundary was not for their protection but for His benefit. The restriction revealed not loving care but selfish insecurity.

This is slander in its purest form. The serpent was not merely lying about the consequences of sin. He was lying about God Himself. He was attributing to the all-good, all-loving Creator the petty motivations of a threatened tyrant. He was turning providence into paranoia, wisdom into wickedness.

And the tragic reality is that this lie still works. I have sat across from countless believers who secretly suspect God is holding out on them. They wonder if His commands are really for their good or if He is keeping them from something better. They question whether His timing is truly perfect or if He is making them wait unnecessarily. They doubt whether His plan for their life is really the best option or if they are missing out on superior alternatives.

These doubts flow from the same poisoned well that the serpent opened in Eden. They assume God's character is fundamentally suspect, that His Word might not be trustworthy, that His intentions toward us might be less than completely good.

But notice the particular form this accusation took. "You will be like God." The serpent promised divine status through human effort. You can transcend your creatureliness. You can escape dependence. You can be self-sufficient, self-determining, self-creating. You do not need God to define good and evil for you. You can make those determinations yourself.

This was the ultimate deception. They were already like God in the only way that mattered. They bore His image. They enjoyed intimate fellowship with Him. They exercised delegated authority over creation under His sovereign rule. They lacked nothing that was good for them to possess.

But the serpent dangled before them likeness to God in a way that would actually destroy their humanity. Autonomy instead of dependence. Self-rule instead of joyful submission. Knowledge obtained through rebellion rather than revelation. A likeness to God that required them to stop being what God had made them to be.

Every sin promises the same lie. You can be your own god. You can determine your own truth. You can create your own meaning. You can establish your own morality. The uniform that I wore as a Marine had the Eagle, Globe, and Anchor. When I put it on, I did not become an admiral or general. I became a Marine, and that identity came with both privileges and responsibilities, freedoms and constraints. The serpent's promise was like telling a private that true freedom meant rejecting the chain of command, that real fulfillment required going AWOL, that authentic self-expression demanded desertion.

The promise is always freedom but delivers slavery. The Bible's diagnosis remains true: "They promise them freedom, but they themselves are slaves of corruption. For whatever overcomes a person, to that he is enslaved." (2 Peter 2:19)

The Psychology of Temptation

"So when the woman saw that the tree was good for food, and that it was a delight to the eyes, and that the tree was to be desired to make one wise, she took of its fruit and ate, and she also gave some to her husband who was with her, and he ate." (Genesis 3:6) The serpent had done his work well. Eve's perception had shifted completely. The tree that had stood as a simple boundary marker now appeared as the source of everything she lacked. Where previously she had seen God's generous provision in all the other trees, now her focus narrowed to the one thing prohibited. Desire spiraled into obsession.

Three elements converged at that devastating moment. Physical appetite: the tree was good for food, promising satisfaction of bodily hunger. Aesthetic pleasure: it was a delight to the eyes, offering visual beauty that stirred her senses. Intellectual aspiration: it was to be desired to make one wise, appealing to her longing for knowledge and understanding. Body, soul, and mind; the whole person, all enlisted simultaneously in the service of disobedience. This threefold assault represents the complete anatomy of temptation, revealing how desire becomes twisted and corrupted when it turns inward toward autonomous self-fulfillment rather than outward toward God-directed worship and obedience.

The pattern would prove enduring. Centuries later, the Apostle John would identify these same categories when warning believers in 1 John 2:16: "For all that is in the world—the desires of the flesh and the desires of the eyes and pride of life—is not from the Father but is from the world." The template established in Eden continues to recur throughout the entirety of human experience, echoing across generations and cultures. Temptation rarely comes in a single dimension, approaching us from only one angle. Instead, it appeals to multiple aspects of our nature simultaneously, creating a powerful convergence of desire that feels overwhelming, inevitable, and even irresistible.

But notice what Eve did not do. She did not consult Adam. She did not seek God's counsel. She did not pause to weigh the consequences. The text gives no indication of internal struggle or hesitation. The serpent's lies had so thoroughly reframed reality that what was actually cosmic treason appeared as a natural, reasonable, even desirable action.

This is how deception works. It does not feel like deception in the moment. The alcoholic genuinely believes one more drink will solve his problems. The adulterer truly thinks this relationship will bring the fulfillment of his marriage lacks.

The embezzler convinces himself the money is owed to him, anyway. Sin makes perfect sense to the sinner.

During my wife's cancer battle, I discovered this truth through profound pain. We confronted innumerable choices regarding treatment approaches, and decisions about her care. In those shadowed hours, I experienced enormous pressure to seize control, to discover the answer, to repair what couldn't be repaired. The lure was to rely on my own understanding, my own investigation, my own resolve rather than abiding in God's sovereign rule.

The serpent's voice was crafty: God has granted you intellect and means. Certainly, He anticipates you'll employ them. Assuming command isn't rebellion but stewardship. And concealed beneath lay a more sinister falsehood: God might not provide, so you must guarantee your own result.

I needed to retreat repeatedly to the reality that God is good, that His Word is reliable, that His purpose is flawless even when it encompasses affliction. The struggle wasn't merely about medical choices but about whom I would depend upon amid circumstances that seemed to be careening beyond my grasp.

Where Was Adam?

The text drops a bombshell that we easily miss on casual reading at the end of verse 6. Eve "gave some to her husband who was with her, and he ate." Adam was there. He was present throughout the entire exchange with the serpent. He heard the lies. He watched Eve's growing fascination with the forbidden fruit. He stood by while she took it and ate it.

And he said nothing.

This silence is deafening. Adam, who had received God's command directly, who had been placed in the garden to work it and keep it, who had been given responsibility to lead and protect, stood mute while the enemy assaulted his wife with lies and led her into rebellion. He offered no correction, no resistance, no defense.

Was he confused? Had the serpent's deceptiveness tangled his thinking so thoroughly that he could not formulate a response? Was he curious? Did he want to see what would happen, treating the situation as an experiment rather than spiritual warfare? Was he weak? Did he lack the courage to confront evil even when it threatened everything he loved?

The text does not tell us his internal state, but it clearly shows his external failure. When leadership was required, he was passive. When the truth needed defending, he was silent. When his wife needed his strength, he was absent even though physically present.

This passivity was itself a sin, perhaps the deeper sin underlying the actual eating. Adam's calling was to guard the garden, and the garden included Eve. The serpent was an intruder, a threatening presence that should have been driven out. But Adam allowed the enemy to operate unchallenged, to spread his poison, to destroy what God had made good.

And when Eve offered him the fruit, he took it. Not after agonizing deliberation. Not after being worn down by persistent persuasion. The text suggests immediate compliance. She gave. He ate. The head, who should have led in righteousness, became a follower in rebellion.

I have seen this same dynamic play out in countless marriages and churches. Men who abdicate their responsibility to lead, to protect, to speak truth. They stand by while error infiltrates their homes and congregations. They remain silent when they should speak, passive when they should act, absent when they should engage.

Sometimes this passivity masquerades as kindness or respect. I do not want to be controlling. I believe in equality. Who am I to impose my views? But biblical headship is not about control or superiority. It is about sacrificial responsibility, about standing between those you love and the dangers that threaten them, about being willing to spend yourself in service of their flourishing.

Adam's failure was not primarily in eating the fruit. It was in failing to fulfill his calling as covenant head, as guardian, as protector. And that failure had devastating consequences not just for him and Eve but for every human being who would descend from them.

The Nature of Spiritual Warfare

Genesis 3 pulls back the curtain on a reality that permeates all of human history. We are in a war. The battlefield is cosmic, but the tactics are intensely personal. The enemy is real, intelligent, and committed to our destruction. And his primary weapon is deception.

Paul would later write to the church at Ephesus, pulling no punches about the nature of the conflict we face: "We do not wrestle against flesh and blood, but against the rulers, against the authorities, against the cosmic powers over this present darkness, against the spiritual forces of evil in the heavenly places" (Ephesians 6:12). These are not the words of a man trafficking in metaphor or engaging in poetic exaggeration. Paul understood something that many modern believers have forgotten or never learned. This warfare is not merely symbolic language designed to help us think about our struggles in dramatic terms. It is actual combat against an actual enemy.

The apostle chose his words with precision. He did not write that we struggle or face challenges or encounter difficulties. He wrote that we wrestle. Anyone who has ever grappled with an opponent, whether in athletic competition or life-and-death combat, knows the intimacy and intensity that word conveys. Wrestling is personal. It is exhausting. It demands every ounce of strength, every tactical advantage, every reserve of endurance you can muster. There is no room for passivity or abstraction when someone is trying to pin you to the mat or take you to the ground.

But the nature of the combat is not what we might expect. The enemy rarely attacks with obvious evil. He comes as an angel of light, making darkness appear bright, poison seem nutritious, death look like life. His strategy has not changed since Eden. Question God's Word. Distort God's character. Promise divine status through human autonomy. Make sin seem reasonable, beneficial, even righteous.

Understanding this strategy is essential for resisting it. The devil is not a creative strategist. He has no need to be. The old lies still work just fine. So he recycles them endlessly, adjusting only the packaging to fit contemporary sensibilities.

"Did God actually say the Bible is reliable?" The question now comes dressed in scholarly garb, citing manuscript variants and cultural accommodation, but it amounts to the same ancient doubt.

"Did God actually say sexual expression should be limited to marriage between a man and woman?" The challenge now appeals to authenticity and personal fulfillment, but it rests on the same foundation of making God's boundaries seem arbitrary and cruel.

"Did God actually say Jesus is the only way to salvation?" The objection now invokes inclusivity and respect for diverse spiritualities, but it denies the same exclusive truth claims that have always offended human pride.

The tactics remain constant because human nature remains constant. We want autonomy. We desire to determine our own truth. We chafe under divine authority. We resent limitations on our freedom. And the enemy knows exactly which buttons to push.

Effective spiritual warfare requires that we recognize these patterns. When we feel that familiar urge to question God's clear revelation, we can identify the source. When Scripture's teaching suddenly seems unreasonable or outdated, we can recognize the serpent's fingerprints. When God's character comes under suspicion, we can see through the slander to the slanderer.

But recognition is only the beginning of our response. The Apostle Paul, writing to believers facing very real spiritual opposition, instructs us with military precision to "take up the whole armor of God, that you may be able to withstand in the evil day, and having done all, to stand firm" (Ephesians 6:13). Notice the comprehensiveness of his command, the whole armor. This is not ceremonial dress for religious pageantry. This is functional equipment for actual combat, each piece carefully designed by divine wisdom for spiritual warfare.

Consider what Paul lists with such deliberate care: the belt of truth, the breastplate of righteousness, the shoes of the gospel of peace, the shield of faith, the helmet of salvation, and the sword of the Spirit, which is the Word of God. These are not random metaphors pulled from a Roman soldier's equipment. Each piece addresses a specific vulnerability that the enemy consistently targets in his attacks against believers.

Truth counteracts the deception we've been examining. Righteousness, both imputed and lived, resists the accusations that would paralyze us with guilt and shame. The gospel provides firm footing when our circumstances shift like sand beneath our feet. Faith extinguishes the flaming darts of doubt that the enemy hurls at us in moments of weakness and uncertainty. The helmet of salvation protects our minds from the fear and despair that would overwhelm us if we forgot whose we are. And God's Word provides the only offensive weapon we need because it is, as Hebrews tells us, "living and active, sharper than any two-edged sword" (Hebrews 4:12) powerful enough to penetrate every defense the enemy might raise.

I learned to appreciate this armor during my time in the Marines. Physical armor only works if you actually wear it. The best body armor in the world provides zero protection if it sits in your locker while you walk into combat. The same principle applies spiritually. God has provided everything we need for victory, but we must intentionally put it on daily, deliberately, completely.

Recognizing the Enemy's Voice

One of the most important skills in spiritual warfare is learning to distinguish God's voice from the enemy's. Both speak. Both make claims. Both promise outcomes. But they are utterly different in character and content.

God's voice brings clarity. The enemy's voice produces confusion. God speaks in line with His revealed Word. The enemy contradicts or distorts Scripture. God's promises align with His character. The enemy's promises require us to doubt that character.

God convicts of specific sin and points toward Christ. The enemy accuses generally and drives toward despair. God's correction is surgical, targeting particular issues. The enemy's condemnation is comprehensive, declaring us worthless and hopeless.

God opens pathways to repentance and restoration. The enemy closes doors and whispers that change is impossible. God reminds us of Christ's finished work. The enemy insists we must earn acceptance through performance.

These distinctions matter enormously. I have counseled people who were convinced God was telling them to do things that directly contradicted Scripture. A woman who believed God was leading her to divorce her husband even though he had not committed adultery or abandoned her. A man who thought God was calling him to leave his church because he felt hurt by criticism. A student who insisted God wanted him to drop out of seminary because the academic work felt too difficult.

In every case, they had confused their own desires or the enemy's suggestions with divine guidance. God does not contradict His Word. He does not lead us away from commitment and toward convenience. He does not tell us to abandon responsibility when it becomes challenging.

Learning to test the spirits requires nothing less than deep, sustained immersion in the pages of Scripture, not casual reading or occasional sampling, but the kind of engagement that shapes our thinking and informs our discernment at the most fundamental level. We simply cannot identify counterfeits if we remain fundamentally unfamiliar with the genuine article. A bank teller learns to spot counterfeit currency not by studying forgeries but by handling authentic bills until their weight, texture, and appearance become second nature. In the same way, believers develop spiritual discernment by saturating themselves in God's Word until they instinctively recognize what sounds true and what rings false.

This is precisely why the great Reformers of the sixteenth century insisted with such unwavering conviction on both the primacy and the all-sufficiency of Scripture. They understood that God has spoken clearly, authoritatively, and comprehensively in His written Word. The Bible is not merely one voice among many that we must weigh and consider; it is the supreme and final authority that judges all other claims to truth. Any voice, whether it seems to come from within our own hearts, from other people, from spiritual experiences, or even from supernatural sources, that contradicts or undermines that divine revelation, no matter how compelling or emotionally satisfying it may feel in the moment, simply cannot be from God. The God who inspired Scripture will never contradict what He has already revealed.

Chapter Ten

Humanity's Rebellion: The Anatomy of Sin

The Nature of Disobedience

When Eve took the fruit and ate, and when Adam, standing beside her, followed her lead, something catastrophic happened. This was not merely a mistake or a lapse in judgment. This was not simply poor decision making that required a course correction. What occurred in that moment was nothing less than cosmic treason, a deliberate rebellion against the sovereign Creator who had given them everything.

The text of Genesis 3:6 describes the action with devastating simplicity: "So when the woman saw that the tree was good for food, and that it was a delight to the eyes, and that the tree was to be desired to make one wise, she took of its fruit and ate, and she also gave some to her husband who was with her, and he ate." Twenty-nine words in English that changed everything. Twenty-nine words that ushered death into a world that had known only life. Twenty-nine words that fractured the perfect harmony between Creator and creature.

But we must understand what actually happened in those few seconds. This was not a simple act of eating forbidden fruit, as though God had arbitrarily selected one tree among thousands and declared it off-limits to test human obedience through some capricious divine game. The prohibition against eating from the tree of the knowledge of good and evil represented something far more profound. It established the fundamental structure of reality itself, the acknowledgment that God alone determines what is right and wrong, what is good and evil, what brings life and what brings death.

By eating from that tree, Adam and Eve were not simply breaking a rule. They were asserting their independence from God. They were claiming the right to decide for themselves what was true and false, good and evil, right and wrong. They were, in effect, dethroning God and enthroning themselves. They were rejecting His loving authority and establishing their own autonomous judgment as the final arbiter of reality.

I have watched this same pattern play out in countless lives over my years in ministry. The specific temptations vary. The particular sins differ. But the underlying dynamic remains constant. At the heart of every sin lies the same basic impulse that drove Adam and Eve to eat the forbidden fruit: the desire to be our own god, to live according to our own wisdom rather than submit to divine authority, to trust our own judgment rather than believe God's Word.

A young couple I once counseled decided to move in together before marriage despite clear biblical teaching against sexual immorality. Their reasoning sounded sophisticated and practical. They needed to make sure that they were compatible. They wanted to save money. They saw no reason to follow an outdated cultural norm that no longer made sense in the modern world. But underneath all these rationalizations lay the same fundamental rebellion. They had decided that their wisdom exceeded God's. They had determined that their assessment of what would bring happiness and fulfillment carried more weight than the Creator's design for human sexuality and marriage.

A businessman in my congregation convinced himself that certain questionable practices were acceptable because everyone in his industry engaged in them. He had developed an entire theological framework to justify actions that clearly violated biblical principles of honesty and integrity. He could quote Scripture. He could explain how grace covered his shortcomings. He could argue that God cared more about his heart than his actions. But again, the root issue was the same. He had placed his own judgment above God's revealed will.

This is what Reformed theology means when it speaks of the radical nature of sin. Sin is not primarily about breaking rules or failing to meet standards. Sin is fundamentally relational. It represents the rupture of the relationship between Creator and creature. It is the creature saying to the Creator, "I will not have you rule over me. I will be my own master. I will determine my own path."

The Federal Headship of Adam

Understanding what happened when Adam sinned requires grasping a concept that many modern Christians find troubling: federal headship. This doctrine, firmly rooted in Scripture and clearly articulated in Reformed theology, teaches that Adam acted not merely as an individual but as the representative of all humanity. When he sinned, he sinned on behalf of all his descendants. His guilt became our guilt. His condemnation became our condemnation.

Paul makes this doctrine explicit in Romans 5:12-19, a passage that demands careful attention. "Therefore, just as sin came into the world through one man, and death through sin, and so death spread to all men because all sinned" (Romans 5:12). The apostle is not simply observing that death is universal or that everyone commits individual acts of sin. He is explaining a theological reality that governs how sin entered the human race and how its effects spread to every person ever born.

He continues in verses 18-19: "Therefore, as one trespass led to condemnation for all men, so one act of righteousness leads to justification and life for all men. For as by the one man's disobedience the many were made sinners, so by the one man's obedience the many will be made righteous." The parallel could not be clearer. Just as Christ's obedience is credited to all who are united to Him by faith, Adam's disobedience was credited to all who are united to him by natural descent.

This strikes many people as profoundly unfair. Why should I be held accountable for something Adam did thousands of years before I was born? Why should his sin be counted as my sin when I had no choice in the matter, no opportunity to make a different decision?

These objections, while understandable from a human perspective, miss several crucial points. First, federal representation is not foreign to human experience. We accept it in numerous contexts. When a nation goes to war, the decision is made by representatives, yet the consequences affect every citizen. When a CEO signs a contract binding the company, individual employees did not negotiate those terms, yet they must abide by them. When parents make decisions for their minor children, those children bear the results whether they would have chosen differently or not.

Second, and more importantly, the principle of federal headship is the very mechanism by which salvation becomes possible. If we reject the idea that Adam's sin can be imputed to us, we must also reject the idea that Christ's righteousness can be imputed to us. The two doctrines stand or fall together. Paul's entire argument in Romans 5 depends on this parallel. If the first Adam could not act as our representative in bringing condemnation, then the second Adam cannot act as our representative in bringing justification.

Third, we must honestly acknowledge that given the same circumstances, everyone of us would have made the same choice Adam made. We know this because we continue to make that choice every single day. Presented with God's clear commands, we regularly choose to disobey. Faced with the option of trusting God's wisdom or following our own understanding, we consistently choose autonomy over submission. The problem is not that we inherited a bad decision we would not have made ourselves. The problem is that we inherit a nature that inevitably produces the same rebellion that characterized our first parents.

During my time of teaching theology, I watched students wrestle with this doctrine. Many came from church backgrounds that emphasized human free will and individual choice to such an extent that federal headship seemed to contradict everything they had been taught about personal responsibility. I remember one particularly earnest young man who argued passionately that it violated basic justice for God to hold him accountable for Adam's sin.

I asked him a simple question: "Have you sinned?" He admitted he had. "Did anyone force you to sin, or did you choose it freely?" He acknowledged that his sins were of his own choice. "Then you are not actually objecting to being punished for Adam's sin. You are objecting to the doctrine of original sin, the teaching that you inherited a sinful nature from Adam. But the evidence of that inheritance is found in your own behavior. You sin because you are a sinner. You are a sinner because you descended from Adam. But you are also personally guilty because you have ratified Adam's choice through your own repeated acts of rebellion."

The doctrine of federal headship, properly understood, does not excuse our personal guilt. It explains our universal guilt. It answers the question of why every human being, in every culture, in every time period, chooses sin. We do not become sinners by sinning. We sin because we are sinners. And we are sinners because we stand in Adam.

The Doctrine of Original Sin

This brings us to one of the most contested yet thoroughly biblical doctrines in all of Christian theology: original sin. This teaching holds that Adam's sin corrupted not just his own nature but the nature of all his descendants. Every person born into this world, with the sole exception of Jesus Christ, enters life bearing a sinful nature inherited from Adam.

David expresses this reality in Psalm 51:5: "Behold, I was brought forth in iniquity, and in sin did my mother conceive me." He is not suggesting that the act of conception itself is sinful or that his mother engaged in immoral behavior. He is confessing that from the very moment of his existence, from conception itself, he possessed a nature inclined toward sin.

Paul develops this doctrine systematically in Romans 3:10-12, quoting from the Psalms: "None is righteous, no, not one; no one understands; no one seeks for God. All have turned aside; together they have become worthless; no one does good, not even one." The universality of sin is absolute. The corruption is comprehensive. The bondage is complete.

Original sin does not mean that every person is as evil as they could possibly be. We are not utterly depraved in the sense that we are incapable of any action that appears good or that we always choose the worst possible option in every situation. Reformed theology has always distinguished between total depravity and utter depravity. We are totally depraved in that sin has affected every part of our being, our minds, our wills, our emotions, our bodies, our relationships, but we are not utterly depraved in the sense that we are as evil as we could possibly be.

I have known unbelievers who were kind, generous, and moral by external standards. I have watched atheists demonstrate remarkable integrity in business dealings. I have seen people with no professed faith in Christ sacrifice their own interests for the sake of others. These actions are genuine. They produce real good in the world. They reflect the fact that all human beings, even after the fall, retain the image of God, however defaced and distorted it has become.

But here is the crucial point that must not be missed: from God's perspective, from the standpoint of what pleases Him and earns His acceptance, even these apparently good works are tainted by sin. They proceed from hearts that do not love God supremely. They are performed by people who are in rebellion against their Creator. They may be externally commendable, but they cannot merit salvation or earn divine favor.

Paul addresses this directly in Romans 8:7-8, and his words cut to the very heart of humanity's fundamental problem: "For the mind that is set on the flesh is hostile to God, for it does not submit to God's law; indeed, it cannot. Those who are in the flesh cannot please God." Notice the progression of Paul's argument here, the careful way he builds from one devastating truth to the next.

The problem is not merely that we fail to keep God's law perfectly, that we occasionally stumble or fall short of the standard. The problem runs far deeper than moral failure or ethical inadequacy. The problem is that in our natural state, in the condition we inherit from Adam, we are fundamentally incapable of pleasing God at all. Our minds, the very center of our thinking and reasoning, are hostile to Him, not neutral, not indifferent, but actively opposed. Our wills, which govern our choices and direct our actions, are set against Him. We cannot submit to His law, not because we lack sufficient willpower or moral strength, but because our very nature, our fallen human nature, rebels against His authority at the most foundational level.

I once had a conversation with a colleague who taught ethics at a secular university. He considered himself a good person. He gave to charity. He treated his students with respect. He maintained strong ethical standards in his research and teaching. He could not understand why Christians insisted that people needed to be "saved." From what? He was not murdering people or committing terrible crimes. He was a contributing member of society, living a morally upright life.

I did not dispute his external morality. But I asked him about his relationship with God. Did he worship God? Did he love God with all his heart, soul, mind, and strength? Did he acknowledge God's authority over his life? Did he live in submission to God's revealed will?

His answer was illuminating. He did not believe in God, at least not in the personal God revealed in Scripture. He saw no need for religious commitment. He determined his own values and made his own moral choices based on reason and empathy. In other words, despite his external morality, he stood in fundamental rebellion against the Creator. His "good works" proceeded from a heart that denied God's very existence. From God's perspective, regardless of how commendable his actions appeared to other people, he remained in a state of hostility toward his Maker.

This is what the doctrine of original sin teaches. We are not neutral beings who sometimes choose good and sometimes choose evil, with our eternal destiny determined by which choices predominate. We are rebels who, apart from God's transforming grace, remain in a state of hostility toward God regardless of how moral our external behavior appears.

Total Depravity and the Bondage of the Will

The doctrine of total depravity, properly understood, maintains that sin has affected every aspect of human existence. There is no part of us that remains untouched by the corruption that entered the world through Adam's sin. Our minds are darkened. Our wills are bound. Our affections are disordered. Our bodies are subject to death and decay.

This does not mean we are incapable of any good action or that we always choose the worst possible option. What it means is that we are incapable of choosing God, incapable of saving ourselves, incapable of doing anything that merits His acceptance apart from His grace.

Paul explains this in Ephesians 2:1-3: "And you were dead in the trespasses and sins in which you once walked, following the course of this world, following the prince of the power of the air, the spirit that is now at work in the sons of disobedience, among whom we all once lived in the passions of our flesh, carrying out the desires of the body and the mind, and were by nature children of wrath, like the rest of mankind."

Notice the language Paul uses. We were dead. Not sick. Not weakened. Not in need of assistance. Dead. A dead person cannot contribute to their own resurrection. A corpse cannot help the one attempting to revive it. In our natural state, we are spiritually dead, completely unable to respond to God or choose Him apart from His intervention.

This doctrine of the bondage of the will became a central point of controversy during the Reformation. Martin Luther wrote his great work "The Bondage of the Will" in response to Erasmus, who argued that human beings retain free will even after the fall. Luther insisted that apart from grace, our wills are enslaved to sin. We are free in the sense that we choose according to our desires, but our desires are corrupt. We are not free to choose God because we do not desire God. We cannot turn to Christ because we have no inclination to turn to Him.

Jesus Himself taught this in John 6:44: "No one can come to me unless the Father who sent me draws him." He does not say that some people find it difficult to come unless the Father helps them. He says no one can come unless the Father draws them. The inability is absolute. The need for divine intervention is universal.

This creates what seems like an impossible situation. We are commanded to repent and believe. We are held responsible for our unbelief. We are condemned for our sins. Yet we are incapable of repenting, believing, or choosing God apart from His grace. How can God command what we cannot do? How can He hold us responsible for what we are unable to perform?

The answer lies in understanding the nature of our inability. We are not unable in the sense that we lack the physical or mental capacity to believe. We are unable in the sense that we lack the desire to believe. Our inability is moral, not mechanical. It flows from our hatred of God, not from any deficiency in our faculties.

Imagine a man who hates classical music. He finds it boring and pretentious. Someone offers him a free ticket to the symphony. He is physically capable of attending. His schedule is free. The concert hall is accessible. But he will not go because he has no desire to go. His failure to attend is his own fault, the result of his own preferences, even though in another sense he "cannot" bring himself to sit through something he despises.

In the same way, we are responsible for our unbelief because it flows from our own corrupt desires and preferences. We do not believe because we do not want to believe. We do not choose God because we hate God. Our inability is the result of our own rebellion, not some external constraint imposed upon us against our will.

I learned this truth in profound ways during my military service. I watched young Marines make decisions that revealed their true character under pressure. Some demonstrated extraordinary courage. Others crumbled. But in every case, people acted according to their nature. The brave Marine did not become brave in the moment of crisis. The crisis revealed bravery that was already there. The coward did not become cowardly when the situation grew dangerous. The danger exposed the cowardice that had always existed beneath the surface.

In the same way, our choices reveal our nature. We sin because we are sinners. We rebel because we are rebels. We reject God because we are, by nature, hostile to God. The doctrine of total depravity simply acknowledges this reality and traces it back to its source in Adam's fall.

The Fracture of Every Dimension of Life

Sin's effects are not limited to our vertical relationship with God, though that is certainly the primary fracture. Sin shatters every dimension of human existence. It corrupts our relationship with ourselves, with other people, with creation itself, and with the cultural mandate God gave us to exercise dominion over the earth.

Consider first our relationship with ourselves. Before the fall, Adam and Eve experienced perfect harmony between their various faculties and desires. Reason, emotion, will, and body all functioned in perfect coordination. There was no internal conflict, no divided heart, no struggle between what they knew to be right and what they desired to do.

After the fall, this harmony shattered. We experience constant internal warfare. Paul describes this in Romans 7:15-20: "For I do not understand my own actions. For I do not do what I want, but I do the very thing I hate. Now if I do what I do not want, I agree with the law, that it is good. So now it is no longer I who do it, but sin that dwells within me. For I know that nothing good dwells in me, that is, in my flesh. For I have the desire to do what is right, but not the ability to carry it out.

For I do not do the good I want, but the evil I do not want is what I keep on doing. Now if I do what I do not want, it is no longer I who do it, but sin that dwells within me."

This is the experience of every Christian who honestly examines their own heart. We know what is right. We desire to do what is right. Yet we find ourselves repeatedly doing what we know to be wrong. There is a war within us, a conflict between the new nature given to us in Christ and the remnants of the old nature that clings to us until we are finally glorified.

But even for unbelievers, who lack this new nature, there is internal conflict. The conscience, though seared and suppressed, continues to testify to moral reality. People violate their own standards. They fail to live up to even their own ideals. They experience guilt, shame, and self-loathing. All of this flows from the fracture within the self that resulted from Adam's sin.

Consider next our relationship with other people. The first human relationship, between Adam and Eve, was characterized by perfect unity and harmony. They were naked and not ashamed. They experienced complete transparency, trust, and intimacy. There was no competition, no manipulation, no conflict.

Immediately after the fall, this changed. When God confronted Adam about his sin, Adam's first response was to blame Eve: "The woman whom you gave to be with me, she gave me fruit of the tree, and I ate" (Genesis 3:12). Notice the shift. Adam, who had previously celebrated Eve as bone of his bones and flesh of his flesh, now distances himself from her. She becomes "the woman whom you gave to be with me," as though she were an unwanted burden imposed upon him rather than the perfect complement to his existence.

Eve, for her part, blamed the serpent: "The serpent deceived me, and I ate" (Genesis 3:13). Both of them sought to escape responsibility by shifting the blame to someone else. Both of them placed self-protection above honest acknowledgment of their own guilt.

This pattern has characterized human relationships ever since. We use people rather than love them. We compete rather than cooperate. We manipulate rather than serve. We hide rather than reveal ourselves authentically. Marriage, which should be the deepest human relationship, becomes a battleground. Families fracture. Friendships dissolve. Nations go to war.

All of this flows from sin. The suspicion, the competition, the conflict that mark human society are not original to creation. They are corruptions of what God intended. They are the bitter fruit of the tree from which Adam and Eve ate.

I have spent countless hours in counseling sessions listening to the wreckage that sin produces in relationships. Husbands and wives who can barely speak to each other without hostility. Parents and children locked in bitter conflict. Friends who have become enemies over trivial offenses that neither party can quite remember how they started. Congregations split by pride and division.

In every case, the same dynamics appear. Self-interest trumps love for others. Pride prevents reconciliation. The desire to be right outweighs the commitment to maintain relationship. Sin that fractures our relationship with God inevitably fractures our relationships with each other.

The Corruption of Work and Vocation

Before the fall, work was pure joy. God gave Adam the task of working and keeping the garden. This was not burdensome labor but a fulfilling vocation. Work was the expression of human creativity and capability. It was the means through which Adam exercised dominion and partnered with God in caring for creation.

After the fall, work became cursed. God said to Adam: "Cursed is the ground because of you; in pain you shall eat of it all the days of your life; thorns and thistles it shall bring forth for you; and you shall eat the plants of the field. By the sweat of your face you shall eat bread, till you return to the ground, for out of it you were taken; for you are dust, and to dust you shall return" (Genesis 3:17-19).

Work itself is not the curse. The curse is the frustration that now accompanies work. The ground resists cultivation. Thorns and thistles grow where we want productive plants. What should be fulfilling becomes exhausting. What should bring satisfaction often brings frustration.

But the corruption goes deeper than mere difficulty. Sin distorts our motives for work. We work to gain wealth that we can use to secure our own comfort and status rather than to serve God and benefit others. We find our identity in our accomplishments rather than in our relationship with God. We compete ruthlessly with others rather than seeking mutual flourishing.

Work becomes an idol when we look to it for the meaning, purpose, and satisfaction that can only be found in God. Or work becomes drudgery when we reduce it to mere necessity, losing sight of its original dignity as the expression of our God-given creativity and dominion.

I have watched people at both extremes. I have known men who sacrificed their families on the altar of career advancement, men who convinced themselves that they were serving their wives and children by providing materially while they destroyed their relationships through neglect. I have known others who hated their work so thoroughly that they spent forty or fifty hours a week in misery, viewing their jobs as nothing more than necessary evils to be endured until retirement.

Both extremes flow from the corruption of work that resulted from the fall. We have lost sight of what work was meant to be: the joyful exercise of our gifts and abilities in service to God and others, the means by which we participate in God's ongoing work of bringing order, beauty, and productivity to His creation.

The Distortion of Worship

Perhaps the most tragic consequence of sin is the distortion of worship. We were created to worship God, to find our highest joy in contemplating His perfections and celebrating His goodness. Before the fall, worship was as natural as breathing. Adam and Eve walked with God in the cool of the day. They lived in constant awareness of His presence. Their entire existence was an offering of praise.

After the fall, we became worshipers of false gods. Paul describes this in Romans 1:21-23: "For although they knew God, they did not honor him as God or give thanks to him, but they became futile in their thinking, and their foolish hearts were darkened. Claiming to be wise, they became fools, and exchanged the glory of the immortal God for images resembling mortal man and birds and animals and creeping things."

We are still worshipers. We cannot help but worship because we were created to worship. But we worship the wrong things.

We worship ourselves, seeking to be the center of our own universe. We worship created things, looking to money, sex, power, and pleasure to provide the satisfaction that can only be found in God. We worship false gods, creating deities in our own image that approve of our rebellion rather than calling us to repentance.

I learned about idolatry in unexpected ways during my years as a pastor. I discovered that the most dangerous idols are often the good things we turn into ultimate things. A man who makes his family an idol will actually harm his family by placing demands on them that only God can meet. A woman who makes her career an idol will find that professional success leaves her feeling empty and unfulfilled. Young people who make romance an idol discover that no human relationship can bear the weight of expectations that belong to God alone.

True worship, worship that pleases God and satisfies the human heart, requires that God be God. It requires that we acknowledge His sovereignty, submit to His authority, trust His goodness, and find our ultimate satisfaction in Him alone. Sin corrupts this by turning our worship in other directions, by causing us to seek in created things the joy that can only be found in the Creator.

The Impossibility of Self-Salvation

All of this leads to the conclusion that scripture states clearly but that human pride constantly resists: we cannot save ourselves. The damage is too deep. The corruption is too comprehensive. The bondage is too complete.

If the problem were merely that we had made some mistakes that needed correction, we could perhaps fix ourselves through better choices. If the problem were simply that we needed more information or better education, we could perhaps learn our way to righteousness. If the problem were only that we needed to try harder, we could perhaps achieve salvation through greater effort.

But the problem is none of these things. The problem is that we are dead in our trespasses and sins. Dead people cannot make themselves alive. The problem is that we are slaves to sin. Slaves cannot free themselves. The problem is that we are enemies of God. Enemies cannot reconcile themselves.

Paul makes this absolutely clear in Ephesians 2:8-9: "For by grace you have been saved through faith. And this is not your own doing; it is the gift of God, not a result of works, so that no one may boast." Salvation is entirely God's work, from beginning to end. It is not a cooperative effort where God does His part and we do ours. It is not a transaction where God makes salvation available and we accept it through our own free will. It is a gift, from start to finish, that we receive rather than achieve.

This is where many people stumble. Modern culture celebrates self-sufficiency and personal achievement. We are taught from childhood that we can accomplish anything if we just work hard enough, believe in ourselves, and never give up. The idea that we are helpless to save ourselves, that we are utterly dependent on God's grace, that we contribute nothing to our salvation except the sin that made it necessary, strikes us as demeaning and offensive.

But this is precisely what the biblical doctrine of sin requires us to acknowledge. We are not sick people who need medicine. We are dead people who need resurrection. We are not lost people who need directions. We are enslaved people who need liberation. We are not confused people who need clarification.

We are rebels who need reconciliation with the King against whom we have committed treason.

I have watched people wrestle with this truth throughout my ministry. Some never fully accept it. They continue to believe at some level that their salvation depends partly on their own effort, their own decision, their own cooperation with God's grace. This leaves them perpetually uncertain about their standing before God because they can never be sure they have done enough, believed strongly enough, or cooperated fully enough.

Others, by God's grace, come to embrace their complete helplessness and find in that acknowledgment a strange but genuine freedom. When we finally stop trying to save ourselves and rest entirely in Christ's finished work, when we acknowledge that we bring nothing to God except our need and our sin, when we trust completely in His grace rather than partially in our own efforts, we discover a peace that surpasses understanding.

The Depth of Human Corruption

Scripture does not soften its assessment of human sinfulness. The prophet Jeremiah declares: "The heart is deceitful above all things, and desperately sick; who can understand it?" (Jeremiah 17:9). We are not merely mistaken or misguided. Our hearts are deceitful, so twisted that we cannot even fully understand our own corruption.

Jesus taught this as well. In Mark 7:21-23, He said: "For from within, out of the heart of man, come evil thoughts, sexual immorality, theft, murder, adultery, coveting, wickedness, deceit, sensuality, envy, slander, pride, foolishness. All these evil things come from within, and they defile a person." The problem is not primarily external, though external influences certainly contribute to sin. The problem is internal. Evil comes from within, from the heart itself.

This means that moral reform, while valuable in limiting the external effects of sin, cannot solve the fundamental problem. Making people behave better does not change their hearts. Teaching better ethics does not transform their nature. Creating better social structures does not eliminate their rebellion against God.

We need something far more radical than reformation. We need regeneration. We need new hearts. We need to be born again. This is precisely what Jesus told Nicodemus in John 3:3: "Truly, truly, I say to you, unless one is born again he cannot see the kingdom of God."

Nicodemus, a teacher of Israel, could not understand this. He asked how a person could be born when they are old. Could they enter their mother's womb a second time? Jesus explained that He was talking about spiritual birth, not physical birth: "That which is born of the flesh is flesh, and that which is born of the Spirit is spirit. Do not marvel that I said to you, 'You must be born again'" (John 3:6-7).

This new birth is entirely God's work. We do not generate it. We do not contribute to it. We do not cooperate with it. God, by His Spirit, gives life to those who are dead in sin. This is sovereign grace, God acting to save those who cannot and will not save themselves.

The doctrine of original sin and total depravity is not pessimistic. It is realistic. It honestly assesses the human condition without the rose-colored glasses of human pride and self-deception. And precisely because it is realistic about the depth of the problem, it drives us to the only solution that can actually save us: the grace of God in Jesus Christ.

The Universality of Sin's Effects

One of the remarkable things about the biblical doctrine of sin is its explanation for the universal patterns we observe in human behavior. Why does every culture, in every time period, struggle with the same basic moral failures? Why do greed, violence, dishonesty, and sexual immorality appear everywhere humans exist? Why do parents in every society find themselves having to teach their children not to lie, not to steal, not to hit other children?

The answer is not primarily cultural or environmental. While cultures certainly shape how sin expresses itself, they do not create the underlying tendency toward sin. That tendency is part of our nature, inherited from Adam.

We do not have to teach children to be selfish. Selfishness comes naturally. We do not have to instruct them in deception. They discover lying on their own. We do not have to model violence for them. They manifest aggressive tendencies without any example.

This is precisely what we would expect if the doctrine of original sin is true. If we inherit a corrupt nature from Adam, then we should see evidence of that corruption from the earliest moments of life. And we do.

I recall observing my own children as they matured. We labored faithfully to instruct them in biblical principles, to demonstrate godliness before them, to establish a nurturing and steady household. Yet every child, in their particular manner and at their individual rate, displayed the identical fundamental sinful inclinations. They required no lessons in rebellion. They needed no training in self-centeredness. These qualities emerged spontaneously because they received a fallen nature just as certainly as they received physical traits.

This acknowledgment does not minimize sin or imply that children bear no accountability for their choices. It merely recognizes the truth that scripture proclaims: we enter this world with a disposition that leans toward transgression from our earliest days.

The Connection Between Sin and Death

Genesis 2:17 recorded God's warning to Adam: "But of the tree of the knowledge of good and evil you shall not eat, for in the day that you eat of it you shall surely die." This was not an arbitrary punishment but a natural consequence. Sin and death are inseparably linked.

Paul makes this connection absolutely explicit in Romans 6:23: "For the wages of sin is death, but the free gift of God is eternal life in Christ Jesus our Lord." Death is precisely what sin earns. It is the payment, the wages, the natural and inevitable result of rebellion against the very source of life itself. Sin does not produce death as some arbitrary divine decree, as though God capriciously decided to punish disobedience with something unrelated to the offense. Rather, death flows from sin as naturally as darkness follows the extinguishing of a light. To turn from the living God is to turn toward death, for there is no life apart from Him.

But we must understand that death in scripture has multiple dimensions, layers of meaning that unfold the full horror of what sin has accomplished in God's good creation. There is spiritual death, which is the separation of the soul from God, the severing of that vital connection between the creature and the Creator who alone gives life. This happened immediately when Adam sinned. Though he continued to live physically for many years, indeed, for nine hundred and thirty years according to Genesis 5:5, he died spiritually the moment he disobeyed. His perfect fellowship with God was broken instantaneously. The intimate communion he had enjoyed in the garden, walking with God in the cool of the day, was shattered beyond human repair.

There is physical death, the separation of the soul from the body. This did not happen immediately but became inevitable. Adam's body, which had been sustained by the tree of life, began the long process of deterioration that would eventually lead to physical death. And every one of his descendants inherited this mortality.

There is eternal death, which scripture calls the second death, the final and permanent separation of the sinner from God in hell. This is the ultimate consequence of sin for those who die outside of Christ, the eternal wages that sin earns apart from God's intervening grace.

All three dimensions of death entered the world through Adam's sin. And all three continue to plague humanity. We are born spiritually dead, alienated from God. We live under the sentence of physical death, our bodies deteriorating and eventually failing. And we face the prospect of eternal death unless we are united to Christ by faith.

This is why the gospel is truly good news. Christ came to reverse every dimension of death. Through faith in Him, we are made spiritually alive. "And you, who were dead in your trespasses and the uncircumcision of your flesh, God made alive together with him, having forgiven us all our trespasses"

(Colossians 2:13). We are promised resurrection bodies that will never die. "For this perishable body must put on the imperishable, and this mortal body must put on immortality" (1 Corinthians 15:53). And we are guaranteed eternal life in God's presence. "Truly, truly, I say to you, whoever hears my word and believes him who sent me has eternal life. He does not come into judgment, but has passed from death to life" (John 5:24).

The Justice of God's Response

Some people question whether the punishment for sin is proportionate to the crime. Does eating forbidden fruit really deserve death? Does Adam's disobedience truly warrant eternal punishment? Is God's response to human sin excessive?

These questions reveal a fundamental misunderstanding of both the nature of sin and the character of God. Sin is not merely breaking a rule. It is an act of cosmic treason against the infinite Creator. It is the creature declaring independence from the source of all life, goodness, and truth. It is rebellion against infinite majesty.

The severity of a crime is determined partly by the dignity of the one against whom it is committed. Insulting a stranger is wrong, but not criminal. Insulting a judge in their courtroom can result in contempt charges. Threatening the President of the United States is a federal crime. Why? Because the dignity of the offended party matters in assessing the severity of the offense.

God is infinitely majestic, infinitely glorious, infinitely worthy of honor and obedience. Therefore, sin against Him is infinitely serious. It deserves infinite punishment because it is committed against an infinite being.

Moreover, God's justice is not arbitrary or excessive. It is perfect. He does not punish too severely or too leniently. His judgment is always precisely what righteousness requires. When scripture says that "all his ways are justice" (Deuteronomy 32:4), it means that we can trust His assessments and His sentences completely.

The real question is not why God punishes sin but why He saves anyone at all. Justice demands that rebels face the consequences of their rebellion. What calls for explanation is not divine judgment but divine mercy, not God's wrath against sin but His grace toward sinners.

Our Only Hope

This chapter has painted a dark picture, and rightly so. Sin is serious. Its effects are devastating. Our condition apart from grace is hopeless. We are dead in trespasses and sins, unable to save ourselves, deserving nothing but judgment.

But the biblical story does not end in Genesis 3. Even in the very chapter where sin enters the world, God promises a solution. He tells the serpent: "I will put enmity between you and the woman, and between your offspring and her offspring; he shall bruise your head, and you shall bruise his heel" (Genesis 3:15).

This is the first gospel promise, what theologians call the protevangelium, the first announcement of good news. The offspring of the woman, ultimately fulfilled in Christ, will crush the serpent's head even though it will cost Him His life.

Everything in Scripture from Genesis 3:15 forward points toward this promised Savior, building a crescendo of expectation through the centuries until it reaches its fulfillment in the person and work of Jesus Christ. The sacrificial system established through Moses teaches with unmistakable clarity that sin requires a substitute, an innocent victim must die in place of the guilty party. The blood of bulls and goats covered sin but could never truly take it away; these sacrifices pointed forward to a greater sacrifice yet to come. The prophets, speaking God's word across generations, announce with increasing clarity that One is coming who will bear our iniquities, who will be wounded for our transgressions and crushed for our iniquities, upon whom the chastisement that brings us peace will fall (Isaiah 53:5). The entire Old Testament, from the Passover lamb whose blood protected Israel from judgment to the Day of Atonement ceremonies that pictured the removal of sin, creates an expectation of deliverance that can only be fulfilled in Christ.

And when Christ finally comes, stepping into human history as the eternal Son of God made flesh, He does what we could never do for ourselves. He lives the perfect life that Adam failed to live, walking in complete obedience to the Father's will every moment of His earthly existence. He resisted temptation where Adam fell, refusing Satan's offers in the wilderness even after forty days of fasting. He obeys fully where Adam rebelled, saying in the garden of Gethsemane, "Not my will, but yours, be done" (Luke 22:42). And then, in the greatest act of love the world has ever witnessed, He takes upon Himself the punishment that our sins deserve. He dies the death we should have died, experiencing not merely physical death but spiritual separation from the Father as He bears the full weight of divine judgment. He bears God's wrath in our place, drinking the cup of judgment to its dregs so that we might drink the cup of blessing forever. He purchased our redemption with His own blood, paying the price that justice demanded but that we could never afford.

This is our only hope, the only remedy for our terminal spiritual condition. Not moral improvement, though Christ transforms our character. Not religious effort, though true faith always produces obedience. Not human achievement, though believers are called to good works. Christ alone can save us. His perfect life is credited to us, so that we stand before God clothed in His righteousness rather than our own filthy rags. His sacrificial death pays for our sins in full, satisfying divine justice and removing our guilt completely. His resurrection power gives us new life, raising us from spiritual death and uniting us to Him in an unbreakable bond.

The doctrine of sin, properly understood, does not lead to despair but to Christ. It strips away our pride, our self-reliance, our confidence in our own ability. It forces us to acknowledge our desperate need. And in doing so, it drives us to the only One who can meet that need, the Lord Jesus Christ, who came not to call the righteous but sinners to repentance.

Chapter Eleven

The Curse and Its Consequences

When our first parents sinned in the garden, the consequences were immediate and devastating. The moment they disobeyed, they plunged themselves and all their descendants into a state of guilt, corruption, and misery. But God did not leave them in silence. He came to the garden and pronounced judgment, not in hasty anger but in righteous response to their rebellion. These judgments, recorded in Genesis 3:14-19, reveal the seriousness of sin while simultaneously pointing toward redemption.

Many Christians today struggle to understand divine judgment. We live in an age that emphasizes God's love while minimizing His holiness, an age that celebrates His mercy while ignoring His justice. But Scripture presents us with a God who is perfectly just, whose righteousness demands that sin be punished, and whose holiness cannot coexist with evil. The judgments pronounced in Genesis 3 are not arbitrary or cruel. They are the necessary consequences of human rebellion against a holy God, the natural outworking of sin's destructive power in God's good creation.

Understanding these judgments helps us make sense of our present experiences. Why does life feel so hard? Why is work often frustrating and exhausting? Why do relationships break down? Why does our world groan under the weight of suffering and death? The answer lies here, in Genesis 3, where God explains how sin has corrupted every aspect of human existence.

Judgment on the Serpent

God begins with the serpent, the one who initiated the deception and led our first parents into sin. "The LORD God said to the serpent, 'Because you have done this, cursed are you above all livestock and above all beasts of the field; on your belly you shall go, and dust you shall eat all the days of your life'" (Genesis 3:14).

This curse is both literal and symbolic. The serpent, whatever its original form, is reduced to crawling on its belly, eating dust, subjected to perpetual humiliation. But the judgment extends beyond the physical creature to the spiritual power behind it. Satan, who used the serpent as his instrument, is himself cursed and condemned. His defeat is certain, his doom is sealed, his power is limited.

The next verse contains what I mentioned earlier as the first gospel promise: "I will put enmity between you and the woman, and between your offspring and her offspring; he shall bruise your head, and you shall bruise his heel" (Genesis 3:15). This is the protevangelium, the first announcement of the gospel. In the very moment of pronouncing judgment, God declares His plan of redemption.

The promise contains several crucial elements. First, God Himself will create enmity between the serpent and the woman. This is grace. Left to ourselves, we would remain in league with Satan, comfortable in our rebellion. But God intervenes, placing hostility between the seed of the woman and the seed of the serpent. Throughout human history, there has been a cosmic conflict between those who belong to God and those who belong to the evil one.

Second, the promise speaks of offspring, or seed. The woman will have descendants who will oppose the serpent's descendants. This conflict will span generations, continuing throughout human history until its final resolution.

Third, and most significantly, the promise points to a particular offspring who will deliver the decisive blow. "He shall bruise your head, and you shall bruise his heel." This is prophecy in its earliest form, pointing forward to Christ. The offspring of the woman, born of a virgin, fully God and fully man, will crush the serpent's head. Satan will wound the Messiah, striking His heel at the cross, but that wound will not be fatal. Christ will rise from the dead, triumphant over sin, death, and Satan himself.

This promise sustained God's people throughout the Old Testament. Every time a godly son was born, there was hope that he might be the promised seed. Abel, Seth, Noah, Abraham, Isaac, Jacob, Judah, David. Each generation looked forward to the One who would finally defeat the ancient enemy. And when Christ came, He accomplished what no other could do. Through His death and resurrection, He crushed the serpent's head, destroying the one who has the power of death (Hebrews 2:14).

The judgment on the serpent teaches us several vital truths. First, Satan is a defeated foe. Though he still prowls about like a roaring lion seeking someone to devour (1 Peter 5:8), his ultimate defeat is certain. Christ has already won the victory. Second, spiritual warfare is real. We are engaged in a cosmic conflict that began in the garden and will continue until Christ returns. We must take seriously the reality of our enemy and his schemes. Third, God's judgment is sure. Satan will not escape. Justice will be done. The one who introduced sin and death into God's creation will himself be cast into the lake of fire forever (Revelation 20:10).

Judgment on the Woman

Having addressed the serpent, God turns to the woman with words that would shape the experience of every daughter of Eve who would follow. "To the woman he said, 'I will surely multiply your pain in childbearing; in pain you shall bring forth children. Your desire shall be contrary to your husband, but he shall rule over you'" (Genesis 3:16).

This divine pronouncement affects two fundamental and defining aspects of the woman's existence: her calling to motherhood and her relationship in marriage. Both of these are precious gifts from the hand of a loving Creator, integral parts of His good and perfect design for human flourishing and the continuation of His image-bearers upon the earth. Yet both are now tragically corrupted by the entrance of sin into God's creation, and both will henceforth be marked by pain, struggle, and frustration. The very relationships and roles that were meant to bring the deepest satisfaction and joy would now be experienced through the dark lens of fallen human nature, twisted from their original purpose yet not entirely destroyed.

Pain in Childbearing

The first part of the judgment addresses childbearing. God will multiply the woman's pain in this process. The Hebrew word for pain, *itsabon*, carries the idea of toil, labor, and hardship. It is the same word used in verse 17 to describe the man's painful toil in working the ground. Childbearing, which should be an unmitigated joy, will now involve significant suffering.

This judgment has been fulfilled throughout human history. Every mother who has given birth knows the reality of labor pain. Medical science has developed ways to manage this pain, and we should thank God for these mercies, but the fundamental reality remains. Bringing forth new life involves suffering.

But we must be careful not to misunderstand this judgment. God is not saying that childbearing itself is a curse, or that children are a punishment for sin. On the contrary, we read is Psalm 127:3: "Behold, children are a heritage from the Lord, the fruit of the womb a reward." The multiplication of pain in childbearing is a consequence of the fall, but it does not negate the goodness of motherhood itself.

Furthermore, this judgment takes on profound new meaning when we view it through the lens of redemption. The apostle Paul, writing to Timothy under the inspiration of the Holy Spirit, declares, "Yet she will be saved through childbearing, if they continue in faith and love and holiness, with self-control" (1 Timothy 2:15). This is admittedly a difficult and much-debated verse, and interpreters throughout church history have wrestled with its precise meaning. Some understand it to refer to the birth of the Messiah through a woman. Others see it as pointing to the godly role of motherhood in the lives of faithful women. Still others interpret it as emphasizing that Christian women will be kept safe through the dangers of childbirth as they walk in faith.

But at a minimum, regardless of which interpretive approach we favor, the verse clearly points to the reality that women participate meaningfully in God's grand redemptive purposes through the bearing and raising of children in the nurture and admonition of the Lord. The very process that was touched by the curse and now involves genuine pain and hardship becomes, in the economy of grace, a means of profound blessing. What sin corrupted, God redeems. What the fall twisted toward sorrow, divine grace transforms into purpose.

Most significant of all, this judgment concerning childbearing points us directly to the incarnation of our Lord Jesus Christ. The promised seed of the woman who would crush the serpent's head had to be born into this world through a woman's body. A human mother had to endure the full reality of painful labor to bring the Savior of the world into human history. Mary, blessed among women and highly favored, experienced this very pain when she gave birth to Jesus in that Bethlehem stable. Through her suffering, through the multiplication of pain in childbearing that resulted from Eve's original transgression, came the One who would ultimately and completely remove sin and break its curse forever. The judgment became the very means by which the remedy arrived.

Conflict in Marriage

The second part of the judgment addresses the woman's relationship with her husband. "Your desire shall be contrary to your husband, but he shall rule over you." (Genesis 3:16) This statement has generated considerable discussion among interpreters, but its basic meaning is clear within a Reformed theological framework.

The word translated "desire" is the Hebrew word *teshuqah*, which appears only three times in the Old Testament. Its most illuminating parallel occurs in the very next chapter, where God tells Cain, "Sin is crouching at the door. Its desire is contrary to you, but you must rule over it" (Genesis 4:7). The parallel is striking. Just as sin desires to master Cain, the woman's desire will be to master her husband. And just as Cain must rule over sin, the husband will rule over his wife.

This is not describing God's original design for marriage. In the garden before the fall, Adam and Eve enjoyed perfect harmony, mutual love, and a complementary partnership. The man exercised loving leadership, and the woman embraced her role with joy. There was no struggle for control, no battle for dominance, no conflict over authority.

But sin corrupted this beautiful relationship. Now, instead of joyful submission to loving headship, there will be a sinful desire to usurp the husband's God-given role. And instead of loving servant leadership, there will be harsh, domineering rule. The very relationship that God designed to reflect His love for His people and Christ's love for the church has been marred by sin.

We see this pattern throughout fallen human history. Women, influenced by sin, resist their husbands' leadership, seeking to control rather than complement. Men, equally corrupted by sin, abuse their authority, becoming tyrants rather than servant leaders. Both sins stem from the Fall; both represent corruptions of God's good design, and both require redemption through Christ.

Understanding this judgment is crucial for biblical counseling and pastoral ministry. When we see conflict in marriages, when we observe power struggles and broken relationships, we are witnessing the outworking of Genesis 3:16. The solution is not to deny gender distinctions or to pretend that men and women are interchangeable. Nor is the solution to reinforce sinful patterns of domination and control. The solution is redemption in Christ, who restores what sin has broken.

In Christ, Christian marriages can begin to reflect God's original design. Husbands can love their wives as Christ loved the church, giving themselves up for them (Ephesians 5:25). Wives can respect and submit to their husbands as to the Lord, not out of fear or compulsion, but out of love and trust (Ephesians 5:22-24). The gospel transforms marriages, enabling couples to overcome the curse and experience the beauty of God's design, albeit imperfectly in this life.

Judgment on the Man

After addressing the woman, God turns His attention to Adam. The judgment pronounced upon him is noticeably longer and more detailed than what was spoken to Eve, a distinction that reflects Adam's unique role as the federal head of the human race and his particular responsibility in the fall. As the representative of all humanity, Adam's sin carried consequences that would reverberate through every generation. What happens to him happens, in a real sense, to all his descendants.

"And to Adam he said, 'Because you have listened to the voice of your wife and have eaten of the tree of which I commanded you, "You shall not eat of it," cursed is the ground because of you; in pain you shall eat of it all the days of your life; thorns and thistles it shall bring forth for you; and you shall eat the plants of the field. By the sweat of your face you shall eat bread, till you return to the ground, for out of it you were taken; for you are dust, and to dust you shall return'" (Genesis 3:17-19).

This divine pronouncement stands as one of the most sobering passages in all of Scripture. God speaks directly to Adam, identifying his sin with precision and announcing consequences that would transform human existence from that moment forward. The curse falls not merely on Adam as an individual, but on the ground itself, on the very creation over which Adam had been given dominion. The judgment is comprehensive, affecting every aspect of human life and labor until death itself brings the final return to dust.

The Nature of Adam's Sin

God begins by identifying with unmistakable precision the specific nature of Adam's transgression. "Because you have listened to the voice of your wife and have eaten of the tree of which I commanded you, 'You shall not eat of it.'" The divine indictment reveals that Adam's sin had two distinct yet interconnected dimensions, each compounding the severity of his rebellion.

First, he listened to his wife rather than to God. We must be careful here to understand what Scripture is and is not saying. This does not mean that husbands should never listen to their wives or that a woman's counsel is inherently suspect. The book of Proverbs commends the noble woman whose husband trusts in her, who opens her mouth with wisdom, and whose teaching is on her tongue (Proverbs 31:26). Throughout Scripture, we see godly women whose voices carried weight and whose wisdom blessed their families and communities.

But Adam's failure was not in listening to Eve's voice; it was in elevating his wife's word above God's word. When faced with the choice between obedience to his Creator and loyalty to his wife, when forced to choose between God's clear command and human relationship, he chose wrongly. He allowed a human voice, however beloved, to drown out the voice of his Maker.

Second, Adam directly violated God's explicit, unambiguous command. He ate from the tree that God had forbidden. This was not a matter of ignorance or confusion about God's will. Unlike Eve, who was deceived by the serpent's cunning arguments and twisted logic, Adam sinned with full knowledge of exactly what he was doing (1 Timothy 2:14). He heard no serpent's lie. He entertained no theological debate about the meaning of God's words. He made a conscious, deliberate, eyes-wide-open choice to rebel against his Creator. His sin was high-handed transgression in its purest form.

This distinction between Adam and Eve's sin matters profoundly because of the doctrine of federal headship. While both our first parents sinned and both bore guilt for their actions, Adam bore particular responsibility as the divinely appointed representative head of the entire human race. His position was unique; his responsibility singular. When he fell, all humanity fell with him. We do not fall individually and independently; we fell corporately in Adam. Paul makes this theological reality unmistakably clear in Romans 5:12-19, where he repeatedly and deliberately emphasizes that sin and death entered the world through one man, Adam. Our condemnation comes through Adam's sin, just as our justification comes through Christ's righteousness. This is not arbitrary or unfair; this is the covenant structure God established from the beginning, a structure that would make possible our salvation through a new and greater Adam.

Cursed Ground and Frustrating Labor

The immediate consequence of Adam's sin extends beyond himself to the very ground from which he was taken. "Cursed is the ground because of you; in pain you shall eat of it all the days of your life; thorns and thistles it shall bring forth for you." (Genesis 3:17)

Before the fall, Adam's work in the garden was pure joy. He tended the garden, cultivated the ground, and enjoyed abundant provision without frustration or difficulty. Work itself was not a curse but a blessing, part of God's good design for human flourishing. God placed Adam in the garden to work it and keep it (Genesis 2:15) before sin ever entered the world.

But now, because of sin, work becomes toilsome and frustrating. The ground that once yielded its fruit readily now resists human effort. Thorns and thistles, which were not part of the original creation, spring up to impede agricultural labor. The very creation that was designed to support human life now seems to work against it.

The word translated "pain" is again *itsabon*, the same word used to describe the woman's pain in childbearing. Both the man and the woman will experience painful toil in their respective callings. For the woman, bringing forth life will involve suffering. For the man, bringing forth food from the ground will involve hardship.

Paul develops this profound theme in his letter to the church at Rome, where he describes creation itself as having been subjected to futility, not by its own choice but by the will of the one who subjected it. He pictures the entire created order as groaning together in the pains of childbirth, eagerly awaiting its liberation from bondage to corruption and its eventual redemption alongside the children of God (Romans 8:19-22). The curse pronounced upon the ground in Genesis 3 represents nothing less than a cosmic catastrophe, a universal disruption that affects not merely humanity in isolation but the entire created order in all its interconnected complexity. The natural world itself bears the ugly scars and deep wounds of human sin, sharing in the consequences of our rebellion.

This divine judgment helps us make sense of the frustration we so often experience in our daily work, whether in the office, the factory, the field, or the home. Why do our most careful plans and best efforts sometimes fail despite our diligence? Why do projects that by all rights should succeed instead encounter unexpected obstacles and inexplicable setbacks? Why does work that should bring satisfaction and fulfillment so often leave us feeling exhausted, discouraged, and wondering if our efforts matter at all? The answer to these troubling questions lies in the curse that God pronounced upon the ground in response to Adam's sin. We live and labor in a world that is fundamentally broken, a world that is no longer functioning as God originally designed it to function in Eden's perfect harmony. Sin has introduced disorder, decay, and death into every sphere of human existence, every corner of creation, leaving nothing untouched by its corrupting influence.

But even this judgment contains a measure of grace. God could have made the ground completely unproductive, condemning humanity to immediate starvation. Instead, He ensures that the ground will still yield its fruit, though only through painful toil. The very fact that we can work and eat and survive demonstrates God's common grace to fallen humanity.

Moreover, this judgment points us toward Christ, who bore the curse for us. When Jesus was crucified, the soldiers placed a crown of thorns on His head (John 19:2). Those thorns, products of the curse, instruments of mockery and pain, represent the curse that Christ bore on our behalf. He became a curse for us (Galatians 3:13) so that we might inherit the blessing.

Toil and Sweat

God continues in Genesis 3:19: "By the sweat of your face you shall eat bread." Work will now require exhausting physical labor. The Hebrew word for sweat appears only here in the Pentateuch, emphasizing the intensity of the toil required. Adam will have to expend tremendous energy just to provide basic sustenance for himself and his family.

This aspect of the curse remains painfully obvious in human experience. Most people throughout history have lived on the edge of subsistence, working long hours in difficult conditions just to survive. Even in wealthy nations with advanced technology, work remains demanding and often exhausting. We may not sweat in fields, but we experience stress in offices, fatigue from long hours, and burnout from constant demands.

The curse on labor affects far more than merely physical exhaustion and bodily fatigue. It extends its reach into the very depths of our souls, touching the frustration we feel when our work seems utterly meaningless and pointless, when our earnest efforts do not produce the results we desperately hope for and pray to achieve, when our hard-won achievements crumble and collapse despite our best intentions and most careful planning. Every entrepreneur who has watched a carefully built business fail and dissolve, every artist who has struggled long and hard to create something beautiful only to fall short of the vision, every parent who has labored faithfully and sacrificially to raise children in the nurture and admonition of the Lord only to see them rebel and turn away, experiences in a deeply personal way the harsh reality of Genesis 3:17-19. This is the curse working itself out in our daily lives, in our vocations and callings, in the very activities that should bring us the greatest satisfaction and sense of purpose.

Yet even here, in the midst of this profound brokenness and frustration, redemption through Christ our Savior offers genuine hope and lasting transformation. In our vital union with Christ, our daily work and vocational calling take on entirely new meaning and eternal significance. We no longer labor merely to eke out our survival in a fallen world, toiling simply to put food on our tables or to maintain our existence. Instead, our work becomes an act of worship, a holy offering presented to our Creator and Redeemer. We labor to glorify the God who redeemed us and to serve sacrificially the neighbors He has placed in our lives. Paul instructs us to work as unto the Lord Himself rather than unto men, knowing with firm confidence and certain assurance that our labor in Him, every effort, every struggle, every small act of faithfulness, is never in vain, never wasted, never meaningless (1 Corinthians 15:58).

This present reality, as glorious as it is, points us forward with eager anticipation of something even more magnificent. We lift our eyes toward the promised new creation that awaits us, that glorious future when the ancient curse will be utterly and completely removed forever. In that day, we will reign alongside Christ in glorified, resurrected bodies that never grow weary or tire, never experience exhaustion or pain. We will joyfully cultivate a renewed and restored earth that yields its abundant fruit without the slightest resistance, without thorns or thistles, without frustration or futility; work as God always intended it to be before sin entered His perfect creation.

The Sentence of Death

God concludes His judgment, in Genesis 3:19, with the most sobering consequence of all: "Till you return to the ground, for out of it you were taken; for you are dust, and to dust you shall return." Adam came from the dust, formed by God's creative power, and to dust he will return. The immortality he enjoyed in the garden, conditioned on obedience, is now forfeited. Death becomes his inevitable destiny.

This is physical death, the separation of soul from body, the disintegration of the unified person into its component parts. God had warned Adam, "In the day that you eat of it you shall surely die" (Genesis 2:17). Adam ate and death entered his experience, though God in His mercy delayed its full execution. Adam lived 930 years after his sin (Genesis 5:5), but he did die, just as God had promised.

But death involves more than physical termination. Scripture speaks of death in multiple dimensions. There is spiritual death, the separation of the soul from God, which occurred immediately when Adam sinned. Paul describes unbelievers as "dead in the trespasses and sins" (Ephesians 2:1), spiritually lifeless and unable to respond to God apart from His regenerating grace. There is eternal death, the final separation from God in hell, which awaits all who die without Christ. And there is physical death, the dissolution of the body, which comes to all humanity as the "last enemy" (1 Corinthians 15:26).

Death was never part of God's original design. He created humanity for life, for fellowship, for eternal existence in His presence. Death is an intruder, an enemy, a consequence of sin that God never intended for His image bearers. Every funeral we attend, every grave we visit, every obituary we read testifies to the devastating consequences of rebellion against God.

The sentence of death levels all human pride. It does not matter how wealthy you are, how powerful you become, or how many achievements you accumulate. "You are dust, and to dust you shall return." Kings and peasants, scholars and fools, saints and sinners all share this common destiny. Death is the great equalizer, the inescapable reminder of our mortality and our need for God.

Yet even this most terrible consequence points us toward redemption. Christ entered into death to destroy death. He died the death we deserved, experiencing not only physical death but the spiritual death of separation from the Father as He bore our sins. And then He rose from the dead, conquering death and opening the way to eternal life for all who believe in Him.

Because Christ lives, we too shall live (John 14:19). Physical death remains for believers, but it has lost its sting (1 Corinthians 15:55). It is no longer a curse but a passage to glory, the doorway through which we enter into the presence of our Savior. We still say with the psalmist, "Precious in the sight of the LORD is the death of his saints" (Psalm 116:15).

The Cosmic Scope of the Curse

The judgments pronounced in Genesis 3 extend far beyond the immediate actors in the drama of the fall. Sin did not only corrupt individual humans but introduced decay and death into the entire created order. Paul describes this cosmic dimension of the curse in Romans 8:20-21: "For the creation was subjected to futility, not willingly, but because of him who subjected it, in hope that the creation itself will be set free from its bondage to corruption and obtain the freedom of the glory of the children of God."

Creation was "subjected to futility." The word futility carries the idea of purposelessness, emptiness, and frustration. The creation can no longer fulfill its original purpose of perfectly reflecting God's glory and providing an ideal environment for human flourishing. Instead, it groans under the weight of corruption, producing thorns and thistles, suffering from natural disasters, manifesting decay and death at every level.

This subjugation happened "not willingly." Creation did not choose to rebel against God. It had no moral agency, no capacity to sin. But it was caught up in the consequences of human sin because of the intimate connection between humanity and the created order. As God's vice-regents, tasked with exercising dominion over creation, our fall necessarily affected the realm we were meant to govern.

Yet the subjection happened "in hope." God did not abandon His creation to permanent corruption. Even in the pronouncement of judgment, we hear the echo of divine mercy. He subjected creation to futility not as a final condemnation but with the promise of future redemption woven into the very fabric of the curse. One day, and this hope sustained the apostle Paul as it sustains us, creation itself will be liberated from its bondage to corruption and will share in the glorious freedom that belongs to God's children. The groaning we hear in creation is not a death rattle but a birth pang, pointing forward to the day when God will make all things new.

We see evidence of this cosmic curse all around us, though our familiarity with a fallen world often dulls our perception of how abnormal it truly is. Natural disasters like earthquakes, hurricanes, and tsunamis reveal a creation out of balance, a world that can turn violent and destructive against the very creatures God placed within it. Animals prey on each other with tooth and claw in ways that seem far removed from the peace and harmony that characterized Eden. Disease and decay affect every living organism, from the microscopic to the magnificent. Entropy increases relentlessly; systems break down with inexorable momentum, and order gives way to chaos at every level of creation.

These are not merely natural processes, neutral facts of existence to be accepted with philosophical resignation. Rather, they are manifestations of the curse, evidence that sin has corrupted God's good creation at the deepest level, reaching into the very structure of physical reality itself.

Understanding the cosmic scope of the curse helps us make sense of natural evil. Why does a tsunami kill thousands of people? Why does a drought bring famine? Why does cancer afflict the innocent? These tragedies are not directly caused by the specific sins of those who suffer. Rather, they result from the fact that we live in a fallen world, a creation subjected to futility because of human rebellion against God.

This understanding should produce several responses in us. First, humility. We should recognize that our sin has consequences that extend far beyond ourselves. Every act of rebellion against God contributes to the corruption of His creation. Second, compassion. When we see others suffering from natural disasters or diseases, we should respond with mercy and help, recognizing that we are all caught up in the same fallen world. Third, hope. The curse is not permanent. God has promised to renew creation, to make all things new (Revelation 21:5). One day, there will be a new heaven and a new earth where righteousness dwells (2 Peter 3:13).

Living Under the Curse: Pastoral Application

How then should we live in a world subjected to futility, a creation that continues to groan and labor under the crushing weight of corruption and decay? The divine judgments pronounced in Genesis 3, those sobering words spoken by God in the garden after the fall, are not merely historical facts to be noted in our study of ancient texts, filed away as interesting artifacts of theological significance from humanity's distant past. No, they are present, pressing realities that shape our daily experience in profound and inescapable ways. Every morning when we wake to face another day of toil, every challenge we encounter in our work and relationships, every frustration we experience in our bodies and in our environment, these are all, in some measure, direct manifestations of what it means to live east of Eden, expelled from paradise and navigating a world that has been fundamentally altered by sin.

We desperately need pastoral wisdom, grounded in the sure foundation of Scripture and refined through the crucible of actual ministry experience, to navigate life in this fallen world without losing the precious hope that anchors our souls to the unchanging character of God. This is no academic exercise, no ivory tower speculation divorced from the realities of human existence. Rather, it is a vital necessity for faithful Christian living in the in-between time, that extended season after the fall and the curse but before the final restoration and the making new of all things. We live in a world that bears the scars of judgment while we wait for the healing that will come when Christ returns.

Acknowledging the Reality of Suffering

First, we must acknowledge the full weight and reality of suffering without minimizing its impact or offering cheap explanations that ring hollow in the ears of those who truly hurt. When a woman experiences the excruciating pain of childbirth, pain that can be overwhelming, terrifying, and utterly exhausting, we do not casually dismiss her agony by saying, "This is no big deal; it is just part of life." Such callous words would betray not only a lack of compassion but also a fundamental misunderstanding of what Genesis 3:16 actually reveals to us about the fallen world we inhabit. Instead, we recognize her suffering as a direct consequence of the fall, a tangible manifestation of the curse that affects all of creation, and we offer genuine comfort and practical support that flows from our understanding of both the brokenness of this world and the hope we have in Christ.

Similarly, when a man finds his work frustrating, exhausting, and seemingly futile, when he comes home day after day feeling defeated by the challenges he faces in his labor, we do not dismiss his struggles as mere weakness or lack of character, as if a stronger man would simply push through without complaint. We acknowledge, based on the clear teaching of Genesis 3:17-19, that work in a fallen world is genuinely difficult, that the ground really does resist our best efforts in ways both literal and metaphorical, that thorns and thistles genuinely impede our labor and make even simple tasks more burdensome than they should be in a world unmarred by sin.

The Bible never sugarcoats the reality of life in a fallen world, never attempts to minimize or gloss over the genuine hardship that characterizes human existence under the curse. The book of Ecclesiastes describes in remarkably stark and uncompromising terms the profound futility and deep frustration that mark human existence apart from God, acknowledging with brutal honesty that much of life seems meaningless, that our best efforts often come to nothing, that death renders all our achievements temporary. The psalms of lament give powerful and visceral voice to genuine suffering, providing God's people with divinely inspired words to cry out for relief from pain, persecution, and death without pretending that such afflictions are anything less than terrible. Jesus Himself wept openly at the tomb of Lazarus (John 11:35), showing us through His own emotional response that it is not only permissible but entirely right to grieve the terrible presence of death in God's good world, to feel the full weight of what sin has brought into creation.

True pastoral ministry, the kind that actually serves hurting people rather than merely protecting the minister's comfort, requires us to sit with suffering people in their pain, to enter into their sorrow rather than maintaining a clinical distance from it. We must learn to weep genuinely with those who weep (Romans 12:15), to offer the deep comfort that comes from God rather than the shallow reassurances of trite platitudes or simplistic solutions that might make us feel better but do nothing to help the sufferer. We must actively resist the powerful temptation to explain away suffering with theological formulas or to suggest, either explicitly or implicitly, that if people just had more faith, prayed harder, or trusted God more fully, their problems would simply disappear. The curse is real, tangible, and undeniable; its effects are genuinely devastating to real people in real situations, and only Christ, through His redemptive work, can ultimately and finally remove it.

Understanding Gender-Specific Struggles

Second, understanding the specific judgments pronounced upon both the man and the woman in the garden helps us minister with greater effectiveness and deeper compassion to the gender-specific struggles that our congregations face daily. Women, bearing the particular weight of the curse pronounced upon Eve, often face a constellation of challenges directly related to these ancient words of judgment that continue to echo through every generation. The pain of childbearing, which God explicitly intensified as part of the curse, extends far beyond the physical labor of delivery to encompass the profound grief of miscarriages that steal away hoped-for children, the monthly disappointment and deep sorrow of infertility that leaves nurseries empty and arms aching, the frightening complications during pregnancy that threaten both mother and child, and the utterly devastating heartbreak of losing children at any age, losses that cut to the very core of a mother's soul and challenge her faith in ways that those who haven't experienced such losses can scarcely imagine. The conflict in marriage that God predicted, where desire would be toward the husband yet he would rule over the wife, often manifests itself in complex and painful ways: some women find themselves struggling persistently against their husbands' God-given authority, resisting the biblical pattern of marital relationships in ways that create ongoing tension and discord; others experience the opposite extreme, suffering abuse from men who have grotesquely distorted the biblical concept of headship, twisting it from Christ-like servant leadership into harsh domination, control, and even violence that bears no resemblance whatsoever to the sacrificial love that should characterize a Christian husband.

Pastoral care for women must take these devastating realities seriously, acknowledging the real consequences of the fall in women's lives. We cannot simply offer platitudes or spiritual band-aids when women face these profound sufferings. Instead, we must weep with those who weep, entering into their pain while pointing them to the God who sees, knows, and cares about their specific struggles.

We should grieve alongside women who experience miscarriages, recognizing these losses not as mere biological events or "tissue" as our callous culture so often labels them, but as genuine deaths of precious children made in God's image, children who were loved, anticipated, and now must be mourned. These mothers need space to acknowledge their grief, permission to name their lost children, and assurance that their maternal love for these babies, however brief their existence, reflects something of God's own heart for His children.

We should compassionately support women struggling with the monthly disappointment and long-term heartache of infertility, acknowledging their deep pain and the sometimes overwhelming sense of failure or emptiness they feel while simultaneously pointing them to God's purposes that transcend biological motherhood, purposes that include spiritual fruitfulness, kingdom impact, and identity found in Christ rather than in parental status. We should neither minimize their longing for children nor allow that longing to become an idol that displaces trust in God's sovereign goodness.

We should courageously and unflinchingly confront abusive husbands who wickedly pervert and distort the biblical concept of headship into domination, control, manipulation, and intimidation, making absolutely clear that such behavior is utterly contrary to Christ's loving example of sacrificial leadership and constitutes serious, grievous sin requiring genuine repentance, sustained accountability through trusted brothers in Christ, and potentially formal church discipline if the abuse continues unabated. The husband who uses Scripture as a weapon to justify cruelty has fundamentally misunderstood the gospel itself and stands in desperate need of correction, confrontation, and, if necessary, the protective intervention of church leadership to shield his wife and children from further harm.

At the same time, we should patiently, carefully, and compassionately teach women the beautiful biblical vision of submission as a joyful, voluntary, and grace-enabled response to Christlike, genuinely sacrificial, truly servant-hearted leadership, not as subjugation to tyranny, not as surrender to abuse, not as compliance with sinful demands that directly contradict God's Word or violate one's conscience. Biblical submission never requires a wife to participate in sin, to endure physical violence, to enable destructive patterns, or to remain silent about behaviors that harm herself or her children.

Men face their own unique, deeply challenging set of struggles intricately related to the curse's ongoing effects in their lives, struggles that often remain unspoken in a culture that demands stoic strength and constant achievement. Work that God originally designed and intended to be genuinely fulfilling, meaningful, and satisfying becomes profoundly frustrating, marked by repeated setbacks, unexpected obstacles, and persistent resistance. Efforts that by all reasonable measures should succeed mysteriously fail despite our best planning, hardest labor, and most careful attention to detail. Careers that initially promised deep meaning, lasting significance, and authentic purpose deliver instead only bone-deep exhaustion, chronic disappointment, crushing pressure, and the nagging sense that all our striving amounts to little of eternal value. Men, shaped by both cultural expectations and something deeper in how God created them, often define themselves almost entirely by their work, finding their core identity, their sense of worth, their very reason for existence in their professional achievements and vocational success, and when that work proves ultimately futile, when projects collapse despite heroic effort, when they fail dramatically in their vocations or find themselves suddenly unemployed through no fault of their own, they experience profound, sometimes devastating crises of meaning that shake the very foundations of who they believe themselves to be.

Pastoral care for men, therefore, must address these deeply rooted struggles with absolute honesty, refusing to offer shallow solutions, quick fixes, or simplistic formulas that minimize the real pain of living under the curse's weight. We should openly, clearly, and without embarrassment acknowledge that work in a fallen, cursed world is genuinely, legitimately difficult, that finding one's job exhausting, frustrating, or disappointing is not a sign of spiritual weakness, moral failure, lack of faith, or insufficient masculinity, but rather the expected experience of laboring in a world that resists our efforts at every turn. We should help men progressively, patiently, persistently find their truest, deepest, most unshakable identity not in their temporal achievements, professional titles, or vocational success, but in Christ alone, carefully and repeatedly teaching them that their fundamental value, their eternal worth, their unchanging significance comes from being beloved sons of God, adopted into His family through union with Christ, not from their job performance, salary level, career trajectory, or any other worldly measure of success that will ultimately fade away. We should earnestly encourage men to lead their families with genuinely servant-hearted, Christlike, sacrificial love that mirrors our Savior's own example of laying down His life for those He loves, while simultaneously warning them against both sinful passivity, the abdication of godly leadership that leaves wives and children without the spiritual direction and protection they desperately need, and sinful domination, the tyrannical assertion of power that crushes rather than cherishes those under their care and fundamentally contradicts everything Scripture teaches about leadership in the home.

Cultivating Proper Expectations

Third, understanding the curse with clear biblical insight helps us cultivate genuinely proper, realistic, scripturally grounded expectations for life in this present age, this time between the fall and the final restoration. Many sincere, well-meaning Christians struggle unnecessarily, wrestling with profound disappointment and deep confusion, precisely because they unknowingly expect far too much from this broken, groaning, deeply fallen world that lies under the weight of divine judgment. They genuinely think, with misplaced optimism that ignores the reality of Genesis 3, that if they simply work hard enough, apply themselves diligently enough, and remain faithful enough in their vocational calling, their careers will inevitably prove deeply satisfying, consistently fulfilling, perpetually meaningful in ways that meet their soul's deepest longings. They sincerely believe, influenced perhaps by romantic notions that bear little resemblance to biblical teaching, that if they carefully choose and marry a truly godly person who loves the Lord and pursues holiness, their marriage will somehow be essentially free from significant conflict, largely immune to the relational friction that marks every other human relationship in this fallen world. They naively assume, shaped by cultural sentimentality rather than scriptural realism, that if they are blessed with children and embrace the calling of parenthood, the experience of raising those children will bring virtually unmitigated joy, uninterrupted delight, and constant satisfaction without the heartache, exhaustion, and disappointment that actually characterize parenting in a world corrupted by sin. When the harsh, unavoidable reality of life under the curse inevitably falls painfully short of these unrealistic, unbiblical expectations that were never grounded in God's Word to begin with, these believers understandably become discouraged, disheartened, even despairing, sometimes seriously doubting God's goodness, questioning His faithfulness, wondering if He has somehow failed them, or anxiously questioning their own faith, wondering if their struggles indicate some profound spiritual deficiency or hidden sin that explains why their experience doesn't match their expectations.

But Genesis 3 teaches us something fundamentally different; it instructs us to expect difficulty, to anticipate struggle, to prepare ourselves for the inevitable friction that marks all of life in this fallen world. The sacred text reveals that marriage will inevitably involve significant conflict, ongoing tension, and persistent challenges precisely because sin has profoundly corrupted the relationship between man and woman, distorting what God designed to be a beautiful partnership of complementary roles into something often marked by power struggles, miscommunication, and competing desires. Work, likewise, will frequently prove frustrating, exhausting, and unsatisfying because the very ground beneath our feet actively resists our efforts, as thorns and thistles symbolize the broader reality that creation itself pushes back against our attempts to cultivate it, to bring forth fruit, to accomplish our purposes. Parenting, too, will be genuinely painful, often heartbreaking, sometimes overwhelming because the very act of bringing forth children in a fallen world, multiplying the human race in a creation groaning under the weight of sin, involves profound hardship, sleepless nights, constant worry, and the anguish of watching those we love most struggle with their own fallenness. This biblical perspective is not pessimism, defeatism, or negativity, but rather honest realism, the courage to face squarely, without flinching or sugar-coating, what God Himself has explicitly told us about the nature of life east of Eden, beyond the garden, in a world where the curse touches everything we do and everyone we love.

Proper, biblically grounded expectations, however, do not lead inevitably to despair, hopelessness, or resignation, but rather to a deeper, more authentic dependence on God, a recognition that we cannot navigate this cursed existence in our own strength or wisdom. When we truly recognize, with clarity born of Scripture rather than experience alone, that this present world in its current state cannot possibly satisfy our deepest longings, our most profound desires, our soul's truest hungers, we gradually stop looking to creation, or to careers, marriages, children, achievements, possessions, for the things only the Creator Himself can provide. When we honestly acknowledge, admitting what our pride resists, that even our best efforts, our most diligent labor, our most careful planning will always ultimately fall short of our hopes in a cursed world where futility marks all human endeavor, we find ourselves relying more fully, more completely, more desperately on God's sufficient grace rather than our insufficient strength. When we finally accept, not with bitter resignation but with humble submission to divine revelation, that suffering is not an aberration but an inevitability in this present age, that pain is the normal experience of God's people between the fall and the final restoration, we fix our hope more firmly, more unshakably, more exclusively on the age to come, when every tear will be wiped away and the curse will be no more.

The Westminster Shorter Catechism asks, "What is the chief end of man?" and answers, "Man's chief end is to glorify God, and to enjoy him forever." Not to enjoy our work, though work can bring satisfaction. Not to enjoy our marriages, though marriage is a good gift. Not to enjoy our children, though children are a blessing. Our ultimate joy, our deepest satisfaction, our truest purpose is found in God Himself. And this God can be enjoyed even in the midst of suffering, even when work is frustrating, even when relationships are difficult, even when we face death itself.

Finding Hope in Redemption

Fourth, we must consistently, faithfully, persistently point people beyond their present suffering to the magnificent hope of redemption found only in Christ Jesus our Lord. Yes, the curse is terrifyingly real and utterly devastating in its effects on every dimension of human existence, touching everything from our most intimate relationships to our daily labor to our final breath. But, and here is the glorious truth that transforms everything, the curse is emphatically not the final word over creation or over God's beloved people. God Himself has spoken a far better word, an infinitely superior word, a word of grace and redemption through His beloved Son, Jesus Christ, who willingly, purposefully entered our cursed and broken world, taking on human flesh and dwelling among us. He came not as a distant observer of our misery but as one who would personally, substitutionally bear the full weight of the curse for us, drinking the cup of God's wrath to its dregs, and through His perfect obedience, His atoning death, and His victorious resurrection, He has inaugurated nothing less than a new creation, a kingdom that is even now breaking into our present darkness and will one day swallow up every trace of the fall.

Every consequence of the fall that we experience points us back to our need for Christ. When women experience pain in childbirth, they are reminded that we live in a fallen world and need a Savior. When men sweat and toil in frustrating work, they are confronted with their inability to create paradise through their own efforts. When we all face death, we must reckon with our mortality and our desperate need for resurrection.

But Christ has addressed every aspect of the curse. He took the curse upon Himself, becoming a curse for us (Galatians 3:13). He wore the crown of thorns, bearing in His own body the consequences of sin. He died the death we deserved, tasting death for everyone (Hebrews 2:9). And He rose from the dead, breaking the power of death and opening the way to eternal life.

In Christ, the curse begins to be reversed even now. Christian marriages can begin to reflect God's original design as husbands love like Christ and wives respect their husbands. Work takes on new meaning as we labor for God's glory rather than merely for survival. Even death loses its terror as we face it with the confidence that to be absent from the body is to be present with the Lord (2 Corinthians 5:8).

And one day, the curse will be completely removed. John describes the new creation in Revelation 22:3: "No longer will there be anything accursed." In the new heaven and new earth, there will be no more pain in childbearing because there will be no more pain at all (Revelation 21:4). There will be no more frustrating labor because we will work in perfect harmony with creation in glorified bodies that never tire. There will be no more death because death itself will have been destroyed (1 Corinthians 15:26).

This hope sustains us through our present sufferings. Paul writes, "I consider that the sufferings of this present time are not worth comparing with the glory that is to be revealed to us" (Romans 8:18). Our struggles under the curse are real and painful, but they are temporary. They are light momentary affliction compared to the eternal weight of glory beyond all comparison (2 Corinthians 4:17).

Practical Wisdom for Daily Life

Finally, understanding the curse provides practical wisdom for navigating daily challenges. When we recognize that work will be difficult, we can prepare accordingly. We set realistic goals, understanding that our efforts will face obstacles. We build margin into our schedules, knowing that things will take longer than expected. We develop perseverance, accepting that meaningful achievements require sustained effort over time despite setbacks.

When we understand that marriage involves conflict because of the curse, we approach our relationships with humility and grace. We do not expect perfection from our spouses or from ourselves. We prepare for difficulties, learning conflict resolution skills and seeking help when needed. We extend forgiveness freely, recognizing that we are both sinners living in a fallen world.

When we accept that parenting involves pain, we enter into it with eyes open. We do not naively assume that if we follow the right formulas, our children will turn out perfectly. We recognize that even godly parenting cannot guarantee godly children because each person bears the corruption of sin and must be transformed by God's grace. We persevere through the difficulties, finding joy in the blessing of children while acknowledging the hardships of raising them in a fallen world.

Understanding the curse also helps us extend grace to ourselves. When we fail, when our efforts fall short, when we struggle with sin, we remember that we are fallen creatures living in a fallen world. This is not an excuse for sin, but a recognition of reality. We are justified by faith in Christ, not by our performance. Our identity rests in what Christ has done for us, not in what we accomplish.

Chapter Twelve

The First Gospel: Hope in the Midst of Ruin

In the midst of judgment, God spoke grace. After pronouncing curses on the serpent, the woman, and the man, after declaring the painful consequences that would mark human existence from that moment forward, God did something unexpected. He announced a promise. Genesis 3:15 stands as the first ray of gospel light piercing the darkness of human rebellion: "I will put enmity between you and the woman, and between your offspring and her offspring; he shall bruise your head, and you shall bruise his heel."

This verse has been called the protoevangelium, the first gospel. It contains in seed form the entire plan of redemption that unfolds across the pages of Scripture. Every promise God made to Abraham, every prophecy delivered by the prophets, every psalm that spoke of a coming deliverer, every sacrifice offered in the temple, all of these find their origin in this single sentence spoken in the garden.

I have spent decades studying this text, and its depths continue to astound me. In my time teaching seminary students, I have watched their faces light up when they grasp what God was doing in this moment. In my pastoral ministry, I saw broken people find hope when they understood that God had planned their rescue before Adam and Eve even left the garden. God had not abandoned humanity to the consequences of sin. He had already set in motion the plan to crush the serpent's head.

The Structure of the Promise

God directed His words to the serpent, but they were spoken for the benefit of Adam and Eve. The promise contains several key elements that establish the framework for understanding redemption history.

First, God declared enmity between the serpent and the woman. This was not merely a description of something that would naturally occur in the aftermath of the fall, but rather a solemn divine decree. God Himself would establish and maintain this hostility between the deceiver and the deceived. This is absolutely crucial to understand because, left to their own devices and fallen inclinations, Adam and Eve had already demonstrated they were quite willing, even eager, to listen to the serpent's whispered lies and align themselves with his rebellious purposes against their Creator.

The enmity God promised was therefore a gracious intervention into the human condition, an act of divine mercy that prevented humanity from sliding completely into the serpent's grasp. It was God's commitment to set humanity in opposition to the very enemy who had so cunningly deceived them in the garden. Without this promised enmity, without God actively working to create this hostility between the woman and the serpent, mankind would have remained in league with Satan, content to follow his lead into deeper darkness. The promise of enmity was itself a promise of grace; God would not allow His image-bearers to remain willing servants of the evil one.

Second, God extended this conflict beyond the immediate participants to encompass the offspring of both parties, a promise that transformed a single encounter in Eden into an ages-long cosmic struggle. The battle would not be confined to that first generation, nor would it conclude when Adam and Eve passed from the scene. Rather, it would continue throughout the entire course of human history, generation after generation, until God's purposes reached their appointed fulfillment.

The serpent would have offspring, not biological descendants, of course, since Satan is a created spiritual being, but spiritual children nonetheless. These would be those who, by choice or by nature, align themselves with his rebellious purposes and follow his deceiving ways. Throughout Scripture, we encounter this dark lineage: those who bear the character of the father of lies, who walk according to the course of this world, following the prince of the power of the air. Jesus Himself would later identify such people when confronting the religious leaders of His day, declaring, "You are of your father the devil, and your will is to do your father's desires" (John 8:44).

Conversely, the woman would have offspring, those whom God would graciously set in opposition to the kingdom of darkness. These would be the sons and daughters of Eve who, by God's sovereign intervention and gracious election, would stand against the serpent's schemes and resist his tyranny. This promised seed would include all those whom God would call out of darkness into His marvelous light, all those who would, by grace through faith, become children of the promise rather than children of wrath.

Third, God predicted a specific outcome to this cosmic conflict between these two opposing lineages. The woman's offspring would strike a devastating blow to the serpent's head, while in the same moment, the serpent would manage only to strike his heel. This imagery is not merely poetic; it reveals the fundamental asymmetry of the conflict. A crushed head represents a fatal, conclusive blow, the kind of wound from which there can be no recovery, no possibility of resurgence. The serpent's power would not merely be diminished; it would be utterly destroyed. A bruised heel, by contrast, is certainly painful, even agonizing in the moment of impact, but it is not mortal. It is a wound that, though it causes real suffering and genuine injury, does not prevent ultimate triumph. The promise, therefore, contains both a sober acknowledgment of coming suffering and an unwavering assurance of ultimate, decisive victory. From the very beginning, even before the first child was born to our fallen parents, God announced that though the conflict would exact a terrible price from the woman's seed, though victory would come through suffering, the final outcome was never in doubt. The serpent would be crushed beneath the heel of the very offspring he sought to destroy.

Fourth, and most remarkably, the promise speaks of "her offspring" in the singular when describing the one who would deliver the decisive blow to the serpent. This might seem like a minor grammatical detail, but it carries profound theological weight. The Hebrew construction allows for both a collective and an individual interpretation, and throughout redemptive history, both dimensions prove to be valid and necessary for understanding God's plan. The woman would indeed have many descendants who would stand against the serpent's kingdom. Yet the singular pronoun in this ancient promise points beyond the collective struggle of humanity toward something far more specific, toward a particular descendant, an individual champion who would accomplish what the collective offspring, in all their cumulative efforts and generations of striving, could never achieve on their own.

This final element of the promise reveals something that should make us pause in wonder; it discloses the fundamentally Christological nature of what God was announcing in that moment of judgment and grace. From the very dawn of human history, even as our first parents stood trembling in their inadequate garments of fig leaves, bearing the weight of their catastrophic rebellion, God's redemptive plan was already centering itself on a single representative, a champion who would accomplish what humanity in its collective strength could never achieve. This promised one would succeed precisely where Adam had so spectacularly and tragically failed, undoing the curse that our first father had brought upon all his children.

Where the first man, created in perfection and placed in paradise, had listened with fatal credulity to the serpent's lies and had chosen the creature's word over the Creator's command, the second Adam, this promised seed of the woman, would face the tempter's cunning and resist every form of temptation with unwavering faithfulness to His Father's will. And where the first man, through his act of willful disobedience in that garden of abundance, had ushered death and decay into God's good creation, bringing ruin upon himself and all who would come after him, the second Adam would accomplish the opposite miracle: bringing eternal life through His perfect, costly obedience to the Father, even unto death on a cross.

The Seed Promise Through Scripture

The theme of the promised seed runs like a golden thread through the entire Old Testament. Each major covenant and promise builds on and develops what God first announced in Genesis 3:15.

When God called Abraham, He promised him offspring as numerous as the stars. But Paul reveals in Galatians 3:16 that the promises made to Abraham and his offspring "does not say, 'And to offsprings,' referring to many, but referring to one, 'And to your offspring,' who is Christ." The covenant with Abraham was not ultimately about physical descendants but about the one Seed who would bring blessing to all nations.

God's promise to David in 2 Samuel 7 continued this theme. The Lord declared that He would establish the throne of David's offspring forever. Solomon built the temple and reigned in splendor, but his kingdom divided after his death. The promise clearly pointed beyond any earthly king to an eternal King whose kingdom would never end.

The prophets spoke repeatedly of this coming figure. Isaiah described a child who would be born, a son who would be given, whose name would be Wonderful Counselor, Mighty God, Everlasting Father, Prince of Peace (Isaiah 9:6). Micah prophesied that from Bethlehem would come forth one "whose coming forth is from of old, from ancient days" (Micah 5:2). Jeremiah announced a righteous Branch who would be raised up for David, a King who would reign wisely and execute justice (Jeremiah 23:5).

Each prophecy added detail to the portrait. The Seed would be born of a virgin (Isaiah 7:14). He would be a prophet like Moses (Deuteronomy 18:15). He would be a priest after the order of Melchizedek (Psalm 110:4). He would suffer and be rejected (Isaiah 53). He would triumph and reign (Psalm 2).

But all of these prophecies trace back to Genesis 3:15. The virgin birth connects to "her offspring." The suffering connects to the bruised heel. The triumph connects to the crushed head. Every messianic prophecy is an expansion and elaboration of what God first promised in the garden.

During my doctoral studies, I traced this theme through every book of the Old Testament. The genealogies that seem so tedious to modern readers were carefully preserving the line of the promised Seed. When Genesis 4:1 records that Eve gave birth to Cain and said, "I have gotten a man with the help of the Lord," she may have hoped he was the promised deliverer. Her hope was misplaced, but it shows how central this promise was to their thinking.

The flood narrative takes on new significance when we see it through the lens of Genesis 3:15. God preserved Noah and his family because through them the line of the Seed would continue. The tower of Babel scattered humanity, but God called Abraham to resume the promise. The patriarchs, Isaac, Jacob, Judah, each represented another link in the chain leading to Christ.

The exodus from Egypt displayed God's commitment to preserve His people through whom the Seed would come. The conquest of Canaan gave them a land where they could flourish and await the fulfillment of the promise. The monarchy established the royal line through which the King of Kings would enter the world. Even the exile and return demonstrated God's faithfulness in maintaining a remnant through whom His purposes would be accomplished.

Christ as the Seed

"When the fullness of time had come, God sent forth His Son, born of woman" (Galatians 4:4). Jesus Christ is the Seed promised in Genesis 3:15. Every aspect of the prophecy finds its fulfillment in Him.

He is uniquely the offspring of the woman. Matthew and Luke both trace His genealogy, but unlike other genealogies that emphasize the father's line, these genealogies highlight the role of women, unusual in ancient records. More significantly, Jesus was conceived by the Holy Spirit and born of a virgin. He had no human father. He was, in the most literal sense possible, the offspring of the woman.

His entire ministry demonstrated the enmity God had established between the woman's seed and the serpent's offspring. From the moment John the Baptist called the Pharisees a "brood of vipers" (Matthew 3:7), the lines were drawn. Jesus consistently confronted and cast out demons, displaying His authority over the forces of darkness. When the scribes accused Him of casting out demons by the power of Beelzebul, Jesus revealed the cosmic conflict: "If Satan casts out Satan, he is divided against himself. How then will his kingdom stand?" (Matthew 12:26).

His temptation in the wilderness recapitulated and reversed the temptation in the garden. Where Adam and Eve faced the serpent in a place of abundance and fell, Jesus faced Satan in a place of deprivation and stood firm. Where the first couple doubted God's word and goodness, Jesus wielded Scripture as a weapon: "It is written, 'Man shall not live by bread alone, but by every word that comes from the mouth of God'" (Matthew 4:4). Where Adam grasped at equality with God, Jesus "who, though he was in the form of God, did not count equality with God a thing to be grasped" (Philippians 2:6).

Throughout His ministry, Jesus proclaimed the kingdom of God and demonstrated its power. Every healing was a reversal of the curse's effects on the human body. Every deliverance was a defeat of demonic forces. Every teaching exposed the lies of the serpent and revealed the truth about God's character and purposes. He was systematically undoing the work of the devil.

But the decisive blow came at the cross. This is where we see the full meaning of Genesis 3:15. The serpent struck Christ's heel, a grievous wound that appeared to be a victory for the forces of darkness. When Jesus hung on the cross, bleeding and dying, it looked like the serpent had won. Satan had stirred up hatred in the hearts of the religious leaders. He had entered Judas and prompted the betrayal. He had incited the mob to cry, "Crucify him!" The prince of this world seemed to have triumphed.

But the serpent did not understand that this was the very means by which his head would be crushed. Colossians 2:13-15 reveals what really happened at the cross: "And you, who were dead in your trespasses and the uncircumcision of your flesh, God made alive together with him, having forgiven us all our trespasses, by canceling the record of debt that stood against us with its legal demands. This he set aside, nailing it to the cross. He disarmed the rulers and authorities and put them to open shame, by triumphing over them in him."

The cross was not Satan's victory but his defeat. Every weapon in his arsenal was rendered powerless. Sin's penalty was paid. Death's sting was removed. The law's condemnation was satisfied. Satan's accusations lost their force because our debt had been canceled. What looked like weakness was the very power of God unto salvation.

I have stood at gravesides too many times to count. I have watched faithful Christians lowered into the ground and seen families weep. But even in those moments of grief, Genesis 3:15 has sustained me. The bruised heel represents the suffering and death of Christ, but it was not the end of the story. Three days later, He rose from the dead, validating His claims and demonstrating His victory over death and the grave.

The resurrection was the public declaration that the serpent's head had been crushed. Jesus "abolished death and brought life and immortality to light through the gospel" (2 Timothy 1:10). He took on flesh and blood "that through death he might destroy the one who has the power of death, that is, the devil, and deliver all those who through fear of death were subject to lifelong slavery" (Hebrews 2:14-15).

The Ongoing Conflict

Yet the promise in Genesis 3:15 also acknowledges an ongoing conflict between two lines of offspring. Throughout history, there have been those who belong to the woman's seed and those who belong to the serpent's brood.

Cain murdered Abel, the first instance of this enmity playing out. The righteous Abel belonged to the woman's seed. Cain, whom John identifies as "of the evil one" (1 John 3:12), belonged to the serpent's offspring. This pattern repeated throughout biblical history. The line of Seth opposed the wickedness of Cain's descendants. Isaac and Jacob were the children of promise while Ishmael and Esau were not. The Israelites faced opposition from pagan nations serving false gods. The prophets confronted false prophets. The faithful remnant stood against the apostate majority.

Jesus Himself drew this distinction sharply in John 8. When the Jewish leaders claimed Abraham as their father, Jesus responded, "If you were Abraham's children, you would be doing the works Abraham did, but now you seek to kill me, a man who has told you the truth that I heard from God. This is not what Abraham did. You are doing the works your father did" (John 8:39-41). When they insisted that God was their Father, Jesus delivered a devastating verdict: "You are of your father the devil, and your will is to do your father's desires. He was a murderer from the beginning, and does not stand in the truth, because there is no truth in him" (John 8:44).

Physical descent from Abraham meant nothing. What mattered was spiritual reality. Those who rejected Christ demonstrated that they belonged to the serpent's offspring. Those who believed in Christ showed themselves to be children of promise, the true seed of Abraham.

This conflict continues in the church age. Paul warned the Galatians about the same dynamic: "But just as at that time he who was born according to the flesh persecuted him who was born according to the Spirit, so also it is now" (Galatians 4:29). The children of the flesh oppose the children of the promise. The seed of the serpent attacks the seed of the woman.

We see this enmity in every age. When the early church preached the gospel, persecution arose. Stephen was stoned. James was killed with the sword. Paul was imprisoned, beaten, and eventually martyred. Throughout church history, believers have faced opposition, ridicule, imprisonment, and death for their faith in Christ. The serpent continues to strike at the heel.

But believers are not passive victims. God has set enmity in our hearts toward evil. We are called to resist the devil, to stand firm against the schemes of the evil one, to fight the good fight of faith. Paul instructs us to "put on the whole armor of God, that you may be able to stand against the schemes of the devil. For we do not wrestle against flesh and blood, but against the rulers, against the authorities, against the cosmic powers over this present darkness, against the spiritual forces of evil in the heavenly places" (Ephesians 6:11-12).

During my time in the Marine Corps, I learned the importance of understanding your enemy. We studied tactics, learned to anticipate attacks, and prepared for various scenarios. The Christian life requires the same vigilance. Peter warns, "Be sober-minded; be watchful. Your adversary the devil prowls around like a roaring lion, seeking someone to devour" (1 Peter 5:8). We must not be ignorant of Satan's designs (2 Corinthians 2:11).

But we fight from a position of victory, not toward it. Christ has already crushed the serpent's head. We are simply working out the implications of His triumph. We cast down arguments and every lofty opinion raised against the knowledge of God (2 Corinthians 10:5). We take every thought captive to obey Christ. We expose the unfruitful works of darkness (Ephesians 5:11). We proclaim the gospel, knowing that God has chosen to continue His assault on Satan's kingdom through the preaching of the cross.

Federal Headship and the Two Adams

To fully appreciate how Christ fulfills Genesis 3:15, we must understand the Reformed doctrine of federal headship. This teaching explains how one person can represent many, how the actions of a single individual can affect entire populations.

Adam stood as the federal head of the human race. When God made the covenant with him in the garden, Adam represented not only himself but all his descendants. His obedience would have secured blessing for all humanity. His disobedience brought condemnation to all. Romans 5:12 makes this clear: "Therefore, just as sin came into the world through one man, and death through sin, and so death spread to all men because all sinned."

This is not arbitrary or unfair. God established the principle of representation because it serves His purposes and reflects the reality of human solidarity. We are not isolated individuals but members of communities and families. What one person does affects others. This is simply how God designed reality to function.

But federal headship also provides the mechanism for our salvation. Just as we were condemned in Adam, we can be justified in Christ. Paul explains in Romans 5:18-19: "Therefore, as one trespass led to condemnation for all men, so one act of righteousness leads to justification and life for all men. For as by the one man's disobedience the many were made sinners, so by the one man's obedience the many will be made righteous."

Christ stands as the second Adam, the new federal head for all who believe. Where the first Adam failed, the second Adam succeeded. Where the first Adam brought death, the second Adam brought life. Where the first Adam was defeated by the serpent, the second Adam crushed the serpent's head.

First Corinthians 15:45-49 develops this parallel: "Thus it is written, 'The first man Adam became a living being'; the last

Adam became a life-giving spirit. But it is not the spiritual that is first but the natural, and then the spiritual. The first man was from the earth, a man of dust; the second man is from heaven. As was the man of dust, so also are those who are of the dust, and as is the man of heaven, so also are those who are of heaven. Just as we have borne the image of the man of dust, we shall also bear the image of the man of heaven."

This is glorious theology with profound practical implications that touch every dimension of our lives as believers. Our identity as Christians depends not on our performance, our progress, or our achievements, but entirely on our representative. In Adam, we were condemned before we ever committed a single personal sin, we inherited guilt through our union with him. In Christ, by contrast, we are justified before we ever perform a single righteous act, we inherit righteousness through our union with Him. The entire ground of our acceptance before a holy God rests completely on what Christ accomplished in His life, death, and resurrection, not on what we achieve through our efforts, no matter how sincere or sustained.

When I taught systematic theology in the seminary classroom, I noticed that students sometimes struggled initially with questions about the fairness of being condemned for Adam's sin. It seemed unjust to them that they should bear the consequences of a decision made by someone else in a garden thousands of years ago. But once they truly grasped the parallel with justification in Christ; once they saw that their salvation operated on the exact same principle of representation, their objections invariably faded. We are saved by the very same principle by which we were condemned. The mechanism is identical; only the representative changes. If we reject the doctrine of representation in Adam, insisting that we should only answer for our own sins, we must also reject representation in Christ, which means we can only claim credit for our own righteousness, a terrifying prospect. But if we joyfully embrace Christ as our federal head, receiving His righteousness as our own though we did not earn it, we must also accept Adam in that representative role, bearing the consequences of his sin though we did not personally commit it.

The profound beauty of Genesis 3:15 is that it announces this glorious solution immediately after the fall, before humanity had time to comprehend the full extent of its tragedy. God did not leave humanity languishing under the condemnation of the first Adam without simultaneously providing the second Adam. Before Adam and Eve were driven from the garden, before they experienced the full crushing weight of the curse upon their lives, before they truly knew the depths of their misery and ruin, God in His mercy promised a deliverer who would undo what the first Adam had done.

The Bruised Heel and Christian Suffering

The promise that the serpent would bruise the heel of the woman's offspring carries implications for all who are united to Christ. If we share in His victory, we also share in His suffering. The bruised heel represents not only Christ's passion but the ongoing afflictions of His people.

Jesus warned His disciples, "If they persecuted me, they will also persecute you" (John 15:20). Paul testified that "all who desire to live a godly life in Christ Jesus will be persecuted" (2 Timothy 3:12). Peter instructed suffering believers not to be surprised at the fiery trial they were experiencing, as though something strange were happening to them (1 Peter 4:12).

The serpent continues to strike, but his blows are not mortal. He can bruise our heel but cannot crush our head. He can afflict our bodies, damage our reputations, take our possessions, even kill us physically, but he cannot separate us from the love of God in Christ Jesus (Romans 8:38-39). His power is limited, and his time is short.

I watched my wife endure surgery, chemotherapy, radiation, and all the brutal realities of fighting cancer. The serpent struck her heel. But even in the midst of that valley, we clung to the promise that he could not touch her soul. Her life was hidden with Christ in God (Colossians 3:3). Whether she lived or died, she belonged to the Lord (Romans 14:8).

By God's grace, she recovered and has been cancer-free for years now. But the experience taught us both the reality of Genesis 3:15. We live in a fallen world where the serpent still strikes. Believers are not exempt from suffering, illness, or death. But these afflictions are temporary and limited. They touch the heel, not the head. And they serve God's purposes of conforming us to the image of Christ and preparing us for eternal glory.

Paul understood this dynamic perfectly. He spoke of carrying in his body the death of Jesus so that the life of Jesus might also be manifested in his mortal flesh (2 Corinthians 4:10-11). He counted his sufferings as light and momentary afflictions producing an eternal weight of glory beyond all comparison (2 Corinthians 4:17). He knew that present sufferings were not worth comparing with the glory to be revealed (Romans 8:18).

This perspective transforms how we face trials. We do not suffer as those who have no hope. We understand our afflictions in light of Genesis 3:15. The serpent strikes, but his doom is certain. Our heel may be bruised, but his head is crushed. We endure for a little while, but we will reign forever with Christ.

The Crushing of the Serpent's Head

The decisive blow has been struck, but its full effects await final consummation. Christ crushed the serpent's head at the cross, but Satan continues to function as a defeated foe whose sentence has been pronounced but not yet fully executed.

Revelation 12:9-12 describes this in-between time: "And the great dragon was thrown down, that ancient serpent, who is called the devil and Satan, the deceiver of the whole world; he was thrown down to the earth, and his angels were thrown down with him. And I heard a loud voice in heaven, saying, 'Now the salvation and the power and the kingdom of our God and the authority of his Christ have come, for the accuser of our brothers has been thrown down, who accuses them day and night before our God. And they have conquered him by the blood of the Lamb and by the word of their testimony, for they loved not their lives even unto death. Therefore, rejoice, O heavens and you who dwell in them! But woe to you, O earth and sea, for the devil has come down to you in great wrath, because he knows that his time is short!'"

Satan has been defeated but not yet destroyed. His head has been crushed, but he has not yet been cast into the lake of fire. He knows his time is short and therefore wages war with increased fury against the woman's offspring.

But his ultimate fate is certain. Revelation 20:10 describes the final judgment: "And the devil who had deceived them was thrown into the lake of fire and sulfur where the beast and the false prophet were, and they will be tormented day and night forever and ever." The serpent who deceived our first parents will receive eternal punishment. The promise of Genesis 3:15 will be completely fulfilled.

Until that day arrives, we find ourselves living in what theologians call the tension between the already and the not yet. Christ has triumphed decisively over Satan at the cross and through the resurrection, yet we still face genuine spiritual warfare in our daily lives. The kingdom of God has broken into history through the first advent of our King, but we still await its full consummation when He returns in glory. We are indeed more than conquerors through Him who loved us (Romans 8:37), yet we must still put on the full armor of God each day and stand firm against the schemes of the devil.

This tension characterized my years in pastoral ministry. I watched faithful believers wrestle with real spiritual battles even while resting in the certainty of Christ's finished work. The victory has been won, yet the war continues until the final trumpet sounds.

Romans 16:20 offers us tremendous encouragement in this ongoing struggle: "The God of peace will soon crush Satan under your feet." Consider carefully what Paul is doing here. He takes the ancient promise of Genesis 3:15, that the seed of the woman would crush the serpent's head, and applies it directly to believers in Rome. By extension, he applies it to all who belong to Christ. We are the woman's offspring, united to Christ by faith and sealed by the Holy Spirit. God promises to crush Satan not only through Christ, our representative and covenant head, but also under our feet as we participate in Christ's victory over evil.

This is not accomplished by our own power or wisdom or strength. We bring nothing to the table except our need and our faith. Yet it is Christ's power working mightily through us, His resurrection life flowing through the members of His body.

And remarkably, gloriously, it is genuinely our participation in His triumph. United to Him, we share in all that is His, including His victory over the ancient serpent who sought to destroy us.

During my pastoral ministry, I often counseled believers struggling with besetting sins, spiritual oppression, or demonic harassment. I reminded them of Genesis 3:15 and Romans 16:20. Yes, the battle is real. Yes, the enemy is formidable. But his head has been crushed by Christ, and God will soon crush him under our feet as well. We fight from victory, not toward it. We stand on the promises of God and resist the devil in the name and authority of Jesus Christ.

The New Creation and the Reversal of the Curse

Genesis 3:15 not only promises the defeat of Satan but also points toward the complete reversal of the fall's effects. When Christ crushed the serpent's head, He set in motion the restoration of all that was lost in the garden.

The curse, in its devastating sweep, brought death into a world that God had declared "very good," physical death, spiritual death, and the shadow of death that hangs over every moment of human existence. But Christ, the last Adam, brings resurrection life that conquers death in all its forms. Where the first Adam's disobedience opened the door to mortality and decay, Christ's obedience opens the door to eternal life. His resurrection is not merely His own triumph over the grave but the firstfruits of a coming harvest in which all who are united to Him will likewise be raised imperishable and immortal.

The curse fractured human relationships at every level: between husband and wife, parent and child, brother and brother, neighbor and neighbor. It turned the intimacy of marriage into a battleground and the community of humanity into warring tribes. But Christ creates a new humanity reconciled to God and to one another through His blood. In Him, the dividing walls of hostility are demolished, and people from every nation, tribe, and tongue are made one body, one family, one new creation in which the old antagonisms and divisions no longer define us.

The curse subjected all of creation to futility, to the frustration of purposes unfulfilled and beauty marred by corruption. The ground itself groaned under the weight of God's judgment. But Christ, through His redemptive work, will liberate the entire creation from its bondage to corruption, setting it free to obtain the freedom of the glory of the children of God (Romans 8:21). What began in a garden will culminate in a garden-city where heaven and earth are joined forever.

Revelation 21-22 describes the final state of redeemed humanity in language that deliberately echoes Genesis 1-3. The Tree of Life, which was lost when Adam and Eve were expelled from the garden, reappears in the New Jerusalem (Revelation 22:2). The curse, pronounced in Genesis 3, is removed: "No longer will there be anything accursed" (Revelation 22:3). God dwells with His people, restoring the intimate fellowship that Adam and Eve enjoyed before the fall: "Behold, the dwelling place of God is with man. He will dwell with them, and they will be his people, and God himself will be with them as their God" (Revelation 21:3).

The serpent, who disrupted paradise, will be forever banished. The dragon, that ancient serpent, will trouble God's people no more. The new creation will surpass even the original creation in glory because it will be populated by redeemed sinners whose salvation has been purchased at infinite cost and who therefore worship with a depth of gratitude that unfallen creatures could never know.

This vision sustained me through the darkest valleys of pastoral ministry. When I sat with parents whose child had died, when I buried young men killed in combat, when I counseled couples whose marriages were disintegrating, when I watched faithful saints suffer with diseases that robbed them of dignity and strength, I clung to the promise that this is not how the story ends.

Genesis 3:15 guarantees that the serpent will be crushed, the curse will be removed, and creation will be restored. We do not grieve as those who have no hope. We know that our Redeemer lives and that at the last He will stand upon the earth (Job 19:25). We wait with patient endurance for the full manifestation of what Christ has already accomplished.

Christ's Obedience Contrasted with Adam's Failure

The promise of Genesis 3:15 finds its fulfillment in Christ's perfect obedience throughout His earthly ministry. Where Adam failed at every point, Christ succeeded.

Adam was placed in a garden of abundance. Christ entered a wilderness of deprivation. Adam had every tree from which to eat except one. Christ fasted for forty days and nights. Adam heard the serpent's suggestion, "Did God actually say?" and doubted God's word. Christ heard Satan's temptations and responded with Scripture: "It is written."

Adam grasped at something God had forbidden. Christ, "though he was in the form of God, did not count equality with God a thing to be grasped, but emptied himself, by taking the form of a servant, being born in the likeness of men" (Philippians 2:6-7). Adam sought glory for himself. Christ humbled Himself and became obedient to the point of death, even death on a cross.

Adam hid from God after he sinned. Christ sought the Father's face even in the agony of the garden of Gethsemane, praying, "Not my will, but yours, be done" (Luke 22:42). Adam blamed his wife and implicitly blamed God: "The woman whom you gave to be with me." Christ took responsibility for sins He did not commit, bearing the guilt of His people.

Adam's disobedience brought condemnation. Christ's obedience brings justification. Romans 5:19 makes the parallel explicit: "For as by the one man's disobedience the many were made sinners, so by the one man's obedience the many will be made righteous."

This is the heart of the gospel. We are not saved by our obedience but by Christ's obedience credited to our account. The doctrine of imputation means that Christ's perfect righteousness becomes ours through faith. God does not lower His standards to accommodate our failure. Instead, He provides in Christ the perfect obedience that His law demands.

Throughout my decades in theological education, first in the seminary classroom and now in the quiet of my study, I have spent countless hours teaching, explaining, defending, and marveling at the doctrine of justification by faith alone. It remains, as the Reformers insisted, the *articulus stantis et cadentis ecclesiae*, the Latin phrase meaning the article by which the church stands or falls. And remarkably, wonderfully, this cornerstone of our faith traces its roots all the way back to that first promise whispered in Eden, to Genesis 3:15.

God promised a Seed who would succeed precisely where Adam failed so catastrophically. That Seed, we now know with the clarity of New Testament revelation, is Christ Himself. His perfect, unwavering obedience, from the manger to the cross, from Bethlehem to Calvary, fully satisfies the righteous demands of the covenant of works that Adam shattered. His substitutionary death on the cross pays in full the terrible penalty we incurred for our violation of that covenant. His glorious resurrection from the dead demonstrates beyond all doubt God's complete acceptance of His sacrifice on our behalf.

When we trust in Christ through faith, that gift of God, not a work of our own, we are vitally, organically, legally, and spiritually united to Him. This union, this blessed reality of being "in Christ," means that His perfect obedience is credited to our account as though it were our own. His death becomes our death to the tyranny and penalty of sin. His resurrection becomes our resurrection to new life, both now and forever. We are in Christ, the second Adam, the long-promised Seed who has crushed the serpent's head beneath His nail-pierced feet.

Participating in Christ's Victory

Genesis 3:15 is not merely historical information about what happened in the past or will happen in the future. It describes a present reality in which all believers participate. We are the woman's offspring, united to Christ the ultimate Seed. God has placed enmity in our hearts toward the serpent and his works. We are engaged in the ongoing conflict between the Kingdom of Light and the kingdom of darkness.

This participation is both positional and experiential. Positionally, we have been transferred from the domain of darkness into the kingdom of God's beloved Son (Colossians 1:13).

We have been raised with Christ and seated with Him in the heavenly places (Ephesians 2:6). We are more than conquerors through Him who loved us (Romans 8:37). These realities are true regardless of how we feel or what circumstances we face.

Experientially, we must work out our salvation with fear and trembling, knowing that God is at work in us both to will and to work for His good pleasure (Philippians 2:12-13). We must resist the devil so that he will flee from us (James 4:7). We must put to death the deeds of the body (Romans 8:13). We must fight the good fight of faith (1 Timothy 6:12).

The Christian life is spiritual warfare. We face a real enemy who seeks to devour us. But we are not fighting alone, and we are not fighting from a position of weakness. Christ has crushed the serpent's head. We fight in His strength, wielding the weapons He has provided.

Prayer is a weapon. When we pray in Jesus' name, we invoke the authority of the One who has triumphed over Satan. Scripture is a weapon. Jesus defeated Satan in the wilderness by quoting the Word of God, and we must do the same. The gospel itself is a weapon. Paul calls it "the power of God for salvation to everyone who believes" (Romans 1:16). When we proclaim the good news of Christ's victory, we are advancing His kingdom and pushing back the darkness.

The church is called to be the instrument through which God displays His wisdom to the rulers and authorities in the heavenly places (Ephesians 3:10). Every time the gospel is preached and someone believes, Satan suffers another defeat. Every time a believer grows in sanctification, the serpent's influence diminishes. Every time Christians love one another and demonstrate the reality of the new creation, the old order passes away.

I have watched this dynamic play out in countless lives. Men and women enslaved to addiction find freedom in Christ. Marriages on the brink of divorce are restored through the gospel's power. Bitter, angry people are transformed into vessels of grace and forgiveness. Fearful, anxious souls discover peace that surpasses understanding. These are not merely psychological changes but evidence that the serpent's head has been crushed and his captives have been set free.

The Hope That Sustains

Genesis 3:15 provides the foundation for Christian hope. Without this promise, the story of Genesis 3 would end in unmitigated tragedy. Humanity would be left under the curse, subject to death, with no possibility of redemption. But God spoke this word of grace, and it changed everything.

Every believer, whether they realize it or not, can trace the story of their salvation all the way back to this remarkable verse in the garden. Long before the foundation of the world was even laid, before time itself began its march through history, God in His sovereign grace chose a people for Himself in Christ, setting His electing love upon them (Ephesians 1:4). Then, standing in that garden amid the wreckage of humanity's rebellion, in Genesis 3:15, He announced to both the serpent and our trembling first parents His gracious intention to redeem those chosen people through the promised Seed who would come.

Throughout the long centuries of the Old Testament, through wars and famines, through the rise and fall of kingdoms, through captivity and return, God faithfully preserved the messianic line through which that promised Seed would ultimately come. He protected it through barren wombs that miraculously conceived, through threats of extinction, through the moral failures of the very people who carried the promise. At precisely the appointed time in history, when the fullness of time had come, He sent forth His Son, born of a woman, born under the law (Galatians 4:4).

This promised Seed, Jesus Christ, lived the perfectly obedient life that we in our fallenness could never live, keeping every jot and tittle of God's righteous law. He died the death that we in our guilt deserved to die, bearing the full weight of divine wrath against sin. And then He rose victorious and triumphant over sin, death, and Satan himself, securing for His people the very salvation that God had promised in the garden so long ago.

Now we await the final consummation when every enemy will be put under Christ's feet and the last enemy, death, will be destroyed (1 Corinthians 15:25-26). We look forward to the new heavens and new earth where righteousness dwells, where there will be no more curse, where the serpent will trouble us no more.

This hope sustained the Old Testament saints who died without receiving the promises but saw them from afar (Hebrews 11:13). This hope sustained the apostles who faced persecution and martyrdom. This hope has sustained believers through every age who have suffered for their faith in Christ. This hope sustains us today as we navigate a fallen world and face our own battles with sin, suffering, and the schemes of the evil one.

Paul writes that hope does not put us to shame because God's love has been poured into our hearts through the Holy Spirit (Romans 5:5). Our hope is not wishful thinking but confident assurance based on God's unchanging promises. He who promised is faithful, and He will bring it to pass.

Genesis 3:15 stands as the first and foundational promise. Everything that follows builds on this declaration that the serpent will be crushed and humanity will be redeemed through the woman's offspring. When we grasp the full weight of this promise and see how it finds its fulfillment in Christ, our faith is strengthened, our hope is renewed, and our love for God deepens.

The gospel was not an afterthought. God did not scramble to devise a rescue plan after the fall caught Him by surprise. Before time began, He determined to display His glory through the redemption of sinful humanity. Genesis 3:15 reveals that plan in seed form. The rest of Scripture traces how that seed grew until it reached its full flowering in the person and work of Jesus Christ.

This is why I have devoted my life to studying, teaching, and proclaiming these truths. This is why I continue to write in my retirement. These are not dry theological abstractions but living realities that transform how we understand ourselves, our world, and our God. Genesis 3:15 connects the garden to the cross, the fall to redemption, the first Adam to the last Adam. It provides the framework for understanding all of Scripture and the foundation for genuine Christian hope.

Chapter Thirteen

Created for Glory, Broken by Sin, Redeemed by Christ

The Christian life cannot be understood apart from these three foundational realities: Creation, Fall, and Redemption. They form the skeleton upon which all biblical truth hangs, the framework through which we interpret every experience, every relationship, every struggle, and every joy. Remove any one of these pillars and the entire structure collapses into incoherence.

I learned this truth not primarily in the classroom, though my years of theological study certainly reinforced it. I learned it in the trenches of pastoral ministry, sitting across from believers who struggled to make sense of their lives. I learned it counseling the young woman who couldn't reconcile her eating disorder with God's love. I learned it talking with the businessman who found his identity in his career success rather than in Christ. I learned it walking alongside my beloved wife through her battle with cancer, watching her cling to truths about who God made her to be, what sin had broken, and what Christ had secured for her.

These three realities answer the fundamental questions every human being asks, whether consciously or unconsciously: Where did I come from? What went wrong? Is there any hope? The secular world offers its own competing narratives, but they crumble under examination. Only the biblical story of Creation, Fall, and Redemption provides a coherent explanation for the glory and horror, the beauty and brokenness, the nobility and depravity we observe in human nature and human history.

The Foundation of Human Dignity

We are created beings. This truth stands first and fundamental. We did not emerge through blind evolutionary processes. We were not cosmic accidents or the unintended byproducts of impersonal forces. The eternal God, who exists in three persons as Father, Son, and Holy Spirit, spoke us into being with intentionality and purpose.

"So God created man in his own image, in the image of God he created him; male and female he created them" (Genesis 1:27). These words carry profound theological weight. Every human being who has ever lived or will ever live bears the image of the Creator. This truth establishes human dignity on an unshakeable foundation that no culture, government, or ideology can rightfully overturn.

When I served in the Marine Corps, I witnessed the best and worst of humanity. I saw men display extraordinary courage, sacrificing their own safety for their brothers. I also saw the devastating effects of sin, the capacity for cruelty that lurks in the human heart. Both realities testified to the biblical truth about human nature. We bear God's image, which accounts for our capacity for love, creativity, moral reasoning, and self-sacrifice. We also bear the corruption of the fall, which accounts for our propensity toward selfishness, violence, and destruction.

The image of God means we were created for relationship with our Maker. Unlike the animals, which were spoken into existence with divine commands, God personally formed Adam from the dust and breathed into his nostrils the breath of life (Genesis 2:7). This intimate act of creation established humanity's unique position in the created order. We alone among all creatures were designed to know God, to commune with Him, to reflect His character, and to exercise dominion over His world as His representatives.

This has staggering implications for how we view ourselves and others. The homeless person on the street corner bears God's image. The unborn child in the womb bears God's image. The elderly person suffering from dementia bears God's image. The political opponent whose views we find abhorrent bears God's image. The criminal on death row bears God's image. Our value does not derive from our usefulness, our productivity, our intelligence, our physical abilities, or our contributions to society. Our value is intrinsic, bestowed by our Creator, indelible despite sin's corruption.

I have watched the church struggle with this truth in various ways throughout my years of ministry, from the pulpit to the classroom, from pastoral counseling sessions to theological discussions with fellow ministers. Some traditions have so emphasized human sinfulness, so focused on our depravity and moral corruption, that they've effectively lost sight of the residual dignity that remains even in fallen humanity. In their zealous efforts to humble human pride and exalt God's sovereignty, they've sometimes painted a picture of humanity as nothing more than worthless worms, utterly without value apart from God's saving grace. This imbalanced view, while rightly recognizing sin's gravity, can inadvertently undermine the biblical truth that we remain God's image bearers even after the fall.

On the opposite end of the spectrum, others have so emphasized human dignity, human potential, and human worth that they've minimized or even denied the devastating effects of sin. They speak of humanity's inherent goodness, our capacity for self-improvement, our ability to overcome our failings through education, effort, or enlightenment. This view, common in much of liberal theology and popular spirituality, fails to reckon seriously with what Scripture teaches about our fallen condition.

Reformed theology, at its best, holds both of these truths in proper biblical tension without compromising either one. Yes, we are totally depraved, not in the sense that we are as evil as we could possibly be, but in the sense that sin has affected every part of our being. We are unable to save ourselves, spiritually dead in our trespasses and sins, incapable of turning to God apart from His gracious intervention. Yet simultaneously, we remain image bearers, creatures of inestimable worth for whom Christ died, beings who retain something of that original glory even in our fallen state.

This understanding of our dual identity as fallen image-bearers fundamentally shapes how we engage in the sacred work of evangelism. We do not approach unbelievers with a spirit of condescension or superiority, as if they were worthless wretches beneath our notice or concern. Rather, we recognize them for what they truly are: precious image bearers of the living God who have tragically rejected their Creator, who stand even now under His righteous judgment, yet who nevertheless retain the profound dignity of creatures originally fashioned for eternal glory. We proclaim the gospel with genuine urgency and heartfelt compassion because we grasp both realities simultaneously, their immeasurable worth as those created in God's image and the terrible danger they face in their rebellion against Him, both their original created purpose to reflect God's glory and their current fallen condition that has left them alienated from their Maker. This balanced perspective prevents us from the twin errors of either dismissing the lost as beyond caring about or minimizing the seriousness of their spiritual peril.

It shapes how we approach the complex and often contentious issues of justice and mercy in our broken world. We cannot remain indifferent or aloof to the grinding realities of poverty that crushes the spirits and bodies of millions, to the insidious poison of racism that denies the fundamental equality of all who share the divine image, to the cruel machinery of exploitation that treats human beings as mere commodities to be used and discarded, or to the manifold forms of oppression that dehumanize and degrade those whom God Himself has crowned with glory and honor. These offenses are not merely social problems to be analyzed with clinical detachment; they are profound moral evils that strike directly against those who bear the very image of the living God. Every act of injustice is ultimately an assault on the One whose image is marred in the victim.

Reformed theology's rich emphasis on common grace, that undeserved favor God extends to all humanity regardless of their spiritual state, means we must recognize with both humility and gratitude that even unbelievers, those who do not acknowledge Christ as Lord, can nevertheless pursue justice with noble intent, create genuine beauty that reflects something of their Creator, and meaningfully advance human flourishing in ways that benefit the common good. They do so imperfectly, of course, for their works are tainted by the same fallen nature that afflicts us all, and they do so without ultimate reference to God's glory as the highest end of all human endeavor. Yet their efforts to retain real value and deserve our recognition and, in many cases, our active partnership. We join them in these worthy endeavors not because we naively believe in the possibility of human perfectibility through social reform or legislative action, not because we imagine we can build the kingdom of God through political activism or humanitarian programs, but because we believe deeply and without reservation in defending the inherent dignity of all image bearers, regardless of whether they acknowledge the God whose image they carry.

It shapes how we view our own lives and callings. Work is not a curse but a gift, established before the fall when God placed Adam in the garden to work it and keep it (Genesis 2:15). We were created for purposeful activity, designed to exercise creativity and dominion as God's representatives. The carpenter who builds a house, the nurse who tends the sick, the teacher who instructs children, the mother who raises her family, all participate in the cultural mandate to fill the earth and subdue it, to bring order out of chaos, to cultivate the potential God embedded in His creation.

The Catastrophe of the Fall

But we must move immediately from Creation to Fall, for the world we inhabit is not the world as God made it. Sin has introduced a rupture of cosmic proportions. What God declared "very good" has been subjected to futility, groaning in the pains of childbirth as it awaits its liberation from bondage to corruption (Romans 8:20-22).

The fall was not simply a minor misstep or an unfortunate mistake. It was high treason against the sovereign God, a declaration of independence from our rightful King, an attempt to seize autonomy that was never ours to claim. When Adam ate the forbidden fruit, he was not merely breaking an arbitrary rule. He was rejecting God's authority, doubting God's goodness, and grasping for equality with God.

The results cascaded through every dimension of human existence. The image of God was not erased but corrupted, defaced though not destroyed. Our capacity for reason became clouded by foolish thinking. Our affections became disordered, loving created things more than the Creator. Our wills became enslaved to sin, unable to choose what is truly good apart from God's regenerating grace.

Paul describes our condition in stark terms: "And you were dead in the trespasses and sins in which you once walked, following the course of this world, following the prince of the power of the air, the spirit that is now at work in the sons of disobedience" (Ephesians 2:1-2). Dead. Not sick, not weakened, not merely in need of assistance. Spiritually dead, unresponsive to God, hostile to His law, incapable of saving ourselves.

I have encountered resistance to this doctrine throughout my ministry. It offends our pride, contradicts our self-perception, challenges our assumption that we are basically good people who occasionally make mistakes. But Scripture knows nothing of this sentimentality. Jesus Himself declared, "No one can come to me unless the Father who sent me draws him" (John 6:44). Paul wrote, "For those who live according to the flesh set their minds on the things of the flesh, but those who live according to the Spirit set their minds on the things of the Spirit. For to set the mind on the flesh is death, but to set the mind on the Spirit is life and peace. For the mind that is set on the flesh is hostile to God, for it does not submit to God's law; indeed, it cannot" (Romans 8:5-7).

The doctrine of total depravity does not mean we are as bad as we could possibly be. God's common grace restrains sin and enables even unregenerate people to perform acts of relative goodness. A mother's love for her child, a soldier's sacrifice for his country, a philanthropist's generosity toward the poor, these are real goods, reflections of the image of God that remains. But they are not saving righteousness. They do not merit God's favor. They do not earn us a place in heaven.

The fall explains the contradictions we observe in human nature and human society. We build hospitals and concentration camps. We compose symphonies and wage genocidal wars. We establish systems of justice and perpetrate horrible injustices. We are capable of breathtaking nobility and shocking depravity, often within the same individual. This is the paradox of being fallen image-bearers.

Sin has corrupted not only our relationship with God but also our relationships with each other. The first murder occurred in the very next chapter after the fall, when Cain killed his brother Abel (Genesis 4:8). Marriage, the first human institution, became a battleground where self-interest competed with covenant love. Work became toil, marked by frustration and futility. Even our relationship with creation itself was ruptured, as the ground brought forth thorns and thistles.

More subtly, sin corrupted our self-understanding. We became strangers to ourselves, unable to see clearly who we are and what we were made for. Pascal wrote of the human being as both the glory and the garbage of the universe, recognizing both our residual greatness and our actual wretchedness. We sense that we were made for something more, yet we find ourselves trapped in patterns of thought and behavior that lead to destruction.

The fall also explains suffering. This world is not as it should be. Disease, natural disasters, death itself, these are intruders, enemies of the good creation God made. They entered through sin, both through Adam's representative sin that brought corruption to all creation and through our own individual sins that compound the damage. When we face cancer or watch a loved one decline with Alzheimer's disease or bury a child, we are experiencing the effects of living in a fallen world under the curse.

This truth provides pastoral comfort even as it confronts us with hard realities. Suffering is not part of God's original design. He did not create cancer, or earthquakes, or pandemics. These are the consequences of sin's entrance into the world. Yet God in His sovereignty uses even these evils for His purposes, conforming His people to the image of Christ, displaying His glory through their faith in trials, and pointing forward to the day when He will make all things new.

I have counseled countless believers who struggled with guilt over their suffering, wondering what they did to deserve it. The doctrine of the fall liberates us from this torment. Yes, some suffering comes as a direct consequence of specific sins. The alcoholic who develops cirrhosis, the adulterer whose marriage crumbles, the embezzler who goes to prison, these reap what they sow. But much suffering simply reflects living in a fallen world where bodies break down, relationships fracture, and disasters strike. Job's friends made the mistake of assuming all suffering must be direct divine punishment for specific sins. God rebuked them for their theological error.

The fall also demands that we take sin seriously, profoundly, soberly, and comprehensively seriously. We live in an age that has largely abandoned the category of sin altogether, preferring instead to speak of mistakes, poor choices, psychological disorders, or social conditioning. The language of transgression and guilt has been replaced with the language of therapy and self-actualization. Even in the church, we often domesticate sin, treating it as a minor problem that a little spiritual effort, a few good decisions, or some positive thinking can overcome. We speak of "issues" rather than iniquities, of "challenges" rather than corruption.

But Scripture presents sin in far starker, more terrifying terms. It is not merely a mistake to be corrected or a habit to be broken. Sin is a tyrant that enslaves us, binding our wills with chains we cannot break. It is a corruption that permeates every part of our being: our minds, our hearts, our affections, our desires. The Reformed tradition has rightly spoken of total depravity, not meaning that we are as bad as we could possibly be, but that sin has touched every aspect of our humanity, leaving no faculty untainted. Most sobering of all, sin is an offense against the infinitely holy God, a cosmic treason that deserves not merely correction but eternal punishment.

I have watched the church's language about sin shift dramatically over my years in ministry, from the seminary classroom, from hospital visits to Sunday morning pulpits. Where previous generations spoke plainly, even boldly, about sin, iniquity, and transgression, using the very words Scripture itself employs, many contemporary Christians now speak in far vaguer, more therapeutic terms about brokenness, woundedness, or struggles. We have traded the sharp precision of biblical vocabulary for the softer, more palatable language of pop psychology. We describe people as "going through a hard time" rather than as rebels against God. We speak of "making mistakes" rather than violating God's holy law.

This linguistic shift is not merely semantic; it reflects a profound theological shift with devastating consequences. When we lose the biblical category of sin in all its horrifying reality, we inevitably lose the biblical solution of redemption in all its glorious sufficiency. The diagnosis determines the treatment. If we are merely wounded, then what we need is healing, perhaps some counseling, some time, some therapeutic intervention. If we are merely confused or misguided, then what we need is education, better information, clearer thinking, and more accurate data. But if we are sinners, rebels against the holy God, deserving of His wrath, enslaved to sin, spiritually dead in our trespasses, then what we desperately need is not therapy or education, but a Savior. We need someone to rescue us from the tyrant we cannot overthrow, to pay the debt we cannot pay, to satisfy the justice we have violated, and to give us the life we do not possess.

The Glory of Redemption

This brings us to the third pillar: Redemption. If the story ended with the fall, we would have no hope. But God, being rich in mercy, intervened. Before pronouncing the curses, before driving Adam and Eve from the garden, He promised that the seed of the woman would crush the serpent's head (Genesis 3:15). This first gospel proclamation set in motion the grand drama of redemption that would unfold across the pages of Scripture and reach its climax at Calvary.

Redemption addresses every aspect of what sin corrupted. Where sin brought spiritual death, redemption brings spiritual life. Where sin enslaved the will, redemption liberates. Where sin corrupted the affections, redemption reorders our loves. Where sin fractured relationships, redemption reconciles them. Where sin subjected creation to futility, redemption promises new heavens and a new earth.

The heart of redemption is the person and work of Jesus Christ. He is the second Adam, who succeeded where the first Adam failed. He is the promised seed who crushed the serpent's head. He is the perfect image of the invisible God who restores the image of God in fallen humanity. He is the mediator who reconciles us to God, the sacrifice who satisfied divine justice, the victor who conquered sin and death.

Paul draws the parallel explicitly: "For as by a man came death, by a man has come also the resurrection of the dead. For as in Adam all die, so also in Christ shall all be made alive" (1 Corinthians 15:21-22). Adam's sin plunged the human race into death. Christ's obedience brings life to all who are united to Him by faith.

This union with Christ stands at the center of Reformed theology's understanding of redemption. We are not merely forgiven sinners who receive Christ's benefits while remaining fundamentally unchanged. We are united to Christ Himself, joined to Him in such a vital way that His death becomes our death, His resurrection becomes our resurrection, His righteousness becomes our righteousness, His life becomes our life.

Paul could say, "I have been crucified with Christ. It is no longer I who live, but Christ who lives in me. And the life I now live in the flesh I live by faith in the Son of God, who loved me and gave himself for me" (Galatians 2:20). This is not metaphorical language or pious exaggeration. It describes the reality of our union with Christ, purchased at Calvary and applied to us by the Holy Spirit through faith.

Redemption begins with regeneration, the Spirit's sovereign work of giving us new life. We who were dead in trespasses and sins are made alive together with Christ (Ephesians 2:5). This is entirely God's work, not the result of human decision or effort. "It is the Spirit who gives life; the flesh is no help at all" (John 6:63). The Spirit awakens us from spiritual death, opens our blind eyes to see Christ's beauty, softens our hard hearts to believe the gospel, and unites us to Christ.

This regenerating work produces faith, which is itself a gift of God (Ephesians 2:8). Through faith we receive justification, the legal declaration that we are righteous in God's sight on the basis of Christ's perfect righteousness credited to us. This justification is not based on our works, our moral improvement, or our religious performance. It is based entirely on Christ's finished work, received through faith alone.

I have spent countless hours explaining justification by faith alone to students and congregation members. It remains one of the most glorious and liberating truths in all of Scripture, yet it continues to be misunderstood even by sincere believers. We are justified not by being made inherently righteous but by being declared righteous, not by our obedience but by Christ's obedience, not by what we do but by what Christ did.

Paul labors this point throughout his epistles because he understands its crucial importance: "For we hold that one is justified by faith apart from works of the law" (Romans 3:28).

"And to the one who does not work but believes in him who justifies the ungodly, his faith is counted as righteousness" (Romans 4:5). "Yet we know that a person is not justified by works of the law but through faith in Jesus Christ, so we also have believed in Christ Jesus, in order to be justified by faith in Christ and not by works of the law, because by works of the law no one will be justified" (Galatians 2:16).

This doctrine liberates us from the crushing burden of trying to earn God's favor through our performance. We stand before God clothed in Christ's righteousness, not our own. Our acceptance by God does not fluctuate based on our daily spiritual temperature. It remains secure because it rests on Christ's perfect work, not our imperfect efforts.

But justification does not standalone. God does not merely declare us righteous and leave us unchanged. He also sanctifies us, progressively conforming us to the image of Christ through the Spirit's ongoing work in our lives. Sanctification is the process by which we actually become in practice what we already are in position: holy, righteous, conformed to Christ.

Paul writes, "And we all, with unveiled face, beholding the glory of the Lord, are being transformed into the same image from one degree of glory to another. For this comes from the Lord who is the Spirit" (2 Corinthians 3:18). This transformation is certain but gradual, assured but not yet complete. We are being sanctified, present progressive tense, indicating ongoing action.

The framework of Creation, Fall, and Redemption illuminates this sanctification process. We are being restored to the glory for which we were created, the image of God that sin corrupted. We are being delivered from the bondage of sin that enslaved us. We are being renewed in knowledge, righteousness, and holiness after the image of our Creator (Colossians 3:10).

This sanctification is both God's work and ours. The same Paul who declared that we are God's workmanship created in Christ Jesus for good works (Ephesians 2:10) also commanded believers to work out their salvation with fear and trembling, for it is God who works in them both to will and to work for His good pleasure (Philippians 2:12-13). We actively pursue holiness, mortifying sin and cultivating virtue, yet we do so in dependence on the Spirit who empowers our efforts.

I have watched many believers struggle with this tension between divine sovereignty and human responsibility in sanctification. Some become passive, waiting for God to change them without engaging in spiritual disciplines or fighting against sin. Others become frantic, trying to manufacture their own transformation through sheer willpower and religious activity. Both miss the biblical balance.

The Puritans spoke helpfully of our "acting faith upon our union with Christ." We draw upon Christ's resurrection power, reckon ourselves dead to sin and alive to God in Christ Jesus, put off the old self and put on the new self. These are real actions we take, yet they are only possible because we are united to Christ and indwelt by His Spirit. Apart from Him we can do nothing (John 15:5), but in Him we can do all things (Philippians 4:13).

Redemption also includes adoption, that glorious truth that we are not merely servants but sons, not merely pardoned criminals but beloved children. "But when the fullness of time had come, God sent forth his Son, born of woman, born under the law, to redeem those who were under the law, so that we might receive adoption as sons. And because you are sons, God has sent the Spirit of his Son into our hearts, crying, 'Abba! Father!'" (Galatians 4:4-6).

This changes everything about how we relate to God. We do not approach Him as slaves cringing before a tyrant, but as children running to a loving Father. We do not serve Him out of fear of punishment but out of love and gratitude. We do not obey to earn His favor, but because we already have His favor through Christ.

I remember counseling a young man who had grown up in a legalistic church environment where God was presented primarily as an angry judge waiting to condemn him for the slightest failure. The doctrine of adoption transformed his entire Christian experience. When he grasped that God was his Father, that he was a beloved son, that his standing before God was secure in Christ, his spiritual life blossomed. He began to pursue holiness not from fear but from love, not to earn acceptance but because he already possessed it.

Redemption will reach its consummation in glorification, when Christ returns and transforms our bodies of humiliation to be like His glorious body (Philippians 3:21). Then we will be completely freed from sin's presence, fully conformed to Christ's image, perfectly restored to the glory for which we were created. Death itself, the last enemy, will be destroyed (1 Corinthians 15:26).

The biblical vision of the new heavens and new earth is not an ethereal, disembodied existence floating on clouds. It is glorified physical existence in a renewed creation where righteousness dwells. The tree of life that stood in Eden will be restored in the New Jerusalem (Revelation 22:2). The cultural mandate to fill the earth and subdue it will reach its perfect fulfillment as we reign with Christ forever.

This hope shapes how we live now. We are not merely waiting to escape Earth for heaven. We are anticipating the day when heaven comes to earth, when God's dwelling place is with man, when He will wipe away every tear and death shall be no more (Revelation 21:3-4). This gives significance to our present labors. Our work in the Lord is not in vain (1 Corinthians 15:58). What we build for God's glory in this age will somehow carry over into the age to come.

Living in Light of This Framework

How then shall we live? How does understanding Creation, Fall, and Redemption shape our daily existence as believers?

First, it shapes our identity. We are not who the world says we are. We are not defined by our sexuality, our ethnicity, our political affiliation, our career, our possessions, or our achievements. We are image bearers of God, fallen sinners, and redeemed children of God in Christ. This identity remains stable regardless of circumstances.

I have watched our culture's obsession with identity intensify over recent decades. Everyone is searching for an identity that provides meaning, significance, and belonging. The secular world offers identities based on race, gender, sexual orientation, or political ideology. These identities promise fulfillment but deliver division, anxiety, and confusion because they are based on shifting foundations.

The Christian's identity rests on the unchanging truth of who God says we are. In Christ, we are chosen, adopted, justified, sanctified, and sealed for the day of redemption. These truths do not fluctuate based on our feelings or circumstances. They anchor us in the storms of life.

This identity also frees us from the exhausting project of self-creation. We do not have to construct our own identity through our choices and self-expression. God has declared who we are. We simply receive and live out this given identity. This is liberation, not oppression; freedom grounded in truth rather than slavery to self-invention.

Second, this framework shapes our understanding of discipleship. Following Jesus is not merely about behavior modification or religious performance. It is about being transformed from one degree of glory to another, being conformed to the image of Christ, being restored to what we were created to be.

Discipleship involves putting off the old self that belongs to our former manner of life and putting on the new self, created after the likeness of God in true righteousness and holiness (Ephesians 4:22-24). This is not superficial change but deep, Spirit-wrought transformation that touches every dimension of our being.

This means addressing specific sins, cultivating specific virtues, developing spiritual disciplines, and growing in grace and knowledge. It means serious engagement with Scripture, regular prayer, faithful participation in the life of the church, and the deliberate pursuit of holiness. These are the means of grace through which the Spirit works to sanctify us.

But it also means understanding that this transformation is not just individual but communal. We were not created for isolation but for relationships. The church is not an optional add-on to Christian faith but the body of Christ, the community of the redeemed where we grow together in maturity.

I have watched the Western church struggle with rampant individualism that treats faith as a private matter between the individual and God. This contradicts the biblical vision of corporate life in Christ. We need each other. We are members of one another (Romans 12:5). What affects one part of the body affects the whole body. We grow together, or not at all.

Third, this framework shapes our engagement with culture. We live as exiles and sojourners in a fallen world, citizens of a heavenly kingdom who are called to seek the welfare of the earthly cities where God has placed us (1 Peter 2:11; Jeremiah 29:7).

We cannot retreat into isolated Christian ghettos, abandoning culture to the forces of darkness. God created this world and declared it good. Though fallen, it remains His world, and Christ has commissioned us to make disciples of all nations. We engage culture with the gospel, seeking to win people to Christ and to see His lordship acknowledged in every sphere of life.

Neither can we naively embrace culture as if the Fall had never happened. We recognize that cultures are always mixed, containing both common grace goods that reflect the residual image-bearing and corruptions that reflect the fall. We affirm what is true, good, and beautiful wherever we find it, while confronting what is false, evil, and ugly.

This requires wisdom and discernment. We must understand both Scripture and culture, knowing what God's Word says and how to apply it to the particular challenges of our time and place. We must be as wise as serpents and innocent as doves (Matthew 10:16).

I have ministered through massive cultural shifts over the past several decades. The sexual revolution, the rise of militant secularism, the explosion of digital technology, the breakdown of family structures, the politicization of nearly everything, these have created challenges the church must address. We require Christians who grasp the cultural moment and discern how God's people should respond (1 Chronicles 12:32).

Fourth, this framework shapes our response to suffering. We do not suffer as those who have no hope (1 Thessalonians 4:13). We understand that suffering entered the world through sin, that this present world is not as it should be, and that we await a restoration that will reverse the curse.

This gives us patience in trials. Our light and momentary afflictions are achieving for us an eternal weight of glory beyond all comparison (2 Corinthians 4:17). We do not minimize suffering or pretend it doesn't hurt. But we see it in perspective, recognizing that it is temporary, purposeful, and ultimately subject to God's sovereign plan.

Walking with my wife through her battle with cancer deepened my understanding of these truths in ways no amount of academic study could achieve. We experienced the reality of living in a fallen world where bodies break down. We also experienced the sustaining grace of God, the comfort of the gospel, the hope of resurrection, and the love of the body of Christ. Theology that had been primarily intellectual became intensely personal.

The framework of Creation, Fall, and Redemption gave us categories for understanding what we faced. This was not God's original design. He did not create cancer. It is an intruder, an enemy, a consequence of living in a fallen world under the curse. Yet God in His sovereignty was using even this evil for His purposes, conforming us to the image of Christ, displaying His glory through our faith in trials, and reminding us that our true hope lies not in this age but in the age to come.

Fifth, this framework shapes our view of marriage and family. Marriage is not a human invention or a mere social construct. It is a creation ordinance established by God before the Fall. The union of one man and one woman in lifelong covenant reflects God's design for human flourishing and points forward to the ultimate marriage between Christ and His church.

The Fall corrupted marriage, introducing conflict, selfishness, and division. Redemption restores marriage, enabling husbands and wives to love each other as Christ loved the church. This does not mean Christian marriages are free from struggles. We are being sanctified, not yet glorified. But it does mean we have resources for navigating those struggles that the world lacks.

Children are not burdens or obstacles to self-fulfillment but blessings and heritage from the Lord (Psalm 127:3). Raising them in the discipline and instruction of the Lord is not optional but commanded (Ephesians 6:4). Family discipleship is not the church's job outsourced to parents, but the parents' job supported by the church.

I have watched the secular vision of marriage and family infiltrate even the church. Marriages treated as temporary arrangements to be dissolved when they stop being fulfilling. Children viewed as lifestyle choices to be planned around careers and personal goals. Family time sacrificed on the altar of individual pursuits.

The biblical vision offers something radically different. Marriage as a covenant, not a contract. Children as gifts, not burdens. Family as the primary context for spiritual formation. This vision swims against the cultural current, which makes it all the more necessary to articulate clearly and live faithfully.

Sixth, this framework shapes our work and vocation. Work is not a curse resulting from the fall. God placed Adam in the garden to work it and keep it before sin entered the world. Work is part of God's good design for human life, a way we exercise dominion, cultivate creation's potential, and serve others.

The fall corrupted work, making it toilsome and frustrating. We experience the sting of thorns and thistles, the vanity of labors that seem to accomplish nothing lasting, the injustice of broken economic systems that exploit workers.

Redemption redeems work. In Christ, our labor is not in vain. We work not ultimately for human employers but for the Lord, who will reward us (Colossians 3:23-24). Whatever we do, whether eating or drinking or working, we do to the glory of God (1 Corinthians 10:31).

This transforms ordinary work into worship. The accountant crunching numbers, the janitor cleaning floors, the salesman making calls, and the engineer designing systems, all can offer their work as service to God and neighbor. There is no sacred-secular divide in the Christian worldview. All lawful work done to God's glory is sacred.

I have counseled many believers who struggled to find meaning in their work. They labored at jobs that seemed insignificant compared to "full-time ministry." But this reflects a faulty theology. The pastor preaching on Sunday and the plumber fixing pipes on Monday both serve the Lord in their callings. Both exercise gifts God gave. Both contribute to human flourishing. Both can glorify God through faithful service.

Seventh, this framework shapes our stewardship of creation. The creation mandate to fill the earth and subdue it, to exercise dominion over God's world, was given before the Fall (Genesis 1:28). We are called to be wise stewards of the resources God has entrusted to us.

The fall subjected creation to futility, introducing death and decay. Creation itself groans in the pains of childbirth, awaiting its liberation from bondage to corruption (Romans 8:19-22). This means creation needs redeeming care, not exploitative abuse. We are caretakers, not owners.

Redemption promises new heavens and a new earth. This is not escapism that treats the present world as disposable. We will inhabit a renewed physical creation, not a disembodied heaven. What we do now in caring for creation, developing its potential, and establishing just systems matters eternally.

This requires balance. We reject both the worship of creation that characterizes much environmentalism and the exploitation of creation that characterizes much industrialism. Creation belongs to God, reflects His glory, and deserves our respectful stewardship. But creation exists for God's purposes and human flourishing, not as an end in itself.

The Gospel in Daily Life

Everything I have written comes down to this: the gospel must be lived, not merely believed. The framework of Creation, Fall, and Redemption is not abstract theology but living truth that transforms how we think, feel, and act in the ordinary moments of daily existence.

When you wake in the morning, you wake as one created in God's image, fallen into sin, and redeemed by Christ. This identity shapes everything that follows. You are not your own. You were bought with a price (1 Corinthians 6:19-20). Your life belongs to the One who created you and redeemed you.

When you face temptation, you face it as one who has died to sin and been raised to new life in Christ. Sin no longer has dominion over you (Romans 6:14). You are not helpless before its power. The same Spirit who raised Jesus from the dead dwells in you, empowering you to put to death the deeds of the body (Romans 8:11-13).

When you interact with others, you interact with fellow image bearers, some redeemed and some not, all deserving respect because of their created dignity, all needing the grace that can only be found in Christ. You love your neighbor not because they are lovable but because God commands it and Christ enables it.

When you work, you work not primarily for human approval or financial gain, but as unto the Lord. Your motivation is gratitude for redemption; your standard is excellence that reflects your Creator; your goal is to glorify God and serve others.

When you suffer, you suffer not as those without hope, but as those who know the end of the story. This world is not our home. We are awaiting a city with foundations, whose designer and builder is God (Hebrews 11:10). Our present sufferings are not worth comparing with the glory that will be revealed in us (Romans 8:18).

When you gather with other believers for worship, you gather as the redeemed community, the bride of Christ, the temple of the Holy Spirit. You celebrate redemption accomplished and anticipate redemption consummated. You encourage one another and build one another up, spurring each other on to love and good works.

I have spent my life studying, teaching, and proclaiming these truths because I am convinced they matter more than anything else. The world offers countless competing narratives about who we are, where we came from, what went wrong, and how to fix it. But only the biblical story rings true to reality; only the biblical diagnosis accurately identifies the disease; only the biblical solution actually heals.

We are created for glory. This gives us dignity, purpose, and hope. We are broken by sin. This explains our misery, our moral failures, and our desperate need. We are redeemed by

Christ. This provides salvation, transformation, and ultimate restoration.

These three truths form the skeleton of biblical Christianity. Everything else hangs on this framework. Remove it and the whole structure collapses. Maintain it, and everything makes sense.

This is why I began this book with Genesis 1 through 3. These opening chapters provide the foundation for all that follows. They explain the origin of humanity, the entrance of sin, and the promise of redemption. They introduce themes that echo throughout Scripture and reach their fulfillment in Christ.

My prayer is that through these pages you have come to see these ancient texts not as outdated myths but as a living truth that speaks directly to the deepest questions of human existence. I pray you understand more clearly who you are as one created in God's image, fallen into sin, and redeemed by Christ. I pray you live more faithfully in light of these truths, glorifying God and enjoying Him forever.

Chapter Fourteen

Foundations for a Faithful Life in a Confused World

The truths of Genesis 1 through 3 are not relics of a bygone age. They are living realities that speak with urgent clarity to the moral and spiritual confusion of our day. Every challenge the modern church faces, every cultural battle we must navigate, every question about identity and meaning, and purpose finds its answer in these opening chapters of Scripture.

I write these words not as a detached scholar but as one who has walked through fire and emerged with his faith intact. My years as a Marine taught me that clarity about mission and identity means the difference between life and death. My years as a pastor showed me that people perish for lack of knowledge, that confusion about foundational truths leads to devastation in daily life. My time as a seminary professor convinced me that the next generation of believers desperately needs solid ground beneath their feet.

The ground is shifting beneath us. What was unthinkable a generation ago is now mainstream. What was universally acknowledged as truth is now dismissed as bigotry. What was celebrated as virtue is now condemned as vice, and what was recognized as vice is now celebrated as virtue. The culture has not merely drifted from biblical moorings but has actively cut the anchor lines and sailed into waters where no lighthouse guides and no compass points true north.

Into this chaos, Genesis speaks with thunderous authority. God created humanity male and female. God instituted marriage as a covenant union between one man and one woman. God placed humanity in a good creation with meaningful work and clear boundaries. God gave commands and attached consequences to disobedience. God responded to sin with judgment and with grace. God promised redemption through a coming Seed who would crush the serpent's head.

These truths equip believers to navigate a confused world. They provide the framework for understanding ourselves, our relationships, our purpose, and our hope. They give us the courage to stand when others fall, the clarity to speak when others stumble, and the compassion to minister when others despair.

The Crisis of Identity

Perhaps no area of modern life demonstrates greater confusion than the question of identity. Who am I? What defines me? Can I choose my own identity or is it given to me? These questions torment our generation.

The world offers answers that shift like sand. You are whoever you feel you are. Your identity is fluid, self-determined, subject to revision. Your body is raw material to be molded according to your inner sense of self. Gender is a social construct. Biology is irrelevant. Feelings trump facts.

This ideology produces misery. Young people who embrace it find not freedom but bondage, not clarity but confusion, not peace but turmoil. Suicide rates soar. Depression becomes epidemic. Anxiety disorders multiply. The promised liberation delivers only deeper slavery.

Genesis offers a radically different answer. Your identity is not self-constructed but God-given. You are a creature made in the image of God. This is the bedrock truth that defines everything else about you. Your value does not depend on your feelings, your achievements, your appearance, or your popularity. Your worth is intrinsic, conferred by your Creator, unchangeable regardless of circumstances.

God made humanity male and female. This is not arbitrary but intentional. Biological sex is not assigned at birth but recognized at birth. It is woven into every cell of your body, expressed in your chromosomes, manifested in your anatomy. Maleness and femaleness are gifts from God, aspects of His good design, reflections of His creative wisdom.

The current cultural confusion about gender represents a rebellion against God's created order. When someone claims to be trapped in the wrong body, they are declaring war on the body God gave them. When someone insists that feelings about gender override biological reality, they are rejecting God's authority over creation. When someone demands that society accommodate their self-perception regardless of truth, they are placing self on the throne that belongs to God alone.

This is not compassion but cruelty. True compassion speaks truth in love. True compassion acknowledges that we are fallen creatures prone to confusion and self-deception. True compassion points people to their God-given identity rather than affirming their feelings-based self-perception.

As a pastor, I counseled people struggling with same-sex attraction. Others simply felt lost, uncertain who they were or what their life meant. In every case, the path to peace began with Genesis. You are created in God's image. God made you male or female. Your body is not a mistake. Your feelings, however powerful, are not infallible guides to truth.

Reformed theology reminds us of a fundamental truth that runs counter to our culture's obsession with self-discovery: sin affects every part of our being, including, perhaps especially, our self-perception. Total depravity means that no aspect of our humanity remains untouched by the Fall. We cannot trust our feelings to tell us who we are. This is not merely a matter of occasional emotional confusion; it touches the very core of our being. Our hearts, as Jeremiah tells us with unflinching clarity, are deceitful above all things and desperately sick (Jeremiah 17:9). Left to ourselves, we will construct identities that serve our rebellion against God while convincing ourselves we are pursuing authentic self-expression. We need an external, objective standard, something outside ourselves that speaks with authority greater than our fluctuating emotions, and that standard is God's inerrant revealed Word in Scripture.

The gospel addresses identity confusion not by validating our feelings but by anchoring our identity in Christ. This is the fundamental shift that changes everything. If you are a believer, your primary identity is not your sexuality, your gender feelings, your race, your nationality, or your occupation. These may describe aspects of your earthly existence, but they do not define who you are at the deepest level. Your primary identity, the truth that supersedes all other self-descriptions, is that you are in Christ. You are a child of God, adopted into His family through the finished work of the Son. You are united to Christ by faith, a union as real as the branch's connection to the vine. You are indwelt by the Holy Spirit, who bears witness with your spirit that you belong to God. You are destined for glory; your future is secured by the One who began a good work in you and will bring it to completion.

This identity transforms everything. When temptation whispers that you should indulge feelings contrary to God's design, you remember that you died to sin and were raised to new life. When confusion clouds your self-understanding, you return to the solid ground of what God says about you. When the culture pressures you to affirm lies, you stand on truth because your identity is secure in Christ, not dependent on cultural approval.

Believers must speak these truths with both clarity and compassion. We do not hate people struggling with identity confusion. We love them enough to tell them the truth. We do not despise those trapped in sin. We remember that we too were slaves to various passions and pleasures until God's mercy saved us. We do not condescend to those blinded by cultural lies. We recognize that apart from God's grace, we would believe the same lies.

But neither can we compromise. The stakes are too high. When we affirm someone's false identity, we participate in their self-destruction. When we use preferred pronouns that contradict biological reality, we bear false witness. When we celebrate what God calls sin, we make ourselves His enemies.

The church must be a place where truth and love coexist, where people hear both the bad news of their sin and the good news of God's grace, where biblical standards are maintained without self-righteousness, where sinners find not condemnation but the call to repentance and faith.

The Sanctity of Human Life

Genesis establishes the foundation for the biblical view of human life. Because humanity bears God's image, human life is sacred. To take innocent human life is to assault God's image and to commit an act of cosmic treason. This truth has profound implications for how we view abortion, euthanasia, capital punishment, war, and the value of the weak and vulnerable.

The modern abortion holocaust stems from rejecting Genesis. When you deny that humanity is created in God's image, you remove the foundation for human rights and human dignity. Life becomes valuable only if someone wants it, only if it meets certain standards of quality, only if it does not inconvenience others. The unborn child is no longer a person but a clump of cells, no longer a gift from God but a problem to be solved, no longer a life to be protected but a choice to be made.

The language of choice itself reveals the bankruptcy of pro-abortion arguments. The choice in question is whether another human being should live or die. But no one has the right to make that choice. God alone is the giver and taker of life. He alone decides who lives and who dies, when life begins and when it ends. To arrogate that authority to ourselves is to play God, and we are not qualified for the role.

I have known women who had abortions and were haunted by guilt for decades afterward. The culture tells them it was just a medical procedure, no different from removing a tumor.

But their hearts know better. They killed their children. They cooperated in an act of violence against the most innocent and vulnerable members of the human family. The guilt they feel is appropriate because they truly are guilty.

But the gospel speaks to this guilt. Christ died for sins, including the sin of abortion. There is forgiveness at the cross for those who repent and believe. There is cleansing for the bloodguilt that stains the conscience. There is restoration for those who have destroyed life. God's grace is greater than our sin, and His mercy triumphs over judgment.

The church must be a place where post-abortive women can find healing. We do not minimize their sin, but neither do we make it unforgivable. We point them to the Savior who receives sinners, who transforms the guilty into the righteous, who makes all things new.

At the same time, the church must actively oppose abortion. We cannot be silent while millions of image bearers are slaughtered. We must speak for those who cannot speak for themselves. We must plead for the unborn. We must work for laws that protect life. We must support alternatives to abortion. We must expose the lies of the abortion industry. We must call abortion what it is: murder.

This will cost us. The culture despises those who defend the unborn. We will be called extremists, misogynists, enemies of women's rights. We will face opposition, ridicule, and perhaps persecution. But truth does not depend on popularity, and righteousness is not determined by majority vote. We must obey God rather than men.

The same principles apply to euthanasia and assisted suicide. Life is a gift from God, not ours to dispose of at will. Suffering does not make life worthless. The elderly, the disabled, and the terminally ill bear God's image just as fully as the young and healthy. To end life because it has become burdensome is to reject God's sovereignty and to deny the sanctity of human existence.

My wife's battle with cancer taught me things about suffering I could never have learned otherwise. I watched her endure pain that would have broken most people. I saw her faith tested in the furnace of affliction. I witnessed her dependence on God deepen as her body weakened. Those months were agony, but they were also holy. God met us in that valley. He sustained us by His grace. He taught us truths about His faithfulness that prosperity could never reveal.

Had we chosen to end her life prematurely, we would have missed those lessons. We would have cut short the sanctifying work God was doing in both of us. We would have robbed ourselves of precious time together. We would have sinned against God by taking into our own hands what belonged to Him alone.

The culture calls euthanasia compassion. It is not. Compassion does not kill. Compassion cares for the suffering, sits with the dying, provides comfort and dignity until natural death comes. Compassion recognizes that every moment of life has value because every human being bears God's image from conception until natural death.

Marriage and Sexual Morality

Genesis 2 establishes God's design for marriage: one man and one woman united in covenant for life. This design has been under sustained assault for decades. First came the sexual revolution with its message that sex outside marriage was liberating rather than destructive. Then came no-fault divorce, making covenant breaking easy and socially acceptable. Then came cohabitation as a mainstream practice. Then came the redefinition of marriage to include same-sex couples. Now comes the normalization of polyamory (practice of engaging in multiple sexual relationships), transgenderism in marriage, and every conceivable deviation from God's design.

Each step away from Genesis has brought misery. Broken homes devastate children. Sexual promiscuity spreads disease and emotional trauma. Pornography enslaves millions and destroys marriages. Divorce ruins families. Same-sex unions cannot provide what God intended marriage to accomplish. The sexual chaos of our age is not freedom but bondage, not enlightenment but darkness, not progress but regression to pre-Christian paganism.

The church must recover and proclaim God's good design for sexuality and marriage. Sex is a gift from God, intended for one man and one woman within the covenant of marriage. This is not prudish repression but wise protection. God's boundaries around sex are not arbitrary restrictions but guardrails that keep us from driving off a cliff.

Sexual sin is serious because it strikes at the heart of God's design for humanity. When Paul warns against sexual immorality, he grounds his warning in creation: "Do you not know that your bodies are members of Christ?" (1 Corinthians 6:15). Sexual sin joins what should not be joined, profanes what should be sacred, and treats as common what God has made holy.

The gospel addresses sexual sin the same way it addresses all sin: by declaring us guilty and then declaring us righteous through faith in Christ. The sexually immoral, the adulterers, the homosexuals, the greedy, the drunkards will not inherit the kingdom of God. "And such were some of you. But you were washed, you were sanctified, you were justified in the name of the Lord Jesus Christ and by the Spirit of our God" (1 Corinthians 6:11).

This text demolishes two errors. First, it demolishes the error that sexual sin is unforgivable or that certain sexual sinners cannot change. The Corinthian church included former homosexuals, former adulterers, former fornicators. They were washed, sanctified, justified. Christ's blood cleanses from all sin, including sexual sin. His power breaks every chain, including the chains of sexual bondage.

Second, it demolishes the error that sexual orientation or gender identity defines who you are in an unchangeable way. Some Corinthians had engaged in homosexual practice. Paul does not say they will always be homosexuals who must manage their orientation. He says they were homosexuals but are no longer so. Their identity changed when Christ saved them. They are now in Christ, and that identity supersedes and transforms their sexual self-understanding.

The church must hold out this hope. People trapped in sexual sin need to hear that change is possible, that Christ transforms desires as well as behavior, that the gospel reaches into the deepest parts of our broken sexuality and makes us new. This is not quick or easy. Sanctification is a lifelong process. But it is real, and the Holy Spirit accomplishes what we could never accomplish on our own.

At the same time, the church must maintain God's standards. We cannot bless what God curses. We cannot call marriage what God does not call marriage. We cannot affirm as good what God declares sinful. When culture demands that we celebrate sexual immorality, we must refuse. When laws compel us to participate in what violates our conscience, we must obey God rather than men.

This will cost us dearly. Christian business owners have already been fined, sued, and driven out of business for refusing to participate in same-sex ceremonies. Christian adoption agencies have been forced to close rather than place children with same-sex couples. Christian counselors have lost their licenses for refusing to affirm transgender ideology. The pressure will only increase.

But we must not compromise. The cost of compromise is greater than the cost of faithfulness. When we compromise biblical truth to avoid cultural backlash, we lose our saltiness and become worthless (Matthew 5:13). When we accommodate lies to maintain respectability, we forfeit our witness. When we seek the approval of the world more than the approval of God, we prove ourselves unworthy of the kingdom.

The Meaning of Suffering

Genesis 3 explains why we suffer. Sin brought the curse into the world. Pain in childbirth, toil in work, conflict in marriage, sickness, aging, death, all these flow from the Fall. The world is broken because humanity broke covenant with God. We groan under the weight of our rebellion and its consequences.

This truth contradicts the prosperity gospel, which promises health, wealth, and happiness to all who have enough faith. The prosperity gospel is a damnable heresy that misrepresents God, misunderstands the gospel, and devastates those who believe it. When suffering comes, as it inevitably does, prosperity preachers leave their followers with only two explanations: either you lack faith or God has failed you. Both conclusions are false and spiritually ruinous.

Reformed theology offers a radically different understanding of suffering. Suffering is not evidence of God's failure or our faithlessness. Suffering is the normal experience of believers in a fallen world. Jesus promised His disciples that in this world they would have tribulation (John 16:33). Paul taught that through many tribulations we must enter the kingdom of God (Acts 14:22). Peter reminded scattered believers that suffering was their calling (1 Peter 2:21).

Suffering serves divine purposes. God uses suffering to conform us to the image of Christ. He uses it to expose idols, to deepen dependence, to cultivate patience, to produce character, to increase hope (Romans 5:3-5). He uses suffering to discipline His children, to purge sin, to refine faith like gold tested in fire.

My years as a Marine prepared me for some aspects of suffering. I learned to endure hardship, to push through pain, to complete the mission regardless of the cost. But military training could not prepare me for watching my wife waste away from cancer. No amount of mental toughness helped when I sat by her bedside and watched her suffer. No battlefield experience equipped me to face the possibility of losing her.

What upheld me was not rigid endurance but biblical truth. I knew that God is sovereign over disease and death. I knew that He could heal my wife if He chose, but I also knew He might not, and His refusal would not mean He loved us less or failed in His promises. I knew that our suffering was not meaningless but served purposes beyond my understanding. I knew that nothing could separate us from the love of God in Christ Jesus our Lord (Romans 8:38-39).

These truths did not make the suffering easy, but they made it bearable. They gave me a framework for understanding what we were enduring. They reminded me that our present circumstances were temporary and our future hope was certain. They anchored me when waves of grief and fear threatened to sweep me away.

The church must teach believers how to suffer well. We must prepare people for trials before the trials come. We must ground them in biblical truth about God's sovereignty, human sin, divine purposes, and eternal hope. We must teach them to lament, to cry out to God in honest anguish, to wrestle with hard questions without abandoning faith.

We must also teach believers how to minister to the suffering. Job's friends started well; they sat with him in silence for seven days (Job 2:13). They failed when they opened their mouths and offered false comfort and bad theology. The suffering need presence more than explanations, companionship more than clichés, prayers more than platitudes.

When believers suffer, we should weep with those who weep (Romans 12:15). We should bear one another's burdens (Galatians 6:2). We should provide practical help, meals, childcare, financial assistance, whatever meets the need. We should point people to Christ and His sufferings, reminding them that our God is not distant from pain but entered into it fully when He took on flesh and went to the cross.

Work, Calling, and Human Flourishing

Genesis reveals that work existed before the Fall. God placed Adam in the garden to work it and keep it (Genesis 2:15). Work is not a curse but a blessing, not punishment for sin but part of God's good design for human flourishing. The curse did not introduce work but made work frustrating, adding thorns and thistles, sweat and toil to what had been joyful.

The modern world has a distorted view of work. Some see work as a necessary evil, something to endure so they can get to the weekend, a means to an end rather than meaningful in itself. Others make work an idol, finding their identity and worth in career success, sacrificing family and health on the altar of professional achievement. Still others despise work altogether, viewing it as oppression, seeking to do as little as possible while extracting maximum benefit from the system.

Scripture presents a different vision. Work is a gift from God, an opportunity to exercise dominion over creation, to serve others, to provide for your family, and to glorify God. Work has intrinsic value, regardless of whether it is prestigious or lucrative. The farmer glorifies God in planting and harvesting. The mechanic glorifies God in repairing engines. The teacher glorifies God in instructing children. The homemaker glorifies God by creating a haven of order and peace.

The doctrine of vocation teaches that God calls people to various occupations and that all legitimate work done for God's glory is sacred. You do not need to be a pastor or missionary to serve God vocationally. You serve Him as an accountant, a nurse, a carpenter, a salesperson, a janitor. Whatever you do, work heartily, as for the Lord and not for men (Colossians 3:23).

This understanding of work transforms daily life. Monday morning is not the dreary aftermath of the weekend, but an opportunity for worship. The office is not merely a place to earn a paycheck but a field for ministry. Difficult bosses and frustrating coworkers become opportunities to display patience, kindness, and integrity. Excellence in work becomes an act of devotion to God rather than a strategy for personal advancement.

The Fall distorted work but did not destroy its meaning. Work remains good even though it is hard. God redeems work just as He redeems every other aspect of life. In Christ, your labor is not in vain (1 Corinthians 15:58). What you do for the Lord has eternal significance, even if the world never notices.

The church must equip believers to see their work as ministry. We must teach people to pray about their jobs, to seek God's guidance in their careers, to view their workplaces as mission fields. We must help Christians think biblically about work-life balance, about ambition, about money, and about integrity in business dealings. We must model healthy attitudes toward work ourselves, neither idolizing productivity nor disdaining honest labor.

Stewardship of Creation

Genesis 1 gives humanity dominion over creation. We are to be fruitful, multiply, fill the earth, and subdue it (Genesis 1:28). This dominion is not exploitation but stewardship. We exercise authority as God's representatives, caring for creation as He would care for it, using resources wisely, protecting what He has made.

The modern environmental movement often errs in two directions. Some treat creation as merely a resource to be exploited with no thought for sustainability or consequences. Strip mines, polluted rivers, extinct species, these represent failures of stewardship. We have not cared for God's creation as we should.

Others elevate creation above humanity, treating animals as having equal rights with people, viewing human presence as inherently destructive, and longing for a return to some imagined pristine state before human civilization. This too is an error. Creation exists for God's glory and human flourishing.

We may use creation's resources. We may alter landscapes. We may domesticate animals. We may develop technology. Humanity is the crown of creation, not an invasive species.

Biblical stewardship navigates between these extremes. We use creation's resources, but not wastefully. We develop technology, but with wisdom. We enjoy the beauty of nature, but do not worship it. We care for animals, but recognize they are not our equals. We work to reduce pollution and protect ecosystems, but not at the cost of human welfare.

The coming new creation should inform our attitude toward environmental issues. God will not abandon this world but will renew it. The earth will be filled with the glory of the Lord as the waters cover the sea (Habakkuk 2:14). This means creation matters. What we do to God's world matters. We are preparing for a renewed earth, not escaping to a disembodied heaven.

At the same time, we must keep environmental concerns in proper perspective. The greatest pollution is not in our rivers but in our hearts. The most urgent crisis is not climate change but human sin. The most devastating destruction is not of forests but of souls. We care about creation, but we care more about the Creator and the people made in His image.

Standing Firm in Babylon

Daniel faced a choice. He could eat the king's food and compromise his convictions, or he could obey God's law and face consequences. He chose faithfulness. He purposed in his heart that he would not defile himself (Daniel 1:8). God honored his courage and blessed his obedience.

Believers today face similar choices. The culture demands that we affirm lies about gender, celebrate sexual immorality, participate in abortion, compromise biblical truth, and remain silent about sin. In many cases, refusing brings real costs: job loss, social ostracism, legal penalties, public vilification.

But we must refuse. We cannot serve two masters. We cannot worship God and mammon. We cannot be faithful to Christ while accommodating the demands of a pagan culture. We must purpose in our hearts that we will not defile ourselves, whatever the cost.

This requires courage. Courage is not the absence of fear, but action in spite of fear. I was afraid many times in combat. I acted anyway because duty demanded it. The mission required it. My fellow Marines depended on it. Fear is natural. Cowardice is sin.

We need courage grounded in theological conviction. We must know what we believe and why we believe it. We must be so convinced of the truth that we would rather suffer than deny it. We must value God's approval more than human approval, eternal reward more than temporal comfort, faithfulness more than safety.

We also need courage supported by the Christian community. Lone Christians often fall under pressure. But when the church stands together, when believers encourage one another, when we remind each other of truth and stiffen each other's resolve, we can endure what would overwhelm us individually.

The early Christians faced far worse than we face. They were thrown to lions, burned as torches, crucified, and beheaded. They lost everything rather than deny Christ. Their courage came from certainty about the resurrection and the reality of eternal life. They knew this world was not their home. They were willing to lose temporal life to gain eternal life.

We need that same eternal perspective. Our citizenship is in heaven (Philippians 3:20). We are exiles and sojourners in this world (1 Peter 2:11). This present age is passing away. A new heaven and a new earth are coming. What we suffer now is nothing compared to the glory that will be revealed.

This perspective does not make us passive. We do not withdraw from culture or abandon our responsibilities as citizens. We engage the culture, speak truth, advocate for justice, work for good laws, serve our neighbors, and seek the welfare of the city where God has placed us (Jeremiah 29:7). But we engage as those whose ultimate allegiance is to God's kingdom, not to any earthly power.

We must be wise as serpents and innocent as doves (Matthew 10:16). We speak truth, but with gentleness and respect (1 Peter 3:15). We contend for the faith, but without becoming quarrelsome or mean-spirited. We stand firm on convictions but treat opponents as people made in God's image who need the gospel. We are warriors but not thugs, advocates but not bullies, truth-tellers but not cruel.

The Call to Holiness

Genesis establishes that God created humanity for a relationship with Himself. Adam and Eve walked with God in the garden in the cool of the day (Genesis 3:8). Sin shattered that fellowship. Redemption restores it. We are called to be holy as God is holy (1 Peter 1:16), to pursue righteousness, to put off the old self and put on the new self (Ephesians 4:22-24).

Holiness is not optional for believers. It is the necessary fruit of genuine faith. Those who are in Christ are new creations (2 Corinthians 5:17). The old has passed away; the new has come. We cannot claim to know God while continuing to walk in darkness (1 John 1:6). We cannot call Jesus Lord while refusing to obey His commands (Luke 6:46).

The Puritan divines understood this better than most modern Christians. They wrote extensively about practical godliness, about mortifying sin, about cultivating virtue, about the daily battle for holiness. They knew that salvation is by grace alone through faith alone, but they also knew that saving faith produces holiness, that justification leads to sanctification, and that those whom God justifies He also sanctifies (Romans 8:30).

We desperately need to recover this emphasis on holiness. The church today is plagued by antinomianism, the error that grace means God no longer cares about obedience. Cheap grace abounds. People claim to be Christians while living like pagans. They attend church but see no need to change their behavior. They profess faith but show no evidence of regeneration.

True grace is not cheap but costly. It cost God His Son. It cost Christ His life. It costs believers the crucifixion of the old self. When Paul says we are saved by grace through faith, not by works (Ephesians 2:8-9), he immediately adds that we are created in Christ Jesus for good works, which God prepared beforehand, that we should walk in them (Ephesians 2:10). Grace produces good works. Faith without works is dead (James 2:17).

Holiness begins with regeneration. The Holy Spirit must give us new hearts before we can live new lives. We cannot manufacture holiness through self-effort or self-discipline. We need the supernatural work of God. But regeneration leads to transformation. We cooperate with the Spirit's sanctifying work through spiritual disciplines, through putting off sin and putting on righteousness, through daily dying to self and living to God.

Holiness requires intentionality. We must be ruthless with sin. Jesus said if your right eye causes you to sin, tear it out (Matthew 5:29). He meant we must be willing to take radical measures to kill sin before it kills us. We cannot coddle pet sins or make peace with besetting sins. We must wage war.

This war involves concrete practices. We flee temptation rather than flirting with it. We avoid situations that weaken our resolve. We fill our minds with truth rather than garbage. We cultivate accountability relationships where others have permission to ask hard questions and challenge us when we stray. We pray for grace to overcome sin. We memorize Scripture to have weapons for spiritual warfare. We confess sin quickly rather than letting it fester. We pursue righteousness as actively as we flee sin.

Holiness is both individual and corporate. I pursue holiness in my personal walk with God. But I also need the church to help me grow in holiness. The church provides teaching that shapes my understanding. It provides accountability that restrains my sin. It provides encouragement that sustains me when I am weary. It provides correction when I go astray. I cannot become holy in isolation. I need the body of Christ.

Hope for the Future

Genesis 3:15 promises that the seed of the woman will crush the serpent's head. This promise found its fulfillment in Christ. He has defeated Satan, sin, and death. He has accomplished redemption. He has made a way for rebels to become children of God.

But the story is not finished. We live between the already and the not yet. Christ has won the victory, but He has not yet consummated His kingdom. Satan is defeated but not yet destroyed. Sin's power is broken but not yet eliminated. Death is conquered but not yet abolished. We wait for Christ's return, when He will make all things new.

This waiting is not passive. We work while we wait. We proclaim the gospel to all nations. We make disciples. We plant churches. We pursue justice. We care for the weak. We resist evil. We live as citizens of the coming kingdom even while we sojourn in a fallen world.

This waiting is filled with hope. Our hope is not wishful thinking but confident expectation grounded in God's promises and Christ's resurrection. Jesus rose from the dead. This is a historical fact, the best-attested event of ancient history. His resurrection guarantees our resurrection. Because He lives, we will live also (John 14:19).

Our hope is not for disembodied existence in an ethereal heaven. Our hope is for bodily resurrection and life in a renewed creation. God will restore what was lost in Eden and more. The new Jerusalem will descend from heaven to earth (Revelation 21:2). God will dwell with His people. He will wipe away every tear. Death will be no more. Mourning, crying, and pain will be no more (Revelation 21:4).

This is the end of the story that began in Genesis 1. God created. Humanity fell. God redeemed. And God will restore. The curse will be lifted. The serpent will be destroyed. The promise of Eden will be fulfilled beyond what Adam and Eve could have imagined.

This hope, this confident, unshakable expectation rooted in God's unchangeable promises and the triumph of Christ's resurrection, sustains believers through every form of suffering, every kind of persecution, and even through the valley of the shadow of death itself. We are not sustained by mere optimism or positive thinking, but by the solid rock of God's Word and the demonstrated power of the empty tomb. When the world threatens to overwhelm us, when circumstances seem to contradict the promises of God, when our faith is tested in the furnace of affliction, this hope anchors our souls.

We know how the story ends. This is not presumption but biblical confidence. We have read the last chapter. We know that evil does not have the final word. We know that suffering is not meaningless. We know that God is sovereignly working all things, even the most painful, confusing, seemingly contradictory things, together for the good of those who love Him and are called according to His purpose (Romans 8:28). This knowledge transforms how we endure. It gives meaning to our struggles. It provides perspective when the present moment feels unbearable.

We know that our labor is not in vain. Every act of obedience, every sacrifice made for Christ's sake, every moment of faithful service; none of it is wasted. Therefore, we can be steadfast, immovable, always abounding in the work of the Lord (1 Corinthians 15:58). We know that our sufferings, these light momentary afflictions that feel so heavy in the present, are producing for us an eternal weight of glory beyond all comparison (2 Corinthians 4:17). The scales are tipped overwhelmingly toward glory. The suffering of this present time cannot even be compared with the glory that is to be revealed to us (Romans 8:18).

We know that the one who began a good work in us will bring it to completion at the day of Jesus Christ (Philippians 1:6). God finishes what He starts. He does not abandon His work halfway through. The God who called us is faithful, and He will surely do it (1 Thessalonians 5:24).

Chapter Fifteen

Foundations That Hold: Living Faithfully in God's Story

The seminary student sat in my office, his face a mixture of frustration and fear. "I believe Genesis is true," he said. "But I feel like I'm standing alone. My professors question it. My friends think I'm anti-science. Even my parents tell me I'm being too rigid. How do I hold onto this when everyone is telling me to let go?"

I understood his struggle more than he knew. I have faced the same pressure throughout my ministry. The temptation to soften Genesis, to make it more palatable, to find an interpretive space that avoids conflict, never goes away. But I have also watched what happens when believers stand firm on these foundational truths. They do not merely survive the cultural chaos. They thrive in it because they know who they are, whose they are, and how their story ends.

This is what I told him, and this is what I want to leave with you as we conclude our time in these three remarkable chapters.

The Story We Need

Genesis 1 through 3 gives us the story that makes sense of everything else. Not just the story of what happened long ago in a garden somewhere in the ancient Near East, but the story of reality itself, the story of how things came to be, why they are broken, and how they will be made whole.

This is the story of a sovereign Creator who spoke worlds into existence by the mere word of His power. Not a distant deity who set things in motion and walked away, but the covenant God who creates with purpose, provides with generosity, and governs with wisdom. He did not need to create. Nothing compelled Him. He created freely, for His glory, because He delights in displaying His perfections through what His hands have made.

This is the story of image-bearers created with dignity, purpose, and responsibility. We are not cosmic accidents or highly evolved animals. We are creatures fashioned deliberately by God, stamped with His image, designed for fellowship with Him and for stewardship over His creation. Male and female He created us, not as interchangeable units but as complementary partners whose union reflects something of His own triune nature. Our embodiment matters. Our sexuality matters. Our work matters. All of it flows from who God made us to be.

This is the story of a catastrophic fall that shattered everything. The serpent came with his ancient lies, questioning God's word, slandering God's character, promising autonomy that would deliver only slavery. Eve was deceived. Adam, standing beside her, chose rebellion with eyes wide open. And in that moment, sin entered the world like a virus, corrupting every relationship, distorting every good gift, introducing death where only life had been.

But this is also, thank God, the story of a promise that could not be broken. Even as God pronounced curses, He spoke grace. The seed of the woman would come. The serpent's head would be crushed. What was lost in Adam would be restored in Christ. Death would not have the final word. The exile from Eden would end in a city where God dwells with His people forever.

This is the gospel in seed form. Everything that follows in Scripture, the covenants with Abraham and David, the law given at Sinai, the sacrificial system, the prophetic promises, the incarnation, the cross, the resurrection, the ascension, the gift of the Spirit, the birth of the church, all of it unfolds from Genesis 3:15. The whole Bible is the story of how God keeps His promise to crush the serpent and restore His people to Himself.

We desperately need this story. Not as mythology that points vaguely toward spiritual truths, but as history that grounds us in reality. When we reduce Genesis to poetry or allegory, we do not make Christianity more credible. We make it incoherent. We lose the foundation that explains why we need a Savior, what He came to accomplish, and how His work connects to our experience.

But when we receive Genesis as God's authoritative word about how things actually are, we gain clarity about everything else. The confusion lifts. The questions find answers. The pieces fit together. We can stand firm because we stand on rock.

The God Who Is There

At the center of Genesis 1 through 3 stands God Himself. This is where we must begin and where we must always return. Not with ourselves, not with our questions or struggles or needs, but with the One who is before all things and in whom all things hold together.

He is the eternal Creator who exists in three persons as Father, Son, and Holy Spirit. He spoke, and it was so. He commanded, and it stood firm. Nothing constrained Him. Nothing limited Him. He created freely, wisely, powerfully, displaying His glory through the vast array of creatures and landscapes and systems He brought into being.

He is the covenant Lord who establishes relationships, sets terms, makes promises, and executes judgments. He did not create humanity and leave us to figure out how to relate to Him. He came to us. He walked with Adam and Eve in the garden. He gave them meaningful work and clear commands. He blessed them with abundance and warned them of danger. He sought them when they hid. He pronounced judgment but also promised redemption.

He is the sovereign ruler whose purposes cannot be thwarted. When Adam sinned, God's plan was not derailed. The Fall did not catch Him by surprise or force Him to improvise a rescue mission. Before the foundation of the world, He had already determined to save a people for Himself through the work of His Son. Adam's sin was humanity's catastrophe, but it fit within God's eternal decree. What Satan meant for evil, God meant for the display of His justice and mercy, His holiness and grace.

He is the holy judge who cannot tolerate sin. When Adam and Eve rebelled, God did not shrug and overlook it. He did not minimize the offense or treat it as a learning experience. He pronounced curses. He executed judgment. He drove them from the garden and placed cherubim with a flaming sword to guard the way to the tree of life. His holiness demands that sin be punished. His justice requires that rebellion face consequences.

But He is also the gracious redeemer who provides what He demands. He made garments of skins to cover Adam and Eve's nakedness, requiring the death of animals to provide covering for their shame (Genesis 3:21). This simple act of provision pointed forward to the greater provision that would come through the blood of Christ. God would not leave His image-bearers in their guilt and shame. He would make a way for rebels to become children, for exiles to come home, for the dead to live.

Everything I have written in this book flows from who God is. If we get God wrong, we get everything else wrong. But if we see Him clearly, sovereign and merciful, holy and gracious, just and loving, then everything else falls into place.

The God revealed in Genesis 1 through 3 is the God we worship on Sunday and trust on Monday. He is the God who sustains you when work is frustrating and marriage is hard. He is the God who forgives you when you fall and sanctifies you as you fight. He is the God who will not let you go, who has bound Himself to you in covenant, who has promised to complete the work He began in you.

How This Shapes How We Live

Theology is not abstract speculation disconnected from the rhythms of daily life, but living truth meant to transform how we actually live from Monday through Saturday, not just how we think on Sunday morning. The doctrines we have examined and unpacked throughout this book, creation, image-bearing, fall, covenant, curse, promise, redemption, these profound realities are not meant to remain locked in our heads as intellectual propositions to be debated in seminary classrooms or argued about in study groups. They must work their way down from our minds into the deepest places of our hearts, transforming our desires and affections. They must shape the mundane routines and sacred rhythms of our homes, where faith is lived out in the thousand small decisions that make up family life. They must inform how we function together as members of our churches, the community of believers where we worship, serve, and bear one another's burdens. And they must fundamentally reshape our engagement with the watching world around us, influencing how we work, how we speak, how we love our neighbors, and how we bear witness to the God who created all things and is making all things new.

In Our Hearts

Genesis teaches us who we are at the most fundamental level. You are not an accident. You are not a mistake. You are not the sum of your achievements or failures. You are a creature made in God's image, fallen into sin, and, if you are in Christ, redeemed by grace.

This identity remains stable regardless of your circumstances, your feelings, or your performance. When you wake in the morning wrestling with shame over yesterday's failures, Genesis reminds you that your value does not depend on moral perfection. You were created good, corrupted by the Fall, and are being restored in Christ. When anxiety about the future threatens to overwhelm you, Genesis anchors you in the sovereignty of the God who numbered the stars and calls each one by name. When depression whispers that your life has no meaning, Genesis declares that you were made for purpose, to know God, to reflect His image, to exercise dominion in whatever sphere He has placed you.

The lies you battle, "I'm worthless," "I'm beyond help," "I'm trapped," "nothing will ever change" all crumble before the truth of Genesis. You are fearfully and wonderfully made (Psalm 139:14). You are known by the God who formed you in the womb. Your life has weight and significance because you bear the image of the eternal God.

But Genesis also confronts our pride. You are a creature, not the Creator. You are accountable to God, not autonomous. You do not get to define reality according to your preferences. You do not determine what is good and evil. You live under authority, and that authority is good, wise, and aimed at your flourishing.

This humility before God liberates us from the crushing burden of trying to be our own gods. You do not have to figure everything out. You do not have to control every outcome. You do not have to create your own meaning or construct your own identity. God has already done these things. You simply receive them with gratitude and live according to His design.

The gospel speaks into our identity confusion with startling clarity. In Christ, you are a new creation. The old has passed away; the new has come (2 Corinthians 5:17). Your identity is no longer "sinner" but "saint," no longer "condemned" but "justified," no longer "slave" but "child." You are united to Christ by faith, and that union defines you more fundamentally than anything else.

This means your past does not determine your future. Your failures do not disqualify you from God's purposes. Your sin, though serious, is not stronger than Christ's blood. You stand before God clothed in Christ's righteousness, and nothing can separate you from His love.

In Our Homes

Genesis establishes the first human institution: marriage between one man and one woman, united in covenant for life. This is not one option among many, but God's design from the beginning. Everything Scripture teaches about marriage and family builds on this foundation.

If you are married, Genesis calls you to honor your covenant. Husbands, love your wives as Christ loved the church. This is not optional. This is not conditional on her performance or your feelings. This is covenant love that serves sacrificially, leads humbly, and gives without counting the cost. Your marriage is a living picture of Christ and His bride. How you love your wife preaches the gospel to your children and to a watching world.

Wives, respect your husbands. Submit to their leadership as the church submits to Christ. This is not degrading but dignifying. You are not diminished by biblical submission but freed to flourish in the role God designed for you. Your trust in your husband's leadership, when he leads as Christ leads, reflects the church's glad submission to her Savior.

Both of you together are called to cultivate your marriage, to work through conflict, and to resist the temptation to quit when things get hard. The Fall brought discord into the marriage. Redemption in Christ makes restoration possible. The Spirit empowers you to love when love is difficult, to forgive when forgiveness costs, to persevere when you want to flee.

And both of you are called to build a home where God is honored. Teach your children the truths of Genesis. Show them that they are created in God's image. Teach them about the Fall and their need for a Savior. Point them to Christ as the seed who crushed the serpent's head. Pray with them. Read Scripture with them. Model faith in the ordinary rhythms of daily life. Your home is the primary context for discipleship, and no institution can replace what God has called parents to do.

If you are single, Genesis speaks to you as well. You are not a half-person waiting to be completed by marriage. You are a whole image-bearer with a calling from God. Marriage is good, but it is not ultimate. Your identity is not "single" but "in Christ." And singleness offers unique opportunities for kingdom service that married people do not have. Paul himself was single and called it a gift (1 Corinthians 7:7).

In your singleness, honor God with your body. Sexual purity matters, not because your body is evil, but because it is good, a temple of the Holy Spirit. Flee sexual immorality. Guard your eyes and your heart. Cultivate same-sex friendships without sexual desire. And if God calls you to marriage, wait for a partner who shares your faith and your commitment to biblical design.

In Our Churches

The church is the community of the redeemed, the assembly of those who have been rescued from the domain of darkness and transferred to the kingdom of God's beloved Son (Colossians 1:13). Genesis shapes how we understand and live as that community.

We gather on the Lord's Day to worship the God who created all things and who rested on the seventh day. Our weekly rhythm of work and worship echoes the pattern established at creation. We cease from our labor to focus on God's work. We rest in His finished work of redemption, just as we are called to rest from our own works. The Sabbath principle, though fulfilled in Christ, continues to guide us toward proper priorities and rhythms.

We preach the word because God's word creates reality. Just as He spoke, and the world came into being, His word continues to accomplish His purposes. When Scripture is proclaimed faithfully, God is speaking, calling sinners to repentance, instructing His people in righteousness, and building up the body of Christ. We cannot have a healthy church without a faithful exposition of God's authoritative word.

We celebrate the sacraments because God uses physical means to communicate spiritual grace. The water of baptism points back to creation when the Spirit hovered over the waters, and forward to the new creation when all things will be made new. The bread and wine of the Lord's Supper point to Christ's body broken and shed blood, to the covenant sealed in His sacrifice, to the marriage supper of the Lamb that awaits us.

We practice church discipline because we are a covenant community accountable to God and to one another. When a member falls into unrepentant sin, we cannot ignore it or pretend everything is fine. We must speak truth in love, call them to repentance, and, if necessary, remove them from membership to protect the purity of the church and to shock them toward repentance. This is not cruelty but covenant faithfulness, not judgment but mercy aimed at restoration.

We pursue holiness together, recognizing that we are being sanctified, not in isolation, but as members of one body. We bear one another's burdens. We confess our sins to one another. We spur one another on to love and good works (Hebrews 10:24). We encourage the discouraged, admonish the idle, and help the weak (1 Thessalonians 5:14).

In the World

Genesis gives us a framework for engaging the culture without either withdrawing into Christian ghettos or capitulating to cultural lies. We are in the world but not of it (John 17:15-16), exiles and sojourners who seek the welfare of the city where God has placed us (Jeremiah 29:7; 1 Peter 2:11).

We work in God's world as His image-bearers, exercising dominion and cultivating creation's potential. Whatever your vocation, whether you work with your hands or your mind, whether in business or education or healthcare or technology, you serve God by doing your work well. Excellence in work glorifies God. Integrity in dealings reflects His character. Service to others mirrors Christ's self-giving love.

We care for creation as stewards rather than exploiters. The dominion mandate has not been rescinded. We still bear responsibility to fill the earth and subdue it, to cultivate its potential and guard it from harm. This means we take environmental concerns seriously without worshipping creation. We use resources wisely without treating nature as sacred. We recognize that creation itself groans for redemption and will share in our liberation from bondage to corruption.

We speak truth in a culture of lies. When the world denies the reality of male and female, we affirm God's design. When society celebrates what God calls sin, we maintain biblical standards. When culture redefines marriage, we proclaim the creation ordinance. When laws compel us to participate in evil, we obey God rather than men.

This will be costly. It already is. But the cost of compromise is greater. When we remain silent about truth to avoid conflict, we fail those who desperately need to hear it. When we accommodate lies to maintain cultural acceptance, we forfeit our witness. When we seek the world's approval more than God's, we prove ourselves unworthy of the kingdom.

Yet we speak the truth with compassion. We remember that we too were once deceived, enslaved to sin, hostile to God. We speak not from a position of moral superiority but from the stance of beggars who have found bread and want to tell other beggars where to find it. We aim for conversion, not just confrontation. We pray for our opponents. We love our enemies. We do good to those who hate us.

Addressing the Tensions

I know some of you have wrestled with questions throughout this book. Let me address a few of them directly before we close.

"What do I do with my doubts and questions?"

First, recognize that questions are not the same as unbelief. Thomas questioned the resurrection until he saw and touched the risen Christ (John 20:24-29). Yet Jesus received him, answered his doubts, and blessed his faith. God is not threatened by honest questions. He invites us to reason with Him (Isaiah 1:18).

But we must distinguish between honest questions and rebellious questioning. Honest questions seek understanding and truth. They come from humility that acknowledges our limitations. Rebellious questioning, by contrast, places ourselves in judgment over God. It assumes we are qualified to assess whether God's ways are right. It demands that God justify Himself to us.

When you question aspects of Genesis, ask yourself: Am I seeking to understand God's word more fully, or am I looking for reasons to dismiss what it clearly teaches? Am I approaching Scripture with humility as a creature before the Creator, or with pride as a judge determining what I will accept?

Bring your questions to Scripture, to faithful teachers, to the community of believers. Study carefully. Think deeply. But recognize that some questions may not be answered fully this side of glory. God has revealed what we need to know, not everything we might want to know. "The secret things belong to the LORD our God, but the things that are revealed belong to us and to our children forever, that we may do all the words of this law" (Deuteronomy 29:29).

"How do I read Genesis faithfully without making it a divisive battleground?"

The truth is, Genesis has become a battleground because the stakes are so high. But we can engage these texts faithfully without unnecessary division.

First, focus on what Scripture clearly teaches rather than disputable matters. Genesis clearly teaches that God created all things, that humanity is made in His image, that male and female are God's design, that marriage is one man and one woman, that sin entered through Adam's disobedience, that death is the consequence of sin, and that God promised a Redeemer. These are non-negotiables.

Second, engage with gentleness and respect. Peter instructs us to be "prepared to make a defense to anyone who asks you for a reason for the hope that is in you; yet do it with gentleness and respect" (1 Peter 3:15). Speak the truth, but do so with humility. Remember that you too are a fallen creature prone to error. Listen to others, even when you disagree. Seek to understand their concerns before demanding they understand yours.

Third, maintain the unity of the Spirit while contending for the faith. Paul commands us to be "eager to maintain the unity of the Spirit in the bond of peace" (Ephesians 4:3). Unity does not mean uniformity on every interpretive question. But it does mean refusing to divide over matters Scripture treats as secondary. Save your strongest stands for the clearest truths. Give grace on the rest.

"How does this help with shame?"

Shame entered the world in Genesis 3. The moment Adam and Eve sinned, they knew they were naked and sewed fig leaves to cover themselves (Genesis 3:7). When they heard God walking in the garden, they hid (Genesis 3:8). Shame made them want to hide from the very One who could help them.

This is what shame does. It isolates us. It makes us believe we are uniquely broken, beyond help, unworthy of love. It whispers that if people knew what we have done or what we struggle with, they would reject us. It drives us into hiding rather than toward the light.

But Genesis also shows God's response to shame. He sought them. He called out to Adam, "Where are you?" (Genesis 3:9). He knew where Adam was, of course. The question was for Adam's benefit, an invitation to come out of hiding and face reality. God did not leave them in their shame. He covered their nakedness with garments He Himself made.

This is the gospel pattern. We try to cover ourselves with fig leaves, our good works, our religious performance, our attempts at self-justification. But these inadequate coverings cannot hide our guilt. God must provide the covering. And He does, through Christ.

When shame threatens to crush you, remember that Christ bore your shame on the cross. He who knew no sin became sin for us (2 Corinthians 5:21). He was stripped naked and exposed publicly, enduring the ultimate shame so that we might be clothed in His righteousness. There is now no condemnation for those who are in Christ Jesus (Romans 8:1). None. Your shame has been dealt with. Your guilt has been removed. You can come out of hiding and stand in the presence of a holy God because Christ has covered you with His own righteousness.

The church must be a place where shame is addressed with the gospel. We cannot pretend sin does not exist, or that everyone is fine. But neither can we leave people in their shame. We must proclaim the good news that Christ removes guilt and restores the shamed to fellowship with God and with His people.

"What about my anxiety and fear?"

We live in an anxious age. Technology has made everything feel urgent. Social media bombards us with worst-case scenarios. The news cycle feeds our fears. Work demands increase.

Financial pressures mount. Relationships fracture. Sickness threatens. The future looms uncertain.

Genesis speaks to this anxiety in several ways. First, it reminds us that God is sovereign over creation. He is not wringing His hands, wondering what will happen next. He holds all things together by the word of His power (Hebrews 1:3). Nothing escapes His control. No crisis catches Him off guard. No problem is too big for His wisdom or power.

Second, it teaches us that God provides for His image-bearers. He planted a garden for Adam before Adam could work. He made provision before there was a need. He continues to provide for His people, giving us daily bread, sustaining us by His grace, working all things together for the good of those who love Him (Romans 8:28).

Third, it shows us that our fundamental security does not depend on our circumstances but on God's covenant faithfulness. Adam and Eve lost the garden, but God did not abandon them. He pursued them. He covered them. He promised redemption. We may lose health, wealth, reputation, or relationships, but we cannot lose God. He has bound Himself to us in Christ, and nothing can separate us from His love (Romans 8:38-39).

The remedy for anxiety is not positive thinking or stress management techniques, though these may have limited value. The remedy is faith, trusting that God is who He says He is and that He will do what He has promised. When Jesus taught His disciples not to be anxious, He grounded His teaching in creation: "Look at the birds of the air: they neither sow nor reap nor gather into barns, and yet your heavenly Father feeds them. Are you not of more value than they?" (Matthew 6:26). The God who provides for sparrows will provide for His image-bearers.

The God who clothes the grass of the field will clothe His children.

"How does this help with broken relationships?"

Sin fractured every relationship. Adam blamed Eve. Eve blamed the serpent. Brothers became murderers. Families divided. Nations went to war. Every broken relationship you experience, the conflict with your spouse, the distance from your children, the betrayal by a friend, the division in your church, flows from the Fall.

But the gospel of redemption offers hope for relationships. Christ came to reconcile us to God, and that vertical reconciliation makes horizontal reconciliation possible. He is making a new humanity where former enemies become brothers, where Jew and Gentile are one body, where slave and free share equal dignity, where male and female complement one another without competition.

This does not happen automatically. Reconciliation requires repentance and forgiveness, confession and grace. You must acknowledge your own contribution to broken relationships rather than merely blaming others. You must extend forgiveness even when the other person does not deserve it, just as God forgave you though you did not deserve it. You must pursue peace actively, taking the initiative to restore what sin has broken.

Some relationships may not be fully restored this side of glory. The other person may refuse to repent. They may continue in patterns of abuse or betrayal. In such cases, you maintain appropriate boundaries while continuing to pray and to forgive. You recognize that full reconciliation may have to wait for the new creation when all things are made right.

But you do not give up on relationships easily. You fight for your marriage. You pursue your wayward children. You work toward reconciliation in your church. You do this because God has reconciled you to Himself at infinite cost, and He calls you to be ambassadors of reconciliation in a fractured world (2 Corinthians 5:18-20).

"What if I've compromised on these truths?"

Many believers have absorbed cultural lies about gender, sexuality, marriage, or the authority of Scripture. They have made peace with ideas that contradict Genesis. Perhaps you are one of them. What now?

Repentance is always the path forward. Acknowledge that you have believed lies. Confess that you have elevated your own wisdom or the culture's consensus above God's word. Return to Scripture with humility, asking God to teach you truth, even when that truth cuts against what you want to believe.

God is gracious to restore those who repent. He does not hold our past errors against us when we come to Him in faith. The same grace that saved you in the first place continues to work in you, conforming you to the image of Christ, sanctifying you progressively through His word and Spirit.

But repentance must be concrete. If you have affirmed same-sex relationships, you must now speak truth about God's design for sexuality. If you have encouraged someone toward gender transition, you must acknowledge that you led them astray and point them toward their God-given identity. If you have performed or supported abortion, you must confess the taking of innocent life and work to protect the unborn going forward.

This may be costly. Changing your position may cost you friendships, job opportunities, or social standing. But obedience to Christ always costs something. The question is whether you value His approval more than human approval, His truth more than cultural acceptance.

The God Who Finishes What He Starts

I want to leave you with one final truth that has sustained me through every trial and that I pray will sustain you: God finishes what He starts.

He created the world and declared it good. Sin corrupted it, but God did not abandon His creation. He promised to redeem it, and He will. He is making all things new (Revelation 21:5). The curse will be removed. Creation will be liberated. The glory of the Lord will fill the earth as the waters cover the sea (Habakkuk 2:14).

He created you in His image. Sin marred that image, but God did not discard you. In Christ, He is restoring the image, conforming you to the likeness of His Son. He began a good work in you, and He will bring it to completion at the day of Jesus Christ (Philippians 1:6). Your salvation is secure, not because you hold onto God, but because He holds onto you.

He promised that the seed of the woman would crush the serpent's head. That promise found its fulfillment in Christ's death and resurrection. But the full outworking of that victory awaits Christ's return. Satan is defeated but not yet destroyed. Sin's power is broken but not yet eliminated. Death is conquered but not yet abolished. We live in the in-between time, the already and the not yet.

But the end is certain. Christ will return. He will raise the dead. He will judge the living and the dead. He will establish His kingdom in fullness. He will make all things new. And we who are in Him will reign with Him forever in a new creation where righteousness dwells.

This confidence allows us to endure whatever comes. Paul could say, "I am sure of this, that he who began a good work in you will bring it to completion at the day of Jesus Christ" (Philippians 1:6). He was sure. Not hopeful. Not optimistic. Sure. Confident. Certain.

This is the faith that Genesis calls us to. Not faith in ourselves, in our understanding, in our ability to figure everything out. But faith in the God who created all things, who governs all things, who redeems His people, and who will bring His purposes to glorious completion.

A Pastoral Charge

As we close, I want to charge you with several responsibilities.

First, guard the foundation. The truths of Genesis 1 through 3 are under sustained assault in our day. You will face pressure to compromise, to soften, to reinterpret these chapters in ways that accommodate contemporary sensibilities. Stand firm. These truths are not negotiable. They are the foundation of everything else you believe. Lose Genesis and you will eventually lose the gospel itself.

Second, teach the next generation. Do not assume your children or the young people in your church will absorb these truths by osmosis. The culture is aggressively teaching them lies about origins, identity, sexuality, and meaning. You must be equally intentional in teaching them truth. Read Genesis with them. Explain it to them. Show them how it connects to the rest of Scripture and to the challenges they face. Ground them in these foundational chapters before the storms of doubt and deception come.

Third, live consistently with what you believe. It is not enough to affirm the right doctrines if your life contradicts them. If you believe God created male and female, live according to biblical manhood or womanhood. If you believe marriage is a covenant, honor your vows even when it is hard. If you believe work is a gift from God, pursue excellence in your vocation. If you believe you are created for God's glory, make His glory your aim in everything you do.

Fourth, extend grace to those who struggle. Not everyone who questions Genesis is a rebel. Some are genuinely confused by conflicting messages from science and Scripture. Some have been taught poorly. Some are working through legitimate questions. Do not write them off. Walk with them. Show them the answers. Point them to resources that address their concerns. Pray for them. Be patient with them. Remember that you too have struggled with doubts and that God was patient with you.

Fifth, hope in the coming renewal. This world is broken, and it will not be fixed this side of Christ's return. Do not place your hope in political solutions or social reform, or technological progress. These may bring temporary improvements, but they cannot reverse the curse or eliminate sin. Our hope is in the new creation, when Christ will make all things new, when the tree of life will be accessible again, when God will dwell with His people, when every tear will be wiped away.

This hope is not escapism. It does not make us indifferent to present suffering or injustice. Rather, it sustains us as we work in a fallen world, giving us strength to persevere, courage to stand for truth, and joy even in the midst of trials. We know how the story ends. We know that our labor is not in vain. We know that God will accomplish all His purposes. And this knowledge enables us to keep going when the way is hard.

Coming Home

I began this book with a woman in my office asking how God could call this good. I end with the same question, but now we can answer it more fully.

God called creation good because it perfectly reflected His wisdom, power, and glory. It was exactly what He intended it to be, a stage for His purposes, a home for His image-bearers, a revelation of His character. Everything worked according to His design. Everything was in harmony. Everything pointed to Him.

Sin did not change God's assessment of what He made. It corrupted the creation, but did not make it evil in itself. God still owns the world. Christ will still redeem it. We still bear His image even in our fallenness. The goodness of God declared over creation in Genesis 1 remains true, though now seen through the dark glass of sin and curse.

But here is the wonder: God will restore what was lost and exceed it in glory. The new creation will be better than Eden. We will be more secure than Adam because we will have been confirmed in righteousness through Christ. We will have greater intimacy with God because we will know Him as Redeemer, not just as Creator. We will have deeper joy because we will have been brought from death to life, from slavery to freedom, from exile to home.

The garden is lost. We cannot go back. Cherubim with flaming swords guard the way. But we can go forward. Through Christ, we have access to the tree of life again. Through Christ, we have fellowship with God restored. Through Christ, we are heading toward a city whose designer and builder is God.

This is how the story ends: not with exile but with homecoming, not with curse but with blessing, not with death but with life, not with separation but with God dwelling among His people forever.

And so we wait with patient hope. We work with faithful diligence. We worship with grateful hearts. We walk by faith, not by sight. We press on toward the goal for the prize of the upward call of God in Christ Jesus (Philippians 3:14).

The foundations hold. They have held through every assault, every challenge, every attempt to undermine them. They held for our fathers in the faith. They will hold for us. They will hold for those who come after us.

Build your life on Genesis 1 through 3. Build your family on these truths. Build your ministry on this foundation. And when the storms come, and they will come, you will stand firm because you stand on rock.

The God who created all things by the word of His power, who made you in His image, who promised redemption when you fell, who sent His Son to crush the serpent's head, who is even now sanctifying you by His Spirit, this God will bring you safely home. He who began a good work in you will complete it. He who called you is faithful.

Genesis tells us where we came from and why things are broken. More importantly, it tells us where we are going and who will bring us there. Trust Him. Follow Him. Rest in Him. And one day, you will stand in the new creation, fully conformed to Christ's image, free from sin and suffering, dwelling in God's presence forever.

That is the hope Genesis gives. That is the foundation that holds. That is the story that makes sense of everything else.

"The LORD bless you and keep you; the LORD make his face to shine upon you and be gracious to you; the LORD lift up his countenance upon you and give you peace." (Numbers 6:24-26)

"Now may the God of peace who brought again from the dead our Lord Jesus, the great shepherd of the sheep, by the blood of the eternal covenant, equip you with everything good that you may do his will, working in us that which is pleasing in his sight, through Jesus Christ, to whom be glory forever and ever. Amen." (Hebrews 13:20-21)

About the author

Bruce served in the United States Marine Corps, retiring with the rank of Gunnery Sergeant after deployments across the globe. His military service instilled in him a deep appreciation for discipline, sacrifice, and the bonds forged through shared hardship; themes that would profoundly shape his understanding of Christian discipleship and the believer's union with Christ.

Following his retirement from the Marine Corps, Bruce pursued theological education, earning a doctorate in theology with a focus on Biblical Studies. His academic journey deepened his conviction that sound doctrine must serve pastoral ministry, not exist in isolation from the real struggles believers face.

Bruce served as a pastor in a Reformed church, shepherding the congregation through seasons of joy and sorrow, growth and conflict, triumph and trial. Careful biblical exposition, compassionate counseling, and an unwavering commitment to the doctrines of grace that sustained him through his own darkest valleys marked his pastoral ministry.

Later in his ministry, Bruce transitioned to seminary education, where he taught Biblical Studies and Theology. His classroom became a bridge between rigorous academic study and practical pastoral application, as he mentored countless students preparing for ministry. Known for making complex theological concepts accessible without compromising their depth, Bruce helped shape a generation of pastors who carry his commitment to Reformed theology and pastoral wisdom into churches around the world.

Throughout his varied career, from the disciplined ranks of the Marines to the halls of academia, Bruce has maintained that the Christian life is fundamentally about union with Christ. This conviction, forged on battlefields and refined in classrooms, tested in hospital rooms and proven in pulpits, shapes every page of his writing.

Bruce and his beloved wife have walked together through the trials that test faith and prove God's faithfulness, including her courageous battle with cancer that deepened their understanding of what it means to be "more than conquerors through him who loved us."

When not writing or teaching, Bruce enjoys the simple pleasures of retirement while remaining active in his writing. He continues to believe that the doctrines of grace are not merely intellectual concepts to be debated but living truths that transform how we face each day, whether in the heat of battle, the quiet of a study, or the ordinary moments where faith becomes sight.

www.ingramcontent.com/pod-product-compliance
Lightning Source LLC
Chambersburg PA
CBHW071645160426
43195CB00012B/1366